Income-poverty and Beyond

Income-poverty and Beyond

Human Development in India

Edited by

RAJA J. CHELLIAH

and

R. SUDARSHAN

Anthem Press
London, UK

First Published by

Social Science Press
69 Jor Bagh, New Delhi 110003
E-mail: beteille@del3.vsnl.net.in

This edition published by

Anthem Press by arrangement with
Social Science Press

Anthem Press is an imprint of the
Wimbledon Publishing Company
P.O. Box 9779, London SW19 7QA
Fax: (+44) 20 8944 0825
E-mail: sales@wpcpress.com

ISBN (hardback) 1 84331 001 5
ISBN (paperback) 1 84431 005 8

Set in Giovanni Book 10/12
Typeset by Eleven Art, Delhi-110035

Printed by
Sanjiv Palliwal, E-9, Green Park Extn.
New Delhi-110016. India at Usha Offset

Contents

Contributors

RAJA J. CHELLIAH
  Professor Emeritus, National Institute of Public Finance and Policy, Delhi and Chairman, Madras School of Economics, Chennai.

R. SUDARSHAN,
  Senior Economist and Assistant Resident Representative, UNDP, India.

SURESH TENDULKAR
  Professor of Economics, Delhi School of Economics, Delhi.

ABUSALEH SHARIFF
  Principal Economist, National Council of Applied Economic Research, Delhi.

R. RADHAKRISHNA
  Former Director, Centre for Economic and Social Studies, Hyderabad and Vice Chancellor, University of Andhra Pradesh.

M.S.S. MEENAKSHISUNDARAM
  Joint Secretary, Prime Minister's Office, New Delhi.

SEETA K. PRABHU
  Professor of Development Economics, University of Bombay, Mumbai.

RAVI SRIVASTAVA
  Associate Professor of Economics, University of Allahabad, Allahabad .

Preface

The eradication of poverty and promotion of sustainable human development are the basic priorities of the United Nations Development Programme (UNDP). Inspired by the decision of the Heads of Government of the SAARC countries to accord poverty eradication the highest priority in the remaining years of this decade, UNDP launched in 1995, a Regional Poverty Alleviation Programme. This programme is now operating in Bangladesh, Maldives, Nepal, Pakistan, India and Sri Lanka. Creating the means to improve capabilities of people who are presently poor, and helping them to create opportunities for sustainable livelihoods and a better future, are the main objectives of the programme. Social mobilization is the principal strategy of the programme's efforts to help the poor in selected locations. As a complement to the action component of the Regional Programme, a South Asia Poverty Monitor was conceived to serve as a tool for establishing benchmarks and providing a yardstick to assess the impact of pro-poor plans and anti-poverty programmes. This book is an outcome of the exercise to prepare a South Asia Poverty Monitor.

The chapters in this volume were originally commissioned by UNDP to serve as background papers making up an India Country Report, along with similar background papers on Bangladesh, Nepal, Pakistan and Sri Lanka. When these papers were discussed at a meeting held in Sri Lanka last year it was apparent that the South Asia Poverty Monitor would be able to use only a limited and summary version of the detailed analysis and information contained in the India Country Report. It seemed worthwhile to edit the papers and make them available to a wider readership with special interest in India.

UNDP is grateful to Raja Chelliah for coordinating the contributions made to the India Country Report, and for taking the lead in editing this volume, together with R. Sudarshan (UNDP Senior Economist).

We are indebted to Nay Htun (Assistant Secretary-General, United Nations, and, Director, UNDP Regional Bureau for Asia and the Pacific) for encouraging this enterprise. Saraswathy Menon, UNDP Regional Programme Manager, provided leadership to the South Asia Poverty Monitor initiative, and supported the publication of this book.

Although this book is the outcome of an initiative sponsored and supported by UNDP, it does not necessarily reflect the views of UNDP, its Executive Board, or its Member Countries. I hope that this book will add value and complement other work on poverty in India by shifting the focus of attention beyond income-poverty. I also hope that it will stimulate debate and discussion, and going beyond that, catalyse even more positive action for poverty eradication and human development.

Brenda Gael McSweeney
United Nations Resident Coordinator,
December 1998   UNDP Resident Representative

Acknowledgements

The editors are indebted to M.S.S Meenakshisundaram, Seeta K. Prabhu, R. Radhakrishna, Abusaleh Shariff, Ravi Srivastava, and Suresh Tendulkar for providing the material on which this book is based. Chapter two draws mainly upon the paper by Suresh Tendulkar; likewise, chapter three, by Abusaleh Shariff; chapter four, by R. Radhakrishna; chapter five, by M.S.S. Meenakshisundaram; chapters six and seven, by Seeta K. Prabhu; and chapter eight, Ravi Srivastava. The editors are grateful to the authors of the background papers commissioned by UNDP on which this book is based. In the interests of coherence and continuity the editors have had to take the liberty of rearranging the original material.

An informal committee comprising five of them provided valuable guidance.

Usha Jayachandran (UNDP Consultant) assisted the editors in the difficult task of rearranging the material contained in the background papers written by different authors. She provided initial drafts for substantial sections of this book.

Elena Borsatti (UNDP Consultant) undertook the arduous and tedious task of cross-checking and verifying the references in the text and the accuracy of the tables, and in the process made valuable contributions towards making the text readable. Without her assistance this book could not have been published.

We also acknowledge the contribution of G. Padmanabhan (UNDP Programme Officer) during all the stages in the production of this book, commencing with the commissioning of the background papers. Saugato Datta copy-edited the script and Jehanara Wasi read the proofs, and helped to introduce a little more economy in the expression of economists! Meera Juneja compiled the index with patience and care.

Esha Béteille, editor and publisher, Social Science Press,

sustained, to an extraordinary extent, her enthusiasm, diligence, and patience, to make this book possible.

Introduction

The foremost objective of development planning in India since Independence has been the reduction and ultimate abolition of poverty and social backwardness. To this end the adopted strategy was two-fold: to promote economic growth and, at the same time, to use state intervention to spread the fruits of growth towards human development. Since the early 1970s, poverty alleviation programmes have been increasingly used to lighten the burden of unemployment and to supplement and augment the trickle-down effects of growth.

There has been much debate about how exactly poverty should be defined. In popular understanding, poverty is identified with lowness of income which prevents a family from obtaining and enjoying the basic necessities of life, including a minimum of food, clothing, shelter and water. This concept is defined as income-poverty. For a more comprehensive picture of poverty those other deprivations, such as in relation to health, education, sanitation and insurance against mishaps, must be taken into account.

The official concept of poverty in India is based on a calorie norm: families which cannot afford to spend enough on food to obtain a stipulated minimum calorie per capita per day are defined to be below the poverty line (BPL). The methodology of calculating the proportion of people below the poverty line from consumer expenditure data has been worked out by an Expert Group of the Planning Commission. Our analysis of poverty has been based on calculations using this methodology.

The broad picture which emerges from a study of the trends and structure of poverty in India and of the policy measures relating to the poor, is that there has been a steady decline in the proportion of people below the poverty line (the head count ratio or HCR) from about 55 per cent in the mid-1970s to 35–36 per cent in 1993–4.

The growth of the economy was relatively slow till the 1970s; however, growth accelerated from then on and per capita income grew at an average of 2.4 per cent per year from the mid-1970s to the mid-1980s. In the decade 1983 to 1993–4, the HCR declined by 16 per cent, poverty gap by 30 per cent, and the severity of poverty by as much as 45 per cent. The decline in the poverty gap and the severity indices show that the people just below the poverty line were not the only ones to have benefitted, but the conditions of those well below the poverty line had also improved. What is important to note is that as average Indian living standards rose during the years since 1951–2, particularly after the mid-1970s, the poor did not get poorer. At the same time, social indicators of well being have also recorded steady progress.

However, poverty reduction and social progress have been slow. The achievements have been far below desirable standards, and much below what has been achieved in many other Asian countries. While the HCR has declined, at latest count, there were around 300 million people living in poverty in 1993–4 compared to 164 million in 1951. Thus, despite reductions in the proportion of the people below the poverty line during the past four decades, the absolute number of poor has increased substantially because of rapid population growth. As a result India contains the largest concentration of poor people in the world.

The impact of population growth or of a reduction in the rate of growth of population on the reduction of poverty cannot be directly established. However, a comparison of the experiences of the various Indian states shows that there is a relationship between reductions in the rate of growth of population during 1981–91 and the percentage of people below poverty line at the end of the period. But since so many other influences are at work, the relationship turns out to be rather weak, as reflected by a low rank correlation coefficient. We know, however, that except for some of the oil rich countries in the Middle East, no country has succeeded in achieving a high per capita income and low poverty ratio whose population is continuing to grow fast. While economic growth and human development will serve to slow down the growth of population, it is equally true that all possible measures to control the growth of population have to be effectively adopted to hasten the removal of poverty.

REGIONAL DISPARITIES

There are pronounced regional disparities within India. The (weighted) average HCR for India masks noticeable interstate variations. The HCRs for five states, Assam, Bihar, Maharashtra, Orissa and West Bengal are well above the average. In Assam and Haryana, all poverty indices increased between 1983 and 1993–4. It is also noteworthy that the highest HCR among the livelihood categories, about 50 per cent, is recorded by rural agricultural labour households followed by other (manual) rural labour households. Similarly, the disadvantaged groups of Scheduled Castes and Scheduled Tribes have a higher HCR than the general population. According to the NCAER Survey, in 1994, the HCRs were 50 and 51 per cent respectively among Scheduled Castes and Scheduled Tribes, who constitute more than 200 million of India's total population.

An analysis of the urban poverty situation in the fifteen major states indicates that the weighted average HCR declined by 8 percentage points, from nearly 40 per cent in 1983 to 32 per cent in 1993–4. The HCR declined by 19 per cent, depth of poverty based on poverty gap index (PGI) by 23 per cent, and the severity of poverty based on relative squared poverty gap (FGT) by 26 per cent over the decade from 1983 to 1993–4. For the individual states too, the decline in the HCR (except Andhra Pradesh which registered a one percentage point increase) was associated with larger percentage reductions in depth and severity indicators of poverty. Also, the prevailing rates for urban poverty are distinctly lower than their rural counterparts. The weighted average HCR for the fifteen major states is lower by 10 percentage points for the urban population for both 1983 and 1993–4. The higher-end urban poverty is much less regionally concentrated than rural poverty. A resident of a slow-growing state such as Bihar, an illiterate rural woman, a member of a Scheduled Caste or Scheduled Tribe, a person who lives in a rural landless household, and one who is dependent on wage earnings in the unorganized sector, are all individuals who face a significantly higher-than-average risk of remaining submerged in poverty.

FOOD SECURITY

Significant progress has been made in meeting the food energy needs of the Indian people during the last decade. The per capita daily availability of food energy, which remained stagnant between 1960 and 1980, increased from 2061 cal in 1980–2 to 2330 cal in 1990–2. The current availability of food energy is just about enough to meet the food needs (about 2200 cal/person/day) of the total population if it were evenly distributed. Given the inequalities in the food energy intake, raising the calorie intake level of the bottom 30 per cent, which was about 1600 cal in 1993–4, to 2200 cal implies that the per capita daily availability of calories at the national level would have to increase to 2800 cal. This is within reach, provided the growth rate experienced in the 1980s is sustained.

Data provided by the National Nutrition Monitoring Bureau (NNMB) for a sample of seven states reveal that the percentage of children suffering from severe malnutrition declined from 15.0 in 1975–9 to 8.7 in 1988–90 and further to 7.5 per cent in 1994. If those classified in moderate and severe malnutrition ranges are considered together, the percentage of children afflicted by malnutrition declined from 62.5 in 1975–9 to 52.5 in 1988–90 and further to 50.9 in 1994. It is evident that inspite of some improvements in nutritional status, nearly half of all rural children suffer from malnutrition. The decline in the percentage of severely malnourished children, however, is very visible across all NNMB sample states except Orissa. The decline is most striking in Kerala and Tamil Nadu.

National Nutritional Monitoring Bureau data also indicate that 46 per cent of the rural adult population suffered from chronic energy deficiency (CED) in 1994, and that the extent of malnutrition among adults was closer to that among children (51 per cent). The regional patterns are similar to those of malnutrition among children. Chronic energy deficiency was found to be lower in Kerala (33 per cent) and Tamil Nadu (37 per cent) and higher in Gujarat, Maharashtra and Madhya Pradesh (above 50 per cent).

There are substantial interstate variations in the malnutrition levels of children under five years; in 1994, the percentage of moderately to severely malnourished children varied between 34 in Kerala and 57 in Gujarat. In terms of the nutritional status of children, middle-income states such as Kerala, Tamil Nadu and Andhra Pradesh performed better than higher-income states like Gujarat and Maharashtra. Not surprisingly, poorer states such as Madhya Pradesh and Orissa showed the worst performance. It is worth noting that despite low food energy intake, Kerala and Tamil Nadu could perform better. National Family Health Survey (NFHS) data also reveal more or less similar patterns except for Gujarat.

An important mechanism for making basic articles available, mainly food items, to the general population at affordable prices is the Public Distribution System (PDS). Till the late 1970s, the main emphasis of the PDS was on price stabilization. It was confined mainly to urban areas and the food-deficit states. The welfare dimension of the PDS gained in importance in the early 1980s and its coverage was extended to rural areas in some states as well as those with a high incidence of poverty. The PDS is a programme based on a support price for producers and a sub-sidized price for consumers. In 1993–4, the food subsidy cost accounted for 0.7 per cent of GDP. In the post economic reform period, PDS is perceived to be the main safety net to protect the poor from potential short-run price increases due to structural adjustments.

Public Distribution System supplies have increased since the mid-1960s. The annual average supply increased from 6.5 million tonnes during 1961–5 to 18.4 million tonnes during 1990–2. The recent large increases in procurement prices in favour of grain surplus farmers in the Green Revolution belt, and the consequen-tial upward revision in the issue prices, have tended to defeat one of the main objectives of the PDS. There has been a more-than-justified increase in the reward to the farmers at the expense of the consumers, adversely affecting the poor. The increases in the issue prices have also led to the slackening of demand which, in turn, has resulted in the buffer stock reaching uneconomic levels. The carrying cost of the larger buffer stock is also an unwarranted burden on the economy. The PDS can be an important ingredient of poverty alleviation strategy, but in reality it has not benefited the poor to a significant extent. Many empirical studies have shown severe biases in the inter-regional distribution of PDS supplies. States with a high incidence of poverty, such as Bihar, Orissa and Madhya Pradesh receive a lower share. Except for a few states, the PDS works mainly in the urban areas. Even in the urban areas, the system often works inefficiently and there seems to be considerable leakage from the fair-price shops. The proposed new scheme of providing 10 kg of cereal per month to identified poor households at half the price would certainly help the poor; but in practice it will be difficult to prevent the non-poor from obtaining undeserved entitlements.

An improvement in the food consumption standard in India is necessary. But such an improvement alone will not be sufficient to overcome the problem of malnutrition. Other important causes, such as the high incidence of gastro-intestinal and respiratory infections, and behavioural factors such as faulty breastfeeding and weaning practices, are also important. These factors contribute to the low absorption of nutrients from the food consumed. Economic growth, left to itself, may not have any dramatic impact on nutritional status in the near future, although it does provide greater opportunities for public intervention. Effective and efficient food and environmental interventions are needed until the poor are freed from food and nutritional insecurity.

POVERTY ALLEVIATION MEASURES

Poverty alleviation has been a part of the Indian planning strategy from the very beginning. Direct poverty alleviation programmes were introduced in the early 1970s. The PDS is a part of these programmes. Apart from this, direct state intervention for poverty alleviation has largely taken place in the rural areas. Two major components of direct poverty alleviation programmes in rural areas are the Integrated Rural Development Programme (IRDP) which is a programme for promoting self-employment, along with training for the rural youth for self-employment (TRYSEM), and the Jawahar Rozgar Yojana (JRY) for the creation of supplementary wage employment together with the employment assurance scheme.

The IRDP was initiated in 1978–9. Its objective is to enable poor families to cross the poverty line by providing them with productive assets and inputs. Since its inception, about 51 million families have been covered under the IRDP. The major constraint in the implementation of IRDP has been sub-critical investments, which have undermined the viability of the projects.

Studies on the implementation of self-employment programmes

have pointed out two major weaknesses: very little interaction
with beneficiaries at the grassroots level, and lack of concern for
responding to actual market demand. While ultimately full employment or near-full employment has to be achieved through
fast economic growth, in the short run, providing supplementary
employment assumes a great importance. For this purpose, the
JRY (which combines two earlier programmes) is in operation.
Two main sub-schemes under the JRY include the Indira Awas
Yojana, a mass housing programme, and the Million Wells
Scheme — the scheme to provide open irrigation wells free of
cost to individual poor, small and marginal farmers belonging
to SCs and STs and freed bonded labourers. The main objective
of JRY is the generation of additional gainful employment through
the creation of rural economic infrastructure. The programme is
intended to provide a means of livelihood to those who are at
the critical level of subsistence. A concurrent evaluation of the
JRY, conducted during 1993–4, revealed that nearly 82 per cent
of the available funds were spent on Community Development
Projects, with construction of rural link roads receiving the highest
priority.

Despite several weaknesses, anti-poverty programmes have
played an important role in reducing both underemployment and
poverty. Not only statistical estimates but also field studies provide
convincing evidence of the beneficial impact of the anti-poverty
programmes. However, it is necessary to identify measures that
might take the existing anti-poverty programmes further. One way
to ensure better utilization of the funds meant for the poor is to
ensure people's participation by actively involving Panchayati Raj
Institutions and NGOs. It is also necessary to devise a programme
of health insurance for the general population. For the rural poor,
such an insurance scheme could be operated on a collective basis
through Panchayats. It is now generally agreed that rapid economic growth is a prerequisite for the gradual reduction and
ultimate near-total abolition of poverty. The results from a World
Bank research project using household surveys covering forty
years indicate that overall growth accounted for the major share
of poverty reduction: 80 per cent of the decline in the percentage
of households below poverty line between 1951 and 1970, and
almost 100 per cent since 1970 (World Bank 1997: 4). There is
little doubt that rapid economic growth will have to be the main

vehicle for poverty reduction. However, in the Indian context, it is important to remember that a fast growth of the economy does not automatically mean a fast growth of all the regions.

The present Planning Commission strategy of planning on a macroeconomic basis for an overall growth of 7 per cent per annum is deficient in the sense that it will not ensure fast growth of backward regions. A disaggregated growth strategy is called for. Special plans for the development of infrastructure in the backward states and special assistance for that purpose as well as for accelerated human development would be important. Such assistance may be made conditional, and a degree of central government intervention would also be necessary. The five states with the lowest per capita domestic product should be enabled to grow at least at 5.5 to 6 per cent per annum. These considerations call for raising the shares of capital formation in these states.

The second ingredient in a policy framework for poverty reduction is a much higher expenditure on human development. Those South-east Asian countries which have achieved remarkable reductions in poverty had invested heavily in human resource development. The right policy for India to follow is to plough back substantial proportions of the fruits of growth into health, education, housing and rural infrastructure. The major responsibility for this should fall on the state governments. Unfortunately, however, although the revenue accruals to the state governments have remained around 12.5 per cent of a fast-growing GDP, the proportion of their expenditure (on revenue account) on social sectors has fallen. The finances of the state governments are, in general, in a sorry state because of high subsidies (often not going to the poorer sections), public enterprises which run at a loss, and a large and growing bureaucracy whose rising emoluments become the first charge on their resources. Hence, along with strenuous efforts to reduce the fiscal deficit of the central government, there has to be a radical restructuring of the finances of the state governments so that they can effectively focus on their main function of providing the infrastructure for spreading education, and improving the health of the population. These tasks are crucial for being able to reduce poverty successfully.

A large part of growth would necessarily have to emanate from private-sector activities. Hence, maintenance of macroeconomic stability and conditions conducive to high investment is the responsibility that the central government has to fulfil. In order to be able to sustain a high growth rate, it is necessary for India to achieve and maintain a fairly high rate of export growth. This requires that India's products be competitive in price and quality. While competition should ensure efforts by the private sector towards these ends, the government also has a large task to fulfil by providing efficient infrastructure, removing irrational cost-enhancing taxes, and cutting down red tape and procedural bottlenecks.

It has been noted that the incidence of poverty is higher in the rural areas and rural agricultural households in particular suffer from poverty more than other livelihood groups. Growth of agricultural productivity as a part of national economic growth is, therefore, an important requirement for reducing rural poverty. There is scope in several states for promoting land reforms by way of distribution of surplus land as well as through tenancy legislation. As the experience of West Bengal and Kerala shows, such reforms help substantially in reducing rural poverty.

In the meanwhile, the ongoing poverty alleviation programmes would have to be strengthened and made more efficient and cost-effective by enlisting the participation of Panchayati Raj institutions and NGOs. Apart from the Indira Awas Yojana, there has to be an emphasis on promoting house-building by private individuals. It is hoped that the recent amendments to the Urban Land Ceiling Act will be beneficial, although a larger network of housing finance institutions has to be created.[1] The government has already launched a literacy mission. An important prerequisite for removing poverty and empowering people is the spread of literacy and education. Given the large disparity in the rates of literacy between males and females in India, there have to be public and private efforts for educating girl children as well as adult women.

Last, but not least, social movements initiated and supported by concerned citizens have to play a large role in breaking down caste barriers and bringing the SC and ST population into the mainstream. Special efforts to empower them through education and employment have to be augmented.

[1] Steps in this direction have recently been initiated by the central government.

COUNTERING POVERTY

The broad picture that emerges from our survey of the poverty and human development situation in India is that there has been considerable progress in both areas although India has a long road to travel before it can be said that the masses have been lifted from the morass of poverty, ignorance and ill-health. It could also be said that there has been somewhat greater progress in reducing income-poverty than in raising the human development index. What is worrying is that there are wide regional disparities, with the concentration of poverty and backwardness in a few large states — rural poverty is more concentrated in some areas than urban poverty.

The lessons that we must learn from our experience in dealing with poverty and backwardness during the last four decades or so are quite clear: there has to be a much faster rate of growth of the economy than in the past and this growth must be more regionally dispersed. It is of utmost urgency to address the problem of regional disparities. Also, a substantial proportion of the fruits of growth should be channelled to the social sectors by way of government expenditure on education, health, nutrition, sanitation and environment. For this purpose, governments have to shift their priorities away from the manufacture of private goods and many concerns with non-priority areas to the tasks of social-sector development. Finally, poverty alleviation programmes, including the public distribution system, have to be effectively targeted and made more efficient.

If these tasks are to be fulfilled and success achieved, there has to be considerable improvement in the quality of governance as well as in the standards of professionalism among service providers. Vested interests and corruption will have to be ruthlessly fought. Although conditions for change appear quite unfavorable, it has been shown that strong commitment and political will can accomplish a lot. The cleaning up of the Surat Municipal Corporation area on the initiative of one earnest and determined officer is a good example. At the state level, we have the examples of the governments of Orissa and Andhra Pradesh embarking upon a comprehensive reform of their respective State Electricity Boards. Administrative improvements have also been initiated in Andhra Pradesh as well as some other states. There has also been a willingness to take the help of voluntary organizations in social-sector development and poverty alleviation programmes. There are thus grounds for optimism about faster progress in the removal of poverty and human deprivation in the next two decades.

Abbreviations

ADPs	Area Development Programmes
BPL	Below Poverty Line
CAG	Comptroller and Auditor General
CAPART	Council for Advancement of People's Action and Rural Technology
CDP	Community Development Projects
CED	Chronic Energy Deficiency
CESS	Centre for Economic and Social Studies
CMNMP	Chief Minister's Nutritious Meal Programme
CMP	Capability Poverty Measure
CPWD	Central Public Works Department
CSO	Central Statistical Organization
DALP	Destitute Agricultural Labourers' Pension
DDP	Desert Development Programme
DDWP	Destitute and Deserted Women's Pension
DPAP	Drought Prone Areas Programme
DWCRA	Development of Women and Children in Rural Areas
DWP	Destitute Widow's Pension
EAS	Employment Assurance Scheme
FAO	Food and Agricultural Organization
FGT	Foster-Greer-Thorebecke Index (Relative Squared Poverty Gap)
GDP	Gross Domestic Product
HADP	Hill Area Development Programme

HAR	Human Allocation Ratio
HCR	Head Count Ratio
HDR	Human Development Report
HI	Household Income
HPE	Human Priority Expenditures
HPI	Human Poverty Index
IAY	Indira Awas Yojana
ICDS	Integrated Child Development Services
IIPS	International Institute for Population Sciences
IRDP	Integrated Rural Development Programme
ISI	Indian Statistical Institute
ITIs	Industrial Training Institutes
JRY	Jawahar Rozgar Yojana
MWS	Million Wells Scheme
NCAER	National Council of Applied Economic Research
NEP	New Economic Policy
NFBS	National Family Benefit Scheme
NFHS	National Family Health Survey
NGOs	Non-governmental Organizations
NIPFP	National Institute of Public Finance and Policy
NMBS	National Maternity Benefit Scheme
NNMB	National Nutrition Monitoring Bureau
NOAPS	National Old Age Pension Scheme
NREP	National Rural Employment Programme
NRY	Nehru Rozgar Yojana
NSAP	National Social Assistance Programme
NSDP	Net State Domestic Product
NSS	National Sample Survey
NSSO	National Sample Survey Organization
OAP	Old Age Pensions
PCTE	Per Capita Total Expenditure
PDS	Public Distribution System
PER	Public Expenditure Ratio
PG	Poverty Gap

PMIUPEP	Prime Minister's Integrated Urban Poverty Eradication Programme
PRAs	Participatory Rural Appraisals
PRIs	Panchayati Raj Institutions
RLEGP	Rural Landless Employment Guarantee Programme
SAR	Social Allocation Ratio
SCs	Scheduled Castes
SDP	State Domestic Product
SEWA	Self-employed Women's Association
SPARC	Society for Promotion of Area Resource Centres
SPR	Social Priority Ratio
SRR	Social Services and Rural Development Expenditure Ratio
SRS	Sample Registration System
STs	Scheduled Tribes
TINP	Tamil Nadu Integrated Nutrition Project
TPDS	Targeted Public Distribution System
TRYSEM	Training for Rural Youth for Self-employment
UNDP	United Nations Development Programme
UT	Union Territory
WEPs	Wage Employment Programmes
WGDP	Western Ghats Development Programme

1

Income-poverty in India

The official measure of poverty in India is based on the concept of income-poverty. However, since estimates of personal or family distribution of per capita consumer expenditure are not available, the poverty line, which serves as the cut-off line for separating the poor from the non-poor, given the size distribution of population by per capita consumer expenditure classes, has evolved after much debate and differences in opinion. Following the recommendations of the Task Force on Projections of Minimum Needs and Effective Consumption Demand (1979), the Planning Commission has been estimating the number and proportion of poor in India, that is, those below the poverty line (BPL), for rural and urban areas, at the national and state levels. This proportion is known as the poverty or the head count ratio (HCR).

Based on a calorie norm, income-poverty estimates the income that would be needed to provide each individual a minimum of 2400 calories of food intake per day in rural areas, and 2100 calories per day in urban areas. At 1973–4 prices, this translated into per capita monthly expenditure of Rs 49.09 in rural areas and Rs 56.64 in urban areas. To estimate the number and proportion of people below the poverty line in different years, adjustments are made for changes in prices; similarly, to derive poverty estimates for different states, adjustments are made for price differentials.

Though the theoretical basis for using the Planning Commission methodology may be endorsed, the actual procedures and assumptions used to define the poverty line are subject to controversy in India. Different opinions exist with respect to the price indices to be used for deflation and for the adjustment of inter-state cost-of-living differentials. A major problem with the use of National Sample Survey (NSS) data for measuring consumption expenditure is that the total of consumption expenditure derived from NSS data falls short of the total consumption estimate derived from the National Accounts.[1] Until recently, the NSS consumption estimates were adjusted upwards uniformly across all expenditure classes so that these aggregated up to consumption figures from the National Accounts. This adjustment has been regarded as arbitrary. An Expert Group appointed by the Planning Commission recommended in 1993, that this mode of adjustment should be given up on the grounds that the National Accounts consumption calculations rely on incomplete information, and are therefore not superior to NSS consumption figures. The Planning Commission accepted this recommendation. The official estimates are now based on the unadjusted NSS consumption figures for calculating the number of people below the poverty line, and previous estimates have been revised.

The Expert Group endorsed the adoption of the per capita intake of 2400 calories in rural areas and 2100 calories in urban areas as the cut-off line for poverty estimation. The adoption of this definition across the country, and 1973–4 as the base year, was strongly recommended. Recognizing the interstate differences, it was suggested to estimate state-level poverty lines by valuing at the prices prevailing in each state in the base year (1973–4) the standardized commodity basket corresponding to the poverty line at the national level. To construct the state-specific consumer price indices, the observed consumption pattern of the 20–30 per cent of the population around the poverty line in 1973–4 should constitute the state-specific weighting diagram.

Here we make use of the official estimates with a caveat. It is incongruous to use NSS estimates for poverty calculation and the National Accounts Statistics (NAS) consumption figure for all other purposes. If the NSS total consumption figure is the most reliable, then either capital formation or the current account deficit figure will have to be adjusted. It is also to be noted that the estimated figure of food availability in the country is usually much larger than the total consumption of food estimated by the NSS. Again, alternative estimates can be derived by using different price deflators. Hence, it should be kept in mind that a high degree of precision should not be attached to the estimate of the proportion of the population that is 'poor'. However, since

---

[1] Currently the difference between the two figures is about 38 per cent.

the same methodology is applied for deriving estimates for successive years, the temporal trends in poverty ratios should be acceptable.

The methodology followed by the Planning Commission for the official estimates of poverty at the national and state levels has generated much debate at the state level. Moreover, the use of state-level poverty estimates for the allocation of plan resources for poverty alleviation programmes has been contentious. State governments have now become more conscious of their poverty estimates, with many questions being raised about the methodology and concepts used for arriving at these estimates. Questions have also been raised about the adoption of uniform calorie norms and fixed consumption baskets, differentials in the base year prices, and uniformity of deflators across states.

In calculating the poverty estimates for the states, the Expert Group recommended that the all-India calorie norms and the relevant consumption baskets at the all-India level be adopted uniformly for all states. But it has been argued that relating poverty to a single set of calorie norms does not allow for interstate variations and intra-person or inter-personal adaptations over time by the same person to varying calorie needs and availabilities. Although such standardization of calorie norms and consumption baskets may have been necessary to enable the aggregation and comparison of state-wise estimates. Guhan (1993) has argued that the 'estimates do not give a full and true picture of poverty at the state level'. Standardization procedures ignore state-wise differences in normative calorie requirements and consumption baskets. These parameters vary considerably across states because of differences in climate and terrain, levels of urbanization, average incomes, income distribution, local availability of cereals, consumer preferences, cultural patterns, etc. These considerations must be kept in mind in interpreting the state-wise estimates of poverty proportions.

For the year 1993–4, the official HCRs (in per cent of total population) are 37.3 for rural areas, 33.7 for urban areas, and 36.3 for India as a whole. As against this, the estimates of the corresponding ratios derived by the World Bank Study Team are 36.7, 30.5, and 35.0 (World Bank 1997). A study sponsored by the Central Statistical Organization (CSO) introduces an alternative poverty line (using price deflators developed at the Indian

Statistical Institute (ISI)) yielding estimates of 36.64 per cent for rural areas, 28.73 per cent for urban areas, and 35.12 per cent for India as a whole (Gangopadhyay, Jain and Dubey 1997). These estimates, derived by using NSS consumption figures, indicate that more than 33 per cent of the Indian population could be counted as poor in the year 1993–4.

Dubey and Gangopadhyay (1998) emphasized that, irrespective of the poverty line used, at the all-India level, there has been a decline in the incidence of poverty and an improvement in the condition of the poor in 1993–4 over that in 1987–8. Reductions in the HCR could either be because people well below the poverty line go over it, or because people close to (but below) the poverty line cross it. In the former case, the average per capita expenditure will rise if those remaining poor do not experience any sharp fall in their per capita total expenditure (PCTE). In the latter case, the average per capita expenditure will fall if those remaining poor do not experience any large increases in their PCTE. As it is more likely that people close to the poverty line move across it, an increased average per capita expenditure suggests an increase in the PCTE of all poor households uniformly. In addition to the decline in HCRs, there has been an overall improvement in the condition of the poor. The average per capita total expenditure has in fact increased by about 3 per cent over the period 1987–8 to 1993–4 (at 1987–8 prices).

Data on poverty incidence reveals sharp disparities across states and regions, between men and women, and between rural and urban areas. Inequalities also exist between caste and ethnic groups and effect women most. Over the period 1987–8 to 1993–4, each social category had more or less made its lot better along with an overall decline in poverty. Rural poverty reduction is seen to be uniformly distributed among social categories, even though the initial correspondence in the relationship between social category and poverty is yet to be corrected. Thus, caste factors play an important role in the incidence of poverty among households (Dubey and Gangopadhyay 1998: 47).

In 1987–8 the Scheduled Tribes (STs) accounted for 14.62 per cent of all poor households in rural areas and 14.40 per cent in 1993–4. Over the same period, the number of poor Scheduled Caste (SC) households in rural areas was higher. In 1993–4, the SC households constituted 28.24 per cent of the poor households,

3.52 more than in 1987–8. The picture in the urban sector is similar to that in the rural sector.

To assess long-term overall trends in poverty in India the World Bank estimates are used (Table 1.1). According to the World Bank's findings there was no clear trend in the level of poverty from the early 1950s to the early 1970s. The average HCR was 53 per cent during 1951–5, which is about the same as the average for 1970–4. From 1971 to 1987–8, however, the proportion of people below the poverty line entered a period of steady decline, with the exception of one year in the post-reform period. Over the period 1970–1 and 1987–8, the incidence of poverty in India declined at the rate of about 2 per cent per year. In rural areas the decline was somewhat greater. The poverty ratio declined from around 38 per cent in 1987–8 to 35 per cent in 1993–4.

TABLE 1.1

POVERTY IN INDIA 1970–1 TO 1993–4

(POVERTY LINE = RS 49 PER CAPITA PER MONTH AT OCTOBER 1973–JUNE 1974 RURAL PRICES)

Survey period	Head-count index		
	Rural	Urban	National
July 70–June 71	54.84	44.98	52.88
October 73–June 74	55.72	47.96	54.10
July 77–June 78	50.60	40.50	48.36
January 83–December 83	45.31	35.65	43.00
July 87–June 88	39.23	36.20	38.47
July 93–June 94	36.66	30.51	35.04

Source: World Bank (1997: 49).

Wide variations in poverty levels in major states are given for the period 1983 to 1993–4 in Table 1.2. Apart from Assam and Haryana, where there has been an increase in the percentage of persons below the poverty line, all other states have shown a decline in the percentage of population living in poverty over the period 1983 to 1993–4. Kerala, Orissa, Tamil Nadu and West Bengal have achieved improvements in poverty levels of 15

TABLE 1.2

PERCENTAGE VARIATION IN PERSONS BELOW POVERTY LINE IN
TOTAL POPULATION (1993–4 OVER 1983)

| (1) | Percentage of persons below poverty line | | Improvement(+)/ deterioration(−) in the period 1983, 1993–94 | Variation in 1993–4 over 1983 |
| | (2) | (3) | (4) | (5) |
	1983	1993–4	(col 2–col 3)	(col 4 as % of col 2)
Andhra Pradesh	28.91	22.19	6.72	23.24
Assam	40.47	40.86	−0.39	−0.96
Bihar	62.22	54.9	7.26	11.67
Gujarat	32.79	24.21	8.58	26.17
Haryana	21.37	25.05	−3.68	−17.22
Karnataka	38.24	33.16	5.08	13.28
Kerala	40.42	25.43	14.99	37.09
Madhya Pradesh	49.78	42.52	7.26	14.58
Maharashtra	43.44	36.86	6.58	15.15
Orissa	65.29	48.56	16.73	25.62
Punjab	16.18	11.77	4.41	27.26
Rajasthan	34.46	27.41	7.05	20.46
Tamil Nadu	51.66	35.03	16.63	32.19
Uttar Pradesh	47.07	40.85	6.22	13.21
West Bengal	54.85	35.66	19.19	34.99
All India[*]	44.48	35.97	8.51	19.13

Notes: a. Col (4) shows the decline in poverty in 1993–4 over 1983 in
percentage points of persons below the poverty line. Negative
figures indicate an increase in poverty during this period.
Col (5) indicates the percentage variation of col (4) over 1983.
　　　b. * Includes all states.
Source: Planning Commission Press Note: Estimates of Poverty (March
1997).

percentage points or more. Specifically, Kerala has reduced its HCR at an average of 2.4 per cent per year, more than 120 times that of Bihar and four times that of Gujarat (World Bank 1997).

In an attempt to analyse the possible impact of the economic reforms undertaken in the 1990s on the nature and incidence of poverty in India, Abhijit Sen (1996) argues that on the basis of a thin sample, for 1986–7 and for 1989–90 to 1992, poverty seems to have increased sharply only during the first eighteen months of the reform period. Partial data for 1993–4 suggest that this increasing trend in poverty was reversed thereafter. The point made is that

Taken together, these data suggest that there was a very large increase in rural poverty in the first eighteen months of reform but that this trend has been moderated thereafter. . . . [and] that the initial impact of the stabilization/structural adjustment package was adverse, that this impinged particularly on the rural sector, with less impact on the urban sector, and that there was some general reversal of the adverse trend subsequently.

To study whether economic reforms did have any impact on poverty, it is important to distinguish between stabilization and structural adjustment-related reforms. The factors that could have contributed towards an increase in rural poverty in the post-reform years could be the stabilization measures undertaken, poor agricultural performance, and increases in foodgrain prices. The stabilization measures, which included reductions in public investment and expenditure on anti-poverty programmes, could have had an adverse impact on rural poverty. Urban poverty, on the other hand, increased slightly till 1993, and declined significantly in 1993–4. Reform-related measures such as the removal of domestic and trade controls may not have been the reason for the increase in poverty. It is more likely that agricultural performance, management of the food economy, food prices, and stabilization measures were the reasons behind the upward movement in the poverty ratios. Thus, in the years immediately after 1991, it is difficult to distinguish completely between the effects on poverty of stabilization measures and those due to structural adjustment measures.

An assessment of the effect of economic reforms on human development in the 1990s is rather difficult. One way of assessing it could be to look at the trends in public expenditure on health and education, especially post-1991. Economic reforms accord priority to reduction in the fiscal deficit and this often results in slower growth in social-sector expenditure. In actual fact, however, the deficit could not be reduced significantly, and interest payments have therefore continued to edge out beneficial expenditure. This indeed signifies the failure to carry out adequate fiscal reform. Although there has been a slight increase in the central government's allocation to the social sectors, the proportion of allocation by the central and state governments taken together to this sector has been adversely affected.

The mid-1980s saw a deceleration in social-sector expenditure, also due to a decline in the per capita real expenditure on health and education. Since 1990–1, the situation seems to have deteriorated further. The total expenditure of central and state governments on rural development and social services decreased falling from 9.1 per cent of GDP in 1989–90 to 8.7 per cent in 1994–5 (Prabhu 1997). A wide interstate variation exists in the level of per capita social expenditure, and a sharp deceleration in the rate of growth of such expenditure has been registered between 1985 and 1992.

To more closely approximate poverty at the state level, normative calorie requirements and differences in consumer baskets could be taken into account while defining the poverty line. Such an exercise will enable state governments and citizens to closely follow levels and trends in poverty in their state.

CHANGE IN POVERTY IN RURAL AND URBAN AREAS, 1983 TO 1993–4, AND ITS RELATIONSHIP TO POPULATION GROWTH

According to the NSS 1993–4 Round and calculations of the poverty line by the Expert Group, 37.3 per cent of India's rural population and 33.7 per cent of its urban population live in poverty.

In the period from the early 1950s to the mid-1970s, poverty fluctuated without a clear trend in either direction. In 1951–5 the average HCR was 53 per cent, close to the average over 1970–4. The data from the various NSS Rounds reveal a steady decline in the poverty rates from 1971 to 1986–7. The decline in poverty was such that it included those whose consumption levels were way below the poverty line. Post-1986-7, poverty seems once again to have entered a phase of fluctuation, although it is below its 1970s level.

Over the period 1970 to 1986-7, the incidence of poverty in India declined at the rate of about 2 per cent per year, from 53 per cent to 38 per cent. The decline was slightly more rapid in rural areas (at 2.2 per cent per year) than in urban areas, where poverty declined at the lower rate of 1.8 per cent. This differential accounts for the gap between the poverty rates prevailing in rural and urban areas. During the forty years since 1951, average Indian living standards rose, and particularly after the mid-1970s, the poor did not get poorer (World Bank 1997).

It is interesting to note that the trend of reduction in poverty coincides with the years of rapid economic growth in the Indian economy. The annual GDP average increases from 3.4 per cent in the first half of the 1970s to 5.9 per cent in the last half of the 1980s. Over the same period of time the three measures of poverty, viz. the HCR, the poverty gap, and the squared poverty gap declined.

At any given moment, it is hard to gauge how a burgeoning population is affecting a nation's economic prospects and poverty levels. In India, despite reductions in the percentage of poor in the past four decades, due to rapid population growth, the absolute number of poor has increased from around 200 million in the 1950s to 312 million in 1993-4. As a result, India has the largest concentration of poor people in the world, with 240 million rural poor and 72 million urban poor.

The impact, which a reduction in the rate of population growth would have had on poverty cannot be directly established. Two possible explanations can be given for the decreases in poverty: a fall in the rate of growth of population and/or an increased GDP growth rate. It is important to inquire whether states with higher growth rates and a lower incidence of poverty experienced a reduction in the rate of population growth. A priori, a negative correlation between the rate of population growth and per capita income growth, and a positive relationship between the rate of population growth and reduction in poverty would be expected to exist.

A rank correlation exercise was undertaken to test whether a relationship exists between

i)   The annual rate of growth of population (1981 to 1991) and
      the annual rate of reduction of persons below the poverty
      line (per cent) (1983 to 1993–4).[2]
ii)   The annual rate of growth of population (1981 to 1991) and
      the percentage of below poverty line persons in 1993–4.[3]

The rank correlation exercise confirms that there is a positive
relationship between the rate of growth of population and reduction of poverty. However, the magnitude of the change is not very
large, as is borne out by the very low rank correlation coefficient,
0.3762. Similar results are obtained with reference to the relationship between the annual rate of growth of population, over the
decade 1981–91, and the percentage of persons below the poverty
line in 1993–4 (Table 1.3). Although reductions in the rate of
growth of population do have a positive effect on reductions in
the percentage of population below the poverty line, the low rank
correlation coefficient (0.1996) implies a weak relationship between the two.

TABLE 1.3
VARIATION IN PERCENTAGE OF PERSONS
BELOW POVERTY LINE IN 1993–4 OVER 1983

	Percentage of persons BPL (in total population) (1993–4)	Annual rate of reduction in persons BPL per cent p.a.	Annual r.o.g of population 1981–91 (per cent)
	(1)	(2)	(3)
Andhra Pradesh	22.19	–2.61	2.19
Arunachal Pradesh	39.35	0.38	2.8
Assam	40.86	0.1	1.19
Bihar	54.96	–1.23	2.14
Gujarat	24.21	–2.99	1.94

[2] The aim of this exercise was to study whether a positive relationship exists
between the rate of growth of population and reductions in poverty.

[3] This exercise examined, whether reductions in rate of growth of population
over the decade 1981–91 have shown up as lower percentages of the population
below the poverty line.

	Percentage of persons BPL (in total population) (1993-4)	Annual rate of reduction in persons BPL per cent p.a.	Annual r.o.g of population 1981-91 (per cent)
	(1)	(2)	(3)
Haryana	25.05	1.6	2.45
Himachal Pradesh	28.44	5.66	1.85
Jammu and Kashmir	25.17	0.38	2.57
Karnataka	33.16	-1.42	1.93
Kerala	25.43	-4.53	1.53
Madhya Pradesh	42.52	-1.56	2.41
Maharashtra	36.86	-1.63	2.32
Orissa	48.56	-2.92	1.84
Punjab	11.77	-3.13	1.91
Rajasthan	27.41	-2.26	2.54
Tamil Nadu	35.03	-3.81	1.44
Uttar Pradesh	40.85	-1.41	2.3
West Bengal	35.66	-4.21	2.23
All India*	35.97	-2.1	2.14

Notes: a. Negative signs in col 2 indicate a reduction in the percentage of population below poverty line.
   b. Rank correlation [col (1) and col (3)] 0.1996.
   c. Rank correlation [col (2) and col (3)] 0.3762.
   d. * Includes all states and UTs.
Source: Planning Commission Press Note, Estimates of Poverty (March 1997).

In Kerala, Gujarat, Orissa, Punjab and Tamil Nadu the annual rate of growth of population, in 1993-4 over 1983, has been less than 2 per cent, and the annual rate of reduction in poverty has been well over 2 per cent. Kerala had the highest reduction in the proportion of people below the poverty line (4.53 per cent). In Andhra Pradesh, Rajasthan and West Bengal, the annual rate of growth of population as well as the annual rate of reduction in poverty have been higher than 2 per cent, West Bengal had the highest annual rate of reduction in poverty (4.21 per cent). Arunachal Pradesh, Haryana and Jammu and Kashmir had an annual rate of increase in the below poverty line population along with a population growth of more than 2 per cent. Among them, only Haryana had a rate of increase in population below the poverty line.

Measures to encourage reduction in family size, especially among poor households, will have a positive anti-poverty impact. The best way of doing this would be to go beyond income-poverty and address the broader human development canvas captured through the concept of human poverty. This aspect is discussed later in this volume.

2

Trends in Income-poverty in India

INTRODUCTION

Poverty in the Rural Areas: Nature and Trends, 1983–94

The vast majority of the poor in India live in rural areas. To assess the changes related to rural poverty in India, the data of the latest quinquennial round of the National Sample Survey (NSS) (for July 1993 to June 1994) is compared with the quinquennial survey of the earlier decade (January to December 1983).

In 1993–4, more than half the rural population was below the poverty line (BPL) in the five states of Bihar (65.5 per cent), Orissa (59.5 per cent), Assam (58 per cent), West Bengal (53 per cent) and Maharashtra (51 per cent).[1] The rural population of these five states was 37 per cent of the total rural population of the fifteen major states. However, the proportion of the rural poor in these five states was 56 per cent of the total rural poor in the fifteen states (Table 2.1). Of these five states, in Assam the head count ratio (HCR) increased by 9 percentage points over the decade 1983 to 1993–4. West Bengal decreased its HCR by 13 percentage points, while Bihar, Maharashtra and Orissa registered declines ranging between 3 to 5 percentage points.

The head count ratios (HCRs) in the remaining ten major states were below the (weighted) average in 1993–4. Five states at the lowest end had HCRs of 30 per cent or less. Punjab had the lowest prevalence of poverty (17 per cent), followed by Rajasthan (26 per cent), Andhra Pradesh (29 per cent), Gujarat and Haryana (30 per cent each). The remaining five states (Kerala, Madhya Pradesh, Tamil Nadu, Karnataka and Uttar Pradesh) had HCRs in the narrow range of 35 to 39 per cent.

1 The figures written in parentheses refer to head count ratios.

TABLE 2.1
POVERTY INDICATORS, SHARES IN TOTAL RURAL POPULATION AND SHARES IN RURAL POOR POPULATION
IN FIFTEEN MAJOR STATES FOR 1983 AND 1993–94

States	Share in rural population (%)		Share in rural poor population (%)		Head-count ratio (HCR)		Poverty gap index (PGI)		Squared poverty gap (FGT*)	
	1983	1993–4	1983	1993–4	1983	1993–4	1983	1993–4	1983	1993–4
1	3	4	5	6	7	8	9	10	11	12
1. Andhra Pradesh	8.0	8.0	5.45	5.31	34.91	28.56	0.0807	0.0563	0.0282	0.0174
2. Assam	3.5	3.6	3.36	5.16	49.21	58.38	0.0977	0.1265	0.0294	0.0380
3. Bihar	12.1	12.9	16.62	19.64	70.43	65.52	0.2355	0.1819	0.1075	0.0670
4. Gujarat	4.6	4.6	3.26	3.22	36.30	30.11	0.0749	0.0607	0.0229	0.0181
5. Haryana	2.0	2.0	0.94	1.40	24.00	30.13	0.0464	0.0630	0.0141	0.0197
6. Karnataka	5.2	4.8	4.08	4.25	40.24	38.13	0.1117	0.0807	0.0429	0.0292
7. Kerala	4.0	4.0	3.68	3.23	47.18	34.79	0.1301	0.0833	0.0491	0.0291
8. Madhya Pradesh	8.2	8.2	8.64	7.00	54.03	36.74	0.1542	0.0821	0.0602	0.0275
9. Maharashtra	8.0	8.0	8.43	9.48	54.02	51.01	0.1527	0.1445	0.0582	0.0565
10. Orissa	4.6	4.5	5.84	6.22	65.04	59.52	0.2078	0.1528	0.0907	0.0549
11. Punjab	2.4	2.2	0.86	0.85	18.44	16.66	0.0358	0.0268	0.0105	0.0069
12. Rajasthan	5.4	5.5	4.42	3.38	41.99	26.42	0.1226	0.0516	0.0496	0.0153
13. Tamil Nadu	6.3	6.0	6.98	5.28	56.82	37.88	0.1842	0.0897	0.0801	0.0312

States	Share in rural population (%)		Share in rural poor population (%)		Head-count ratio (HCR)		Poverty gap index (PGI)		Squared poverty gap (FGT*)	
	1983	1993–4	1983	1993–4	1983	1993–4	1983	1993–4	1983	1993–4
1	3	4	5	6	7	8	9	10	11	12
14. Uttar Pradesh	17.8	17.3	17.28	15.75	49.76	39.18	0.1377	0.0920	0.0525	0.0303
15. West Bengal	7.8	8.2	10.15	10.16	65.86	53.34	0.2238	0.1256	0.1015	0.0409
16. Total (for 15 states)	100.0	100.0	100.00	100.00	–	–	–	–	–	–
17. Weighted average (15 states)	–	–	–	–	51.27	43.03	0.1495	0.1044	0.0609	0.0336
18. All-India	–	–	–	–	49.02	39.65	0.1386	0.0929	0.0545	0.0314

Notes: a. Shares in columns (3) to (6) relate to the total for fifteen states.
    b. Poverty indicators are based on the official rural poverty line at all-India level based on per capita total expenditure (PCTE) per month of Rs 49.09 at 1973–4 prices. This has been adjusted for changes in state-specific middle range consumer price indices to derive the corresponding state-specific poverty lines. Poverty indicators in columns (7) and (12) are based on these adjusted state-specific poverty lines using the state-specific size distribution of population ranked according to the size of PCTE.
    c. Row 17 provides the population-share weighted average of the state-specific poverty indicators.
    d. Row 18 is based on the all-India official poverty line (see note b above) and all-India size distribution of PCTE which includes states and Union Territories other than the fifteen states included in the table.

Source: Cited in Tendulkar (1997).

The most impressive reductions in HCRs were recorded by Madhya Pradesh (17 per cent), Rajasthan (16 per cent), Kerala (12 per cent), Uttar Pradesh and Tamil Nadu (10 per cent each). These five states together account for 37 per cent of the total rural population and 29 per cent of the rural poor.

Two other indices based on the official poverty line are the Poverty Gap Index (PG), reflecting the depth of poverty, and the Foster-Greer-Thorebecke Index (FGT*), involving relative squared poverty gap which is taken to measure the severity of poverty. Apart from Assam and Haryana, all major states registered a decline also in these two measures.

SOCIO-ECONOMIC CHARACTERISTICS OF THE RURAL POOR

The rural poor can be classified in terms of economic and/or social categories. The economic categories classify rural households according to reported major source of income during the preceding year. These categories are:

   i)   Self-employed households in agriculture
   ii) Self-employed households in non-agriculture
   iii) Rural labour households in agriculture
   iv) Rural labour households in non-agriculture
   v)   Others (non-self-employed, non rural-labour households)

The first two categories, the self-employed households in agriculture and non-agriculture, possess physical assets from which they derive their major source of income. The next two categories, viz. the rural labour households in agriculture and non-agriculture, comprise assetless or virtually assetless rural (mostly casual) labourers earning their livelihood from manual labour. The last (residual) category includes those engaged in non-manual and non-self-employed activities in non-agriculture. Households with income earners having regular salaried and wage employment in mostly white-collar or blue-collar jobs come into this category.

In the social stratification of Indian society, two social groups, viz. the Scheduled Castes (SCs) and the Schedule Tribes (STs) are at the lowest end of both the social and the economic hierarchy. Although the social origins of economic backwardness of these two groups are different, both lack the material and human capital base needed for economic advancement and social mobility. In addition, the SCs face social barriers.

The SCs belong to the lowest rung of the birth-determined and occupation-linked caste hierarchy of the numerically dominant Hindu society, and have been subjected to social segregation by the upper castes. In 1993–4, they were estimated to account for 21.1 per cent of the rural population, dispersed all over the major states. The backwardness of the STs, has been brought about and perpetuated by the expropriation of their traditional land base by outsiders. This has invariably compelled them to shift their habitation to remote, inaccessible and underdeveloped areas. They are outside the Hindu caste hierarchy, and are geographically concentrated largely in the north-east and in the hilly and forest regions of ten of the major states. In 1993–4, they accounted for 10.8 per cent of the rural population.

Trends in Rural Poverty Based on Livelihood Categories and Social Groups

The percentage of rural households below the official poverty line, at the all-India level, for each of the five rural livelihood categories is presented in Table 2.2 for the years 1983, 1987–8

TABLE 2.2

PERCENTAGE OF RURAL HOUSEHOLDS BELOW THE POVERTY LINE FOR LIVELIHOOD CATEGORIES AND FEMALE-HEADED HOUSEHOLDS 1983, 1987–88 AND 1993–94

	Livelihood category		1983	1987–8	1993–4
1.	Self-employed:	agriculture	38.99	35.88	27.11
2.	Self-employed:	non-agriculture	42.89	36.11	29.13
3.	Rural labour:	agriculture	63.20	59.63	50.56
4.	Rural labour:	non-agriculture	44.13	43.66	34.62
5.	Others		29.80	25.40	23.27
6.	All households		46.80	42.25	34.70
7.	Female-headed households		N.R.	41.10	32.70

Notes: a. N.R.: Not reported.
　　　　b. Based on tables in the following sources:
Sources:　Cited in Tendulkar (1997). Based on tables
　　　　1. *Sarvekshana,* April 1988 for 1983.
　　　　2. *Sarvekshana,* September 1990 for 1987–8.
　　　　3. NSS Report No. 409 for 1993–4.

and 1993–4. The HCRs in this Table are for *households*, whereas those presented in Table 2.1 are for *persons*)

A gradual reduction occurred in the HCR for each livelihood category over the periods 1983 to 1987–8 and 1987–8 to 1993–4. Despite that, a little over one-third of the rural households were still below poverty line in 1993–4. For all the time points, rural agricultural labour households had the highest HCR, 50 per cent or higher, followed by other (manual) rural labour households. The major cause of their poverty is clearly the uncertain, fluctuating and low-wage employment. Self-employed rural households had the next lower HCRs, with a smaller difference between households involved in agricultural and non-agricultural activities. The residual non-manual-non-self-employed households had the lowest HCR. Interestingly, the HCR for female-headed households was lower than that for all households.

HCRs (in terms of *persons*) for 1993–4, for each of the three social groups (SCs, STs, and others), and within each social group according to rural livelihood categories, are presented in Table 2.3. Comparing the last column of Table 2.3 with the corresponding column of Table 2.2 it can be seen that the HCR in terms of population is uniformly higher than the HCR in terms of households for all the livelihood categories. Data regarding the socially disadvantaged groups of SCs and STs show that these groups face a higher risk of being in poverty than the non-SC, non-ST population for each category of principal means of livelihood. Head count ratios for the members of rural labour SC and ST households are distinctly higher than the average HCR for all households. This could be explained by the fact that in addition to the social disadvantage the rural labour households have the economic disadvantage of being virtually assetless and overwhelmingly dependent on low wage, irregular and fluctuating demand for manual labour. This double disadvantage (economic as well as social) considerably increases their risk of being in poverty. The self-employed SC and ST households (agricultural as well as non-agricultural) also have HCRs above the average for all households. It needs to also be noted that a larger proportion of the ST population than the SC population is poor.

To carry the analysis forward, the distribution of the entire rural poor population, at the all-India level, is cross-classified according

TABLE 2.3

HEAD COUNT RATIOS FOR RURAL POPULATION CROSS-CLASSIFIED
ACCORDING TO SOCIAL GROUPS AND LIVELIHOOD CATEGORIES,
ALL-INDIA 1993–94

	Livelihood category	Social groups			All households in livelihood category
		Scheduled Tribes	Scheduled Castes	Others	
1.	Self-employed households in agriculture	49.5	40.0	27.3	31.1
2.	Self-employed households in non-agriculture	46.6	40.4	31.1	33.6
3.	Agriculture labour households	65.8	62.0	54.4	58.8
4.	Other rural labour households	54.4	43.8	37.4	41.7
5.	Other (residual) households	32.6	30.9	21.3	23.7
6.	All households	54.2	50.3	33.1	39.0

Notes: a. Poverty line is approximated to Rs 210 in terms of per capita total household consumer expenditure per month.

      b. The official poverty line (corresponding to 2400 calories) adjusted by Minhas *et al.* middle range index is Rs 211.3 corresponding to which HCR works out to 39.5.

Source: National Sample Survey Organisation: Report No. 422 (August 1997); cited in Tendulkar (1997).

to economic and social categories for the year 1993–4 (Table 2.4). Confining attention first to the economic and social categories (taken separately), it emerges that nearly 42 per cent of the rural poor fall into the most economically disadvantaged category of agricultural labour. This category accounts for 28 per cent of the total rural population. Nearly one-third of the rural poor population derive their major means of livelihood from self-employment in agriculture. A little over 42 per cent of the rural poor belong to the two socially disadvantaged groups of the SCs and STs,

TABLE 2.4
DISTRIBUTION OF THE RURAL POOR POPULATION
CROSS-CLASSIFIED ACCORDING TO SOCIAL GROUPS
AND LIVELIHOOD CATEGORIES, ALL-INDIA 1993–94

	Livelihood category	Social groups			All households in livelihood category
		Scheduled Tribes	Scheduled Castes	Others	
1.	Self-employed households in agriculture	5.62	4.76	22.490	32.87
2.	Self-employed households in non-agriculture	0.75	2.38	7.70	10.83
3.	Agriculture labour households	6.49	16.19	18.91	41.59
4.	Other rural labour households	1.45	2.40	3.98	7.83
5.	Other (residual) households	0.73	1.46	4.69	6.88
6.	All households	15.04	27.19	57.77	100.00

Notes: a. Poverty line is approximated to Rs 210 in terms of per capita total household consumer expenditure per month.

   b. Memo items:
   Estimated Total Rural Poor Population   228.1 million
   Estimated Total Urban Population   584.9 million

Source: Cited in Tendulkar (1997).

whereas these two groups together account for only about 32 per cent of the total rural population. Finally, even when considered separately, the SCs and STs are over-represented in the rural poor population.

Poverty proportions in the economic categories within the social groups are also presented in Table 2.4. The poor ST population is almost equally divided between agricultural labour and agricultural self-employed households. They account for about 6 per cent each of the total rural poor population. Almost 60 per cent of the SC poor population, accounting for 16 per cent of total rural poor belong to the agricultural labour households. Among the non-SC, non-ST rural poor population, which is about 58 per cent of the total rural poor, two livelihood categories, namely, the self-employed in agriculture and agricultural labour, dominate by accounting for 22 and 19 per cent of the total rural poor respectively.

Size Distribution of Land and Other Physical Assets

A more detailed classification of livelihood categories within each social group is available according to the extent of land possessed, ranging from less than 0.01 hectare to 4.01 hectares and above (six classes).[2] The first category (less than 0.01) is clearly that of the landless households. The next two categories (0.01–0.40 and 0.41–1.00) are usually defined as marginal farmers, while the category 1.01–2.00 is that of small farmers. It may be noted that these categories do not take account of quality of land so that small farmers in assured irrigation or rain-fed farming areas may be better off than large farmers (categories with 2.01–4.00 hectares and 4.01 and above) in arid and semi-arid tropical areas. Table 2.5 presents the distribution of the rural poor population across land possessed categories for four selected target groups of significant rural poor concentration. They are all SC households, all ST households, non-SC and non-ST agricultural labour households and non-SC and non-ST households self-employed in agriculture.

It is seen that a little over 85 per cent of the SC poor and 92 per cent of all non-SC and non-ST poor agricultural labour population are either assetless or marginal farmers. The remaining two categories, all ST poor and non-SC and non-ST agricultural self-employed poor, are more or less evenly spread across all categories of landholdings. It is noteworthy that 19 per cent of the ST poor and 28 per cent of non-SC and non-ST self-employed agricultural poor, numbering a little over 21 million, belong to the category of large farmers. They are below the poverty line because of the likelihood of low productivity of their land, possibly located in arid and semi-arid areas. Since as high as 33 per cent of the rural poor population belong to households that are self-employed in agriculture, their poverty is clearly attributable to low productivity (resulting from the use of traditional technology) and/or the inadequate size of their physical asset base in relation to their labour endowments.

2 Information on some of these categories is based on a very small sample of households and hence the HCR will have a larger sampling error.

TABLE 2.5
DISTRIBUTION OF RURAL POOR POPULATION
ACROSS LAND POSSESSED CATEGORIES FOR SELECTED
TARGET GROUPS: ALL-INDIA FOR 1993–94

		All households		Percentage non-SC–non-ST	
	Land possessed category (hectares)	SC	ST	Ag.Lab.	SE-Ag.
				Households	
1	2	3	4	5	6
1.	Less than 0.01	16.95	11.00	15.82	0.69
2.	0.01–0.40	52.13	27.41	59.72	11.47
3.	0.41–1.00	16.51	22.46	16.49	29.74
4.	1.01–2.00	8.84	20.07	6.09	30.11
5.	2.01–4.00	3.88	14.09	1.72	17.98
6.	4.01 and above	1.69	4.97	0.16	10.51
7.	All categories	100.00	100.00	100.00	100.00
	Memo Items				
8.	HCR for category	50.3	54.2	54.4	27.3
9.	Total estimated rural population in category (millions)	123.4	63.2	79.3	187.9

Notes: a. Column headings use households for classification into social groups/livelihood categories.
b. Percentages in rows 1 to 7 in columns (3) to (6) refer to population located in the corresponding category of households.

Notations: SC: Scheduled Caste.
ST: Scheduled Tribe.
Ag. Lab.: Agricultural labour households.
SE-Ag.: Self-employed households in agriculture.

Source: National Sample Survey Organization: Report No. 422 (August 1977); cited in Tendulkar (1997).

Land being the major physical asset in the rural areas, it is useful to examine the size distribution of land and other physical assets associated with each size group. For changes over time, we examine the entire size distribution at the all-India level (Table 2.6).

TABLE 2.6
DISTRIBUTION OF RURAL HOUSEHOLDS AND AREA OPERATED BY SIZE-CLASS OF HOUSEHOLD OPERATIONAL HOLDINGS: ALL-INDIA 1961–62 – 1991–92

Size-class (in acres)	Households				Area operated			
	1960–1	1970–1	1981–2	1991–2	1960–1	1970–1	1981–2	1991–2
0.00	26.86	27.41	26.06	21.84	–	–	–	–
0.01–0.99	15.10	14.93	23.96	28.22	1.30	1.69	1.45	3.32
1.00–2.49	15.63	17.94	17.19	20.03	5.77	7.56	9.13	12.18
2.50–4.99	16.17	16.44	14.45	14.21	12.75	14.91	16.71	18.55
5.00–19.99	21.78	19.81	16.10	13.97	44.83	46.13	47.61	45.27
20+	4.46	3.47	2.24	1.72	35.35	29.71	24.13	20.67
Average size of holding per household	–	–	–	–	1.84	1.60	1.26	1.08
Concentration ratios of Hhld Op. holding	0.71	0.70	0.73	0.71				

Sources: Cited in Tendulkar (1997).
1. *Sarvekshana*, January–March 1990.
2. Draft Report No. 408.

At the aggregate level, the average operated area per household has declined from 1.84 hectares in 1961–2 to 1.08 hectares in 1991–2. The demographic pressures on agricultural land are obvious. As expected, these are most conspicuous in the open-ended top size class of household operational holdings which exceed 20 acres. The share of land operated by this size class has declined by 14 percentage points over the 30-year period from a little over 35 per cent in 1961–2 to around 21 per cent in 1991–2. There has been a gradual increase in the share of area operated by the bottom three size groups (0.01 to 4.99 acres). The combined share of these three size classes increased by 14 percentage points over the same period from 20 per cent in 1961–2 to 34 per cent in 1991–2. This increased share of the bottom three size classes is accompanied by an increase in their share of total households from nearly 47 per cent in 1961–2 to a little over 62 per cent in 1991–2. The share of rural households operating no land has gone down from 27 per cent in 1961–2 to 22 per cent in 1991–2. Thus, the sliding down at the top appears to be accompanied by a movement of zero-operators into bottom size classes.

The economic characteristics of household operational holdings of size less than or equal to 2 hectares (Table 2.7) reveals that there are nearly two adult members in the labour force per household among the 'zero' operators, and even in the lowest two size groups. The dependency ratio (i.e. those not in labour force

TABLE 2.7

SOME CHARACTERISTICS OF HOUSEHOLDS
OPERATIONAL HOLDINGS: ALL-INDIA RURAL 1991–92

Size-class of holdings (0.00 ha)	NIL	0.02– 0.20	0.21– 0.50	0.51– 1.00	1.01– 2.00	All
Characteristics						
1. Percentage of Hhlds	21.84	20.28	13.31	14.66	14.21	100.00
2. Percentage of operated area		1.18	4.30	10.02	18.55	100.00
3. Operated area per Hhld		0.06	0.36	0.74	1.41	1.08
4. Hhld size	4.1	4.9	5.1	5.3	5.9	5.3
5. Adults in L.F.	1.6	1.7	1.8	2.0	2.2	1.9

Size-class of holdings (0.00 ha)	NIL	0.02– 0.20	0.21– 0.50	0.51– 1.00	1.01– 2.00	All
Characteristics						
6. Livestock owned per 100 Hhlds						
a) cattle-total	14	76	138	206	228	143
-in milk	3	19	24	33	38	26
b) buffaloes-total	8	33	45	59	90	59
-in milk	3	12	16	21	31	20
c) sheep and goats	20	75	77	93	115	85
d) pigs	2	4	3		6	4
e) poultry	49	14	183	203	223	166
7. Irrigation eqpt owned per 100 Hhlds						
a) pump	0.51	1.58	7.04	11.69	22.12	12.78
b) indigenous water-lift eqpt	14.39	28.29	44.85	45.16	53.07	38.44

Sources: Cited in Tendulkar (1997).
1. NSS Draft Report No. 408, *Land and Livestock Holdings Survey*, NSS 48th Round, January–December 1992.
2. *Livestock and Implements in Household Operational Holdings*, October 1996.

as a ratio of household size), varies between 60 and 65 per cent in the selected size classes. If at least two heads of cattle are considered as the minimum necessary for viable farming, the two lowest size groups do not possess this minimum, and even the next two size groups are borderline cases. Even though between 45 and 53 per cent of the marginal and small farmers (0.21 to 2.0 hectares) possess indigenous water-lifting equipment, irrigation pumps are rare. Thus 62 per cent of the rural households operating some land upto 2 hectares are characterized by a low physical asset base and high dependency ratios.

The above analysis, however, does not provide information on the productivity of assets possessed by these households. The characteristics of operational holdings, as distinct from household operational holdings (Table 2.7), need to be studied to get a clearer picture (Table 2.8). More than one household can be associated with one operational holding, which represents a unit of economic enterprise. Data reveal that there is virtually no

TABLE 2.8

SOME CHARACTERISTICS OF OPERATIONAL HOLDINGS
IN RURAL INDIA BY SIZE-CLASS OF OPERATIONAL HOLDINGS: ALL-INDIA 1991-92

Size-class of holdings (0.00 ha)	NIL	0.002-0.20	0.21-0.50	0.51-1.00	1.01-2.00	All
Characteristics						
1. No. of households* (00's)	25,4249	23,6100	15,4991	17,0686	16,5486	1,16,4173
2. No. of operational holdings (00s)	–	23,6010	15,4962	17,1673	16,624	93,4534**
3. Av. area operated (ha)	–	0.06	0.35	0.74	1.41	1.34
4. No. of parcels per holding	–	1.3	2.4	2.9	3.6	2.7
5. Percentage of operated area	–					
a) owned	–	86.98	87.14	88.18	87.30	87.91
b) leased-in	–	6.98	9.04	8.70	8.53	8.25
6. Percentage of area leased-in by terms of lease	–					
a) fixed money	–	24.37	18.51	11.63	15.11	18.97
b) fixed produce	–	7.51	13.58	15.99	19.09	14.51
c) share of produce	–	19.23	38.73	41.60	40.92	34.39
d) from relatives: no specific terms	–	17.98	9.77	5.21	4.33	7.37

Size-class of holdings (0.00 ha)	NIL	0.002–0.20	0.21–0.50	0.51–1.00	1.01–2.00	All
Characteristics						
7. Area operated by land use (%)						
a) unirrigated and cropped once	—	15.84	24.15	28.33	31.86	35.31
b) cropped more than once	—	14.56	13.61	13.34	12.44	11.59
c) irrigated and cropped once	—	9.39	12.15	11.04	11.07	10.93
d) irrigated and cropped twice	—	21.58	28.04	28.21	25.95	22.97
e) irrigated and cropped more than twice	—	2.75	3.25	2.48	1.88	1.49
8. Percentage of irrigated area	—	33.72	43.44	41.73	38.90	35.39

Notes: a. * In same size-class of 'household operational holdings'
     b. ** Includes 2,4225 operational holdings in the size-class, 'less than 0.002 ha'
       Cited in Tendulkar (1997).

Sources: 1. NSS, Report No. 407, *Land and Livestock Holdings Survey*, NSS 48th Round January–December 1992: Report 2
      2. *Some Aspects of Operational Holdings*, September 1996.

difference between the number of households and the number of operational holdings in the bottom four classes of holdings (Table 2.8). We can, therefore, treat operational holdings as virtually the same as household operational holdings.

What can be inferred is that even the smallest size class of holding has more than one parcel, the number gradually rising to nearly four for the small farmers (1.01 to 2.00 hectares). In other words, these holdings comprise non-contiguous plots even in the smallest size-class. Moreover, the bulk of the operated area is owned by the operators. Less than 10 per cent of the operated area is leased-in. Also, for marginal and small holders, crop-sharing is the dominant form of leasing-in. In the smallest-size class, there is diversity in the terms of lease. Also the percentage of irrigated area varies between 33 and 43 per cent. Thus, Tables 2.7 and 2.8 show that 62 per cent of the rural households not only have a high dependency ratio and low physical asset base, but also possess parcelled holdings with irrigation confined to hardly 40 per cent of the operated land. The productivity of their land cannot be high enough to provide them with a sustained livelihood above the poverty line. Possibly, many of them might be engaged in self-employment in non-agriculture-related activities in addition to agricultural activities. Besides, agriculture might not provide a major source of livelihood for many. Others might derive their major source of income from rural agricultural labour. In other words, these rural households might be spread over three of the livelihood categories of rural poor households presented in Table 2.2, namely, self-employed in agriculture, self-employed in non-agriculture and agricultural labour. While exact mapping is not possible from the available tabulations, an indicative piece of evidence can be put together from the cross tabulation of size-classes of land cultivated into per capita total consumer expenditure class. This makes it possible to derive the distribution of below poverty line households classified by the size-class of land cultivated for the year 1993–4 (Table 2.9). Those households which cultivate land upto 2 hectares account for nearly 51 per cent of all rural poor households. Those cultivating no land need to be carefully interpreted, as they account for as much as 42 per cent of the rural poor households. This category would include totally assetless households (mostly earning their livelihood from manual labour) as well as those who own land but do not operate it.

TABLE 2.9
HEAD-COUNT RATIOS OF HOUSEHOLDS AND DISTRIBUTION OF RURAL POOR HOUSEHOLDS ACROSS SIZE-CLASSES OF LAND CULTIVATED: 1993–94

	Size class of land cultivated (hectares)	Head-count ratio of households	Distribution of rural poor households
1.	0.00	37.3	41.63
2.	0.01–0.40	30.3	21.79
3.	0.41–1.00	34.6	17.05
4.	1.01–2.00	31.0	12.01
5.	2.01–4.00	24.4	5.34
6.	4.01 and above	17.4	2.18
7.	All households	37.7	100.00

Source: Cited in Tendulkar (1997).

Poverty Shares of Four Target Groups: Adult Men and Women, Children and Youth

Finally, it is useful to consider the shares of certain target groups belonging to below poverty line households. The four target groups chosen are: adult males, adult females, children (0–14 years) and youth (15–24 years). Table 2.10 provides the available information for three time points 1983, 1987–8 and 1993–4, for these four groups. Consistent with the overall gradual decline in

TABLE 2.10
PERCENTAGE OF CERTAIN TARGET GROUPS OF POPULATION LOCATED IN HOUSEHOLDS BELOW THE POVERTY LINE 1983–1993–94

	Population group	1983	1987–8	1993–4
1.	Adult male	44.64	40.11	34.00
2.	Adult female	46.58	42.30	35.70
3.	Children: male	N.R.	50.26	45.08
4.	Children: female	N.R.	51.59	46.59

Table 2.10 (continued)

Table 2.10 (continued)

Population group		1983	1987–8	1993–4
5. Children:	all	54.02	50.58	45.79
6. Youth:	male	N.A.	N.A.	30.85
7. Youth:	female	N.A.	N.A.	33.83
8. Youth:	persons	N.A.	41.16	32.28

Notes: a. Age group (0–14) years defines children.
        b. Age group (15–24) years defines youth.
        c. Based on official poverty line.
        d. N.R.: not reported.
Sources: Cited in Tendulkar (1997).
        1. Tendulkar, Sundaram and Jain (1993) for 1983 and 1987–88.
        2. NSS Report No. 402 for 1993–4.

the HCRs of persons over time, there has been a similar decline in the percentage of each target group belonging to the households below poverty line. A more than proportionate concentration of children follows from the higher than average dependency ratio among the households below poverty line. The concentration of youth is lower than that of adult males or females. While the gender difference exists, it is conspicuous only in respect of youth.

LABOUR-FORCE CHARACTERISTICS OF THE RURAL POOR

In the previous section, the population or, alternatively, households, have been identified along two dimensions: those below the poverty line, and the socio-economic group most vulnerable to being in poverty. Agricultural labour households were found to belong to the latter category. The labour-force characteristics of the population in these identified categories are considered below. While the social dimension of poverty is as relevant as its economic dimension, non-availability of relevant tabulation for 1993–4 leads us to confine our discussion to the economic categories alone.

Table 2.11 presents the changes in the composition of rural households by principal means of livelihood (used earlier in Table 2.1) between 1983 and 1993 for fifteen major states, and at the all-India level (Table 2.11). At the all-India level, a 3 percentage point decline in the proportion of households self-employed

TABLE 2.11
COMPOSITION OF RURAL HOUSEHOLDS BY PRINCIPAL MEANS OF LIVELIHOOD 1983 AND 1993–94

		Self-employed		Rural labour		Others	Estimated no. of Hhlds ('000s)
		Agri	Non-Agri	Agri	Others		
1. Andhra Pradesh	1983	29.1	13.4	41.6	6.8	9.2	9455.7
	1993–4	27.7	14.5	41.5	8.4	8.0	11028.1
2. Assam	1983	50.9	11.0	19.5	10.2	8.6	2381.1
	1993–4	41.9	11.5	23.0	11.8	11.8	3551.2
3. Bihar	1983	36.4	12.3	37.1	2.8	11.4	10854.0
	1993–4	36.7	10.8	39.2	3.4	9.8	12351.1
4. Gujarat	1983	40.2	8.3	30.7	6.7	14.1	4127.8
	1993–4	32.3	9.2	37.8	10.0	10.7	5155.9
5. Haryana	1983	40.6	11.6	20.3	11.6	15.9	1795.6
	1993–4	38.5	16.8	15.9	14.3	14.5	2293.1
6. Karnataka	1983	39.7	9.5	36.6	6.0	8.1	4815.4
	1993–4	37.0	12.6	37.7	3.8	9.0	5772.5
7. Kerala	1983	23.3	15.0	31.7	17.6	12.4	3622.3
	1993–4	23.0	15.1	28.2	19.6	14.1	3898.6
8. Madhya Pradesh	1983	53.5	6.4	30.2	3.5	6.5	7635.8
	1993–4	48.4	6.3	34.9	5.0	5.4	9560.2

Table 2.11 (continued)

Table 2.11 (continued)

		Self-employed		Rural labour		Others	Estimated no. of Hhlds ('000s)
		Agri	Non-Agri	Agri	Others		
9. Maharashtra	1983	36.3	8.2	38.6	7.1	9.8	7863.0
	1993–4	31.8	8.9	41.2	8.5	9.7	9557.5
10. Orissa	1983	31.4	14.6	36.4	4.6	13.0	4737.7
	1993–4	35.1	17.1	25.5	3.7	18.7	5954.7
11. Punjab	1983	40.6	13.5	25.3	6.3	14.4	2221.5
	1993–4	33.0	15.6	27.7	7.1	16.5	2548.6
12. Rajasthan	1983	64.1	10.4	11.1	6.2	8.3	4907.5
	1993–4	54.0	10.7	10.0	16.4	8.9	5779.8
13. Tamil Nadu	1983	23.6	13.3	42.2	10.2	10.7	7380.3
	1993–4	20.5	13.0	42.1	12.6	11.9	8937.5
14. Uttar Pradesh	1983	56.2	13.1	18.0	4.1	8.6	16880.5
	1993–4	54.2	13.2	15.3	3.9	13.3	19992.0
15. West Bengal	1983	28.1	13.9	38.3	8.1	11.5	8153.5
	1993–4	27.2	19.7	32.6	10.3	10.2	9983.8
16. All-India	1983	40.7	11.7	30.7	6.6	10.3	100530.7
	1993–4	37.8	12.7	30.6	8.0	11.2	119466.9

Sources: Cited in Tendulkar (1997).

1. *Sarvekshana*, for all-India, April 1998.   2. State-wise Draft Reports for states for 1983.

3. NSS Report No. 409 for 1993–4 for percentage composition.

4. For estimated number of households, NSS Report No. 402.

in agriculture is made up by 1 percentage point increase each in households self-employed in non-agriculture, non-agricultural rural labour, and the residual category of 'others', i.e. non-self- employed, non-manual labour households. This change could reflect diversification resulting from either the inability of the agricultural sector to absorb the growing number of households because of limited land availability or a rise in the average living standards, including a shift away from agriculture, or more probably a combination of both. A 9 percentage point reduction in the HCR for the all-India rural population (Table 2.1) suggests that the second cause must have dominated the first.

Such an inference, *ex-post*, becomes difficult at the state level, except possibly in extreme cases. Orissa and Assam can be identified as two such cases where changes in the composition of livelihood sources are consistent with the direction of changes in poverty proportions (using the livelihood category-specific HCRs at the all-India level, Table 2.2, is a reasonable guide).

In Orissa, there has been a significant decline of 11 percentage points in the poverty share of rural labour households (Table 2.11). This was made up by a 6 percentage point increase each in the residual category 'others', and the self-employed households (more in agriculture than non-agriculture). This is consistent with a decline by over 5 percentage points in the HCR (Table 2.1), although Orissa continues to be a high poverty state.

In Assam, on the other hand, a 9 percentage point reduction in the share of self-employed agricultural households was accompanied by a 5 percentage point increase in the share of rural labour households, and a 3 percentage point increase in the share of the residual category 'others'. This is broadly consistent with a 9 percentage point increase in the HCR in Assam, the only state among the fifteen to experience a deterioration in the poverty situation. Clearly, the first cause mentioned above must have dominated over the second, although Assam is also faced with the problem of the influx of migrants from international borders. The state has also been plagued by militancy. This type of *ex-post* inference does not exist either in the other three high-poverty states of Bihar, West Bengal, and Maharashtra, or in the remaining ten major states. This is not surprising as several factors besides the changes in livelihood composition (Table 2.12) influence the outcome on the poverty front.

TABLE 2.12

AVERAGE NUMBER OF PERSON-DAYS PER YEAR PER PERSON IN
USUAL STATUS (PRINCIPAL PLUS SUBSIDIARY) LABOUR FORCE FOR
HOUSEHOLDS BELOW THE POVERTY LINE, FOR 1983, 1987–88 AND
1993–94 RURAL POPULATION, ALL-INDIA

Year	Activity description	Males	Females	Persons
1983	Person-days at work in agriculture	246	179	220
	Person-days at work in non-agriculture	65	35	53
	Unemployed person-days	30	20	26
	Total labour force person-days	341	234	299
1987–8	Person-days at work in agriculture	256	192	231
	Person-days at work in non-agriculture	75	42	62
	Unemployed person-days	16	18	17
	Total labour force person-days	347	252	310
1993–4	Person-days at work in agriculture	257	208	238
	Person-days at work in non-agriculture	67	36	55
	Unemployed person-days	23	15	19
	Total labour force person-days	347	259	312

Notes: Usual status: Employment in the preceeding 180 days. Calculations based on the tables in the following
Sources: Cited in Tendulkar (1997).
1. *Sarvekshana,* January–March 1989 and April 1988 for 1983.
2. *Sarvekshana,* September 1990 and 1987–8.
3. NSS Report No. 409 for 1993–4.

Data on the average number of days of employment per year
in agricultural and non-agricultural activities, along with unemployed person-days per year for the households below poverty
line is presented for the three quinquennial surveys, i.e. 1983,
1987–8 and 1993–4 (Table 2.12). Normalized over persons in the
Usual Status Labour Force (principal plus subsidiary status),
labour-force person-days varied within a narrow range of 341 to
347 days for males between 1983 and 1993–4. However, there
is a distinct increase in the case of women, from 234 days in
1983 to 259 days per year in 1993–4. This is accompanied by

a gradual increase in the work-force person-days in agriculture
from 179 to 208 days for females belonging to below poverty
line households over the period 1983 to 1993–4 coupled with a
reduction in unemployed person-days over the same period. The
reduction in the HCR observed for women appears to be due
at least partly to the improved employment situation for females.

It is now attempted to estimate the number of labour force
person-days per year for the below poverty line households.
Table 2.13 provides the same information as in Table 2.12 for the
persons in agricultural labour households (the livelihood category
with the highest HCR) for the same three time-points. This table
also provides the number of labour-force persons per household
(PPH) to arrive at the estimated number of labour-force person-days
per year (PDPY). As in the case of households below the poverty
line, we find that the number of person-days in agriculture increased
from 225 to 252 days per year for agricultural labour households

TABLE 2.13

AVERAGE NUMBER OF PERSON-DAYS PER YEAR
PER PERSON IN USUAL STATUS (PRINCIPAL PLUS SUBSIDIARY)
LABOUR FORCE AGRICULTURAL LABOUR HOUSEHOLD
1983, 1987–88 AND 1993–94

	Activity description	1983	1987–8	1993–4
1.	Person-days at work in agriculture	225	251	252
2.	Person-days at work in non-agriculture	26	33	24
3.	Unemployed person-days	46	24	30
4.	Labour-force person-days	297	308	306
5.	No. of labour-force persons per household	2.35	2.26	2.22
6.	No. of labour-force person-days per household per year	698	696	679

Notes: Calculation based on the tables given in
Sources: Cited in Tendulkar (1997).
   1. *Sarvekshana,* April 1988 and January–March 1989 for 1983.
   2. *Sarvekshana,* September 1990 for 1987–8.
   3. NSS Report No. 409 for 1993–4.

over the period 1983 to 1993–4. What is more interesting is that
the number of labour-force person-days per household per year
declined from 698 to 679 over the same period. Equally notable
is the combination of (i) a decline in the number of labour-force
persons per household (ii) a decline in the number of labour-force
person-days per household and (iii) a reduction in the HCR
between 1983 and 1993–4 for the agricultural labour households.
This combination could not have emerged without a rise in the
real wages per day for this set of households.

The reduction in labour-force persons per household between
1983 and 1993–4 is possibly indicative of increased participation
in schooling. This inference is confirmed by figures in Table 2.14
which present the percentage distribution of persons in agricultural
labour households across three major usual status (principal plus

TABLE 2.14

PERCENTAGE DISTRIBUTION OF PERSONS IN AGRICULTURAL
LABOUR HOUSEHOLDS ACROSS THREE MAJOR CATEGORIES USUAL
STATUS (PRINCIPAL PLUS SUBSIDIARY) ACTIVITIES: 1983–1993–94

Year		Activity description	Males	Females	Persons
1983	(i)	Work-force participation	66.6	49.0	57.9
	(ii)	Seeking and/or available for work	0.7	0.2	0.5
	(iii)	Attended educational institutions	14.9	6.7	10.9
1987–8	(i)	Work-force participation	56.2	39.9	48.2
	(ii)	Seeking and/or available for work	0.8	1.3	1.0
	(iii)	Attended educational institutions	11.7	6.1	9.0
1993–4	(i)	Work-force participation	57.3	41.4	49.6
	(ii)	Seeking and/or available for work	0.4	0.2	0.3
	(iii)	Attended educational institutions	17.9	11.2	14.6

Sources: Cited in Tendulkar (1997).
1. *Sarvekshana*, January–March 1989 for 1983.
2. *Sarvekshana*, September 1990 for 1987–8.
3. NSS Report No. 409 for 1993–4.

subsidiary) activities for the three quinquennial surveys. Since the problem of non-participation in schooling is generally acute for females, the table provides the information separately by gender. The year 1987–8 was not normal as it was a drought year in which there was a decline (by 9 percentage points) in the percentage of women in the work-force, relative to 1983. The percentage of males attending an educational institution went up from 15 per cent in 1983 to 18 per cent in 1993–4, and from a little under 7 per cent to a little over 11 per cent for females between 1983 and 1993–4.

Distribution of Labour-force Person-days Across Activity Categories

Finally, for designing programmes for poverty alleviation it is important to obtain information on the distribution of labour-force person-days across important activity categories (Table 2.15). Those who are self-employed in agriculture have concentrated employment patterns. As high as 87 per cent of the person-days are reported in self-employment in agriculture. With the possibilities of work-sharing and work-spreading among the members of a household, there is usually considerable underemployment in this category, with the reported daily status rate of unemployment turning out to be the minimum for this category. Those below the poverty line in this group are faced with a double handicap, that of an inadequate physical asset base (in relation to labour endowment) and its low productivity.

Predictably, those self-employed in non-agriculture spend 52 per cent of their labour force person-days in the same activity. What is interesting is that they report regular wages and salaried employment for 24 per cent of the total labour-force person-days. Agricultural labour households spend 63 per cent of person-days in uncertain, fluctuating and low-wage casual labour in agriculture. But they also spend 17 per cent of their time in self-employment in agriculture. Clearly, at least some of these households own or operate land.

The most diversified distribution is obtained for other rural labour households with 39 per cent in rural non-agricultural labour and between 14 and 18 per cent each in agricultural self-employment, agricultural labour and regular wage and salaried employment. The rates of unemployment for both males and

TABLE 2.15

PER THOUSAND COMPOSITION OF LABOUR-FORCE PERSON-DAYS
FOR HOUSEHOLDS BY LIVELIHOOD CATEGORIES AND LEVELS OF LIVING: ALL-INDIA, RURAL, 1993–94

Activity	Self-employment in		Regular wage and salaried employment in		Casual labour in		Per 1000 unless otherwise mentioned
Household type	Ag	Non-ag	Ag	Non-ag	Ag	Non-ag	Unemployed
1. Self-employed in agriculture	867	33	5	18	36	15	26
2. Self-employed in non-agriculture	140	525	2	238	43	22	30
3. Rural agriculture labour	167	26	31	12	627	41	96
4. Other rural labour	179	46	23	145	138	390	79
5. Others	245	58	25	464	97	43	68
6. All households	461	109	15	89	220	53	53
7. Households below poverty line	415	89	16	22	334	61	63

Source: Cited in Tendulkar (1997).

females of agricultural and non-agricultural rural labour households are among the highest. This is because the lack of a
physical asset base for livelihood makes them more dependent
on the labour market than other livelihood categories. Since this
category has one of the highest HCRs, giving them some kind
of employment guarantee would contribute towards their poverty
alleviation, albeit temporarily. In the long-run, sustained improvements in the productivity of land could lead to a shift in the
demand for rural labour and thereby provide a greater quantum
of productive employment with higher real wages.

Another possibility would be to rehabilitate the rural labour
households into self-employment activity by supplying them with
micro-credit. However, the profitability of sustained self-employment critically depends on the local demand for their output.
Any fluctuation in local demand would have an adverse impact
on the viability of self-employment. In addition, lack of previous
experience in asset and enterprise management would raise the
probability of failure for this set of households in comparison
with self-employed households.

The residual category of 'others' consists of households with
principal means of livelihood from non-self-employed and non-
manual labour categories. These households spend 46 per cent of
their person-days in the labour force in regular salaried and wage
employment (Table 2.15). These are mostly white-collar or blue-
collar activities, which are usually better paying than self-employment with much lower variability during the year. However,
one-fourth of the person-days are also spent in self-employment in
agriculture. Predictably, this group has the lowest rate of person-day
unemployment and the lowest HCR (Table 2.2).

The composition of labour-force person-days for all households
below the poverty line needs also to be considered (Table 2.15).
These households are expected to belong mostly to the first
four livelihood categories of self-employed and manual rural
labour. It is not surprising that nearly three-fourths of the
person-days in the labour-force are derived from self-employment
in agriculture (41.5 per cent) and rural agricultural labour (33
per cent). Their person-day rate of unemployment is somewhat
higher than the average for all rural households. Compared to
the average 5.8 per cent rate of unemployment for this group,
the target group of youth belonging to these households

experienced a considerably higher rate of person-day unemployment of 9.7 per cent for males and 8.3 per cent for females in the 15–24 age group.

TRENDS IN URBAN POVERTY: 1983 TO 1993–94

Urban poverty in fifteen major states, measured by a weighted average HCR, declined by 8 percentage points from nearly 40 per cent in 1983 to 32 per cent in 1993. The severity of poverty based on FGT declined by 26 per cent over the decade 1983 to 1993. In individual states too, a decline in HCR (except for Andhra Pradesh registering a 1 percentage point increase) was associated with larger percentage reductions in depth and severity indicators of poverty. These movements in the HCRs show that the prevalence rates for urban poverty are distinctly lower than their rural counterparts. The weighted average for fifteen major states is lower by 10 percentage points for the urban population in both 1983 and 1993–4 (compare Tables 2.1 and 2.16).

In 1993–4, the highest HCRs for the urban population were around 46 per cent in Bihar and Madhya Pradesh. In another four states they ranged between 35 and 40 per cent: Orissa (39 per cent), Tamil Nadu (38.5 per cent), Andhra Pradesh (36 per cent), and Uttar Pradesh (35 per cent). These six states, accounting for a little over 42 per cent of the urban population, contained nearly 51 per cent of the urban poor population of the fifteen major states. The higher-end urban poverty is thus much less regionally concentrated than rural poverty. It may also be noted that the two highly-urbanized states of Maharashtra and West Bengal together contained a little under one-fourth of the urban poor while accounting for 29 per cent of the total urban population. The remaining (mostly small) states, seven in number, accounted for the rest — a little over one-fourth of the urban poor population. At the lowest end are the two agriculturally prosperous states of Punjab (7 per cent) and Haryana (11 per cent) along with Assam (10 per cent).

While all states, except Andhra Pradesh, registered a decline in urban poverty between 1983 and 1993, the most dramatic reduction of 19 percentage points over ten years has been registered in Kerala — from 48 per cent to 29 per cent. Kerala's urban poverty proportions transformed from above the average

TABLE 2.16

STATE-SPECIFIC POVERTY INDICATORS, SHARES IN TOTAL URBAN POPULATION AND SHARES IN URBAN POOR POPULATION IN FIFTEEN MAJOR STATES FOR 1983 AND 1993–94

States	Share in total urban population (%)		Share in urban poor population (%)		Head-count ratio (HCR)		Poverty gap index (PGI)		Squared poverty gap (FGT*)	
	1983	1993–4	1983	1993–4	1983	1993–4	1983	1993–4	1983	1993–4
1	3	4	5	6	7	8	9	10	11	12
1. Andhra Pradesh	8.3	8.2	7.4	9.2	35.49	36.44	0.0868	0.0850	0.0309	0.0287
2. Assam	1.4	1.3	0.7	0.4	21.02	10.18	0.0392	0.0133	0.0110	0.0032
3. Bihar	5.9	6.5	7.6	9.1	51.29	45.86	0.1494	0.1167	0.0575	0.0418
4. Gujarat	7.0	6.5	6.6	5.9	37.34	29.20	0.0743	0.0663	0.0218	0.0212
5. Haryana	1.9	2.3	1.0	0.8	21.30	11.22	0.0409	0.0196	0.0122	0.0052
6. Karnataka	7.2	7.1	6.8	8.3	37.65	33.41	0.1038	0.0842	0.0400	0.0300
7. Kerala	3.2	3.0	3.9	2.7	47.78	29.22	0.1459	0.0669	0.0601	0.0235
8. Madhya Pradesh	7.2	7.9	9.4	11.4	51.95	46.72	0.1363	0.1269	0.0495	0.0470
9. Maharashtra	14.5	13.7	14.7	14.3	40.36	33.67	0.1166	0.0955	0.0466	0.0385
10. Orissa	2.1	2.5	2.8	3.0	52.54	38.94	0.1531	0.1024	0.0596	0.0373
11. Punjab	3.1	3.1	1.7	0.6	21.58	6.98	0.0463	0.0100	0.0141	0.0022
12. Rajasthan	4.9	5.3	4.6	5.2	37.22	31.75	0.0953	0.0732	0.0344	0.0236
13. Tamil Nadu	10.3	8.6	11.7	10.1	45.14	38.51	0.1289	0.0972	0.0515	0.0365

Table 2.16 (continued)

Table 2.16 (continued)

States		Share in total urban population (%)		Share in urban poor population (%)		Head-count ratio (HCR)		Poverty gap index (PGI)		Squared poverty gap (FGT*)	
		1983	1993–4	1983	1993–4	1983	1993–4	1983	1993–4	1983	1993–4
1	2	3	4	5	6	7	8	9	10	11	12
14.	Uttar Pradesh	9.4	8.5	11.4	9.1	48.14	35.15	0.0406	0.0406	0.0231	0.0123
15.	West Bengal	13.6	15.4	9.7	9.9	28.33	20.77	0.1327	0.0893	0.0498	0.0322
16.	Total for 15 states	100.0	100.0	100.0	100.0	–	–	–	–	–	–
17.	15 state weighted average	–	–	–	–	39.81	32.18	0.1079	0.0829	0.0402	0.298
18.	All-India	–	–	–	–	38.33	30.65	0.0995	0.0752	0.0366	0.0264

Notes: a. Shares in columns (3) to (6) relate to the total for fifteen states.
   b. Poverty indicators are based on the official urban poverty line at the all-India level based on per capita total expenditure (PCTE) per month of Rs 56.64 at 1973–4 prices corresponding to the calorie norm of 2100 calories per person per day. This has been adjusted for changes in state-specific middle range consumer price indices to derive the corresponding state-specific poverty line. Poverty indicators in columns (7) to (12) are based on these price adjusted state-specific poverty lines and using state-specific size distribution of urban population ranked according to the size of the PTCE.
   c. Row 17 provides population-share weighted average of the state-specific indicators.
   d. Row 18 is based on the all-India urban poverty line and the all-India urban size distribution of PCTE which includes states and Union Territories other than the fifteen states included in the table.

Source: Cited in Tendulkar (1997).

HCRs for the fifteen states in 1983 to below-average HCRs in 1993. Ten percentage points or higher reductions are also recorded by Punjab (15 points), Orissa (14 points), Uttar Pradesh (13 points), Haryana (10 points) and Assam (11 points) over 1983–93.

SOCIO-ECONOMIC CHARACTERISTICS OF THE URBAN POOR

The livelihood categories into which the urban population are classified in the National Sample Survey (NSS) are as follows:

i) Self-employed households
ii) Regular wage and salaried households
iii) Casual labour households
iv) Other(residual urban) households

As in the context of the rural population, the basis is the major source of income for a household in the 365 days preceding the date of interview. It may be noted that self-employed persons in urban households would include formal sector self-employed professionals (lawyers, businessmen, etc.) with high returns to professional skills, as well as unskilled self-employed households in the urban informal sector with very low levels of physical and human capital and hence low levels of productivity. A similar distinction could also be made in the second category containing skilled and unskilled workers belonging to households whose major source of income is derived from regular wage and salaried employment. The third category has workers with no regular jobs but with irregular intermittent employment depending on the demand for their labour. This would contain mostly unskilled casual workers. The final residual category includes households with major source of income from activities other than the first three.

Social groups for the urban population and the rural population are the same. However, the SC and the ST population in the urban areas consists mostly of migrants from their rural place of origin. Unlike in rural surroundings, their social origins are not distinguishable from others in large and impersonal urban population densities. Their disadvantage in urban surroundings is thus derived from their initial economic handicaps in terms of lack of education and skills.

For the present analysis, the HCRs for the urban population are cross-classified according to (i) social groups and (ii) livelihood categories (Table 2.17). Confining attention first to the individual categories of social groups and livelihood, certain regularities are found. For instance, SCs and STs individually are marked by higher-than-average HCRs in urban areas. In other words, as in the rural population, these two social groups are also over-represented among the urban poor population. It was also found that among the economic categories, casual-labour households are marked by very high HCRs. Self-employed households also have an above-average HCR. The lowest HCR is predictably obtained for regular wage and salaried households followed by other (residual urban) households, also with below-average HCR.

TABLE 2.17

HEAD COUNT RATIOS FOR URBAN POPULATION CROSS-CLASSIFIED
ACCORDING TO SOCIAL GROUPS AND LIVELIHOOD CATEGORIES
ALL-INDIA FOR 1993–94; PERCENTAGE OF TOTAL
URBAN POPULATION IN A CELL

	Livelihood category	Scheduled Tribe	Scheduled Caste	Others	All households in livelihood category
1.	Self-employed households	49.7	51.7	30.8	33.2
2.	Regular wage and salaried households	26.9	32.2	16.8	19.3
3.	Casual labour households	62.6	65.6	57.0	59.1
4.	Other (residual) households	26.7	42.4	24.3	26.6
5.	All households	39.3	46.6	27.1	30.2

Notes: Poverty line is Rs 274.8 in terms of per capita total household consumer expenditure per month. It corresponds to the official urban poverty line (corresponding to 2100 calories) adjusted by middle range consumer price index developed by Minhas et al.

Source: National Sample Survey Organisation, Report No. 422 (August 1997), cited in Tendulkar (1997).

The HCRs for the cross-classified urban population show that non-ST and non-SC other (residual urban) population record lower HCRs for all economic categories than that for either SCs or STs. A similar trend was noted earlier for the rural population (Table 2.5). However, unlike in the rural areas, the urban SC population has higher HCRs than the ST population for all economic categories. Besides, HCRs for the urban SC population records higher than average HCRs for each livelihood category. This was also the case for the rural population. But, this is not true for the STs. The urban ST population belonging to regular wage and salaried households and other (residual) households have *below* average HCRs. In other words most of the migrant Scheduled Tribes possess adequate skills or other means to maintain above poverty line living standards. However, those in self-employed and casual-labour activities do not have HCRs different from the SCs.

Among the non-ST and non-SC population, only casual labour households record considerably higher-than-average HCRs. All the remaining three economic categories have below average HCRs. Scheduled Castes account for 21 per cent of the urban poor population with STs contributing a further 4 per cent (Table 2.18).

TABLE 2.18

DISTRIBUTION OF URBAN POOR CROSS-CLASSIFIED
ACCORDING TO SOCIAL GROUPS, ALL-INDIA 1993–94

Livelihood category	Social groups			All households in livelihood category
	Scheduled Tribe	Scheduled Caste	Others	
1. Self-employed households	1.39	6.04	33.35	40.78
2. Regular wage and salaried households	1.39	6.18	19.69	27.26
3. Casual labour households	1.32	7.96	16.26	25.54
4. Other (residual) households	0.31	1.23	4.88	6.42
5. All households	4.41	21.41	74.18	100.00

Notes: Memo items: Estimated total urban poor population 58.2 million; Estimated total urban population 192.7 million.

Source: National Sample Survey Organisation, Report No. 422 (August 1997); cited in Tendulkar (1997).

Their combined share of 25 per cent is much lower than their 42 per cent share in the rural population. While SCs are quantitatively significant, and have above-average HCRs for all economic categories, this is not true for the STs. In other words, urban SCs can constitute a target group for poverty alleviation programmes irrespective of their livelihood category.

Of the three-fourths of the urban poor belonging to non-SC and non-ST households, casual labour households with above-average HCRs account for a little over 16 per cent of the urban poor. A higher proportion belongs to regular wage and salaried households (20 per cent), and self-employed households (33 per cent), both with lower-than-average HCRs. These self-employed poor are likely to be found mostly in the widely dispersed and diverse urban informal sector. For these reasons, it is not easy to identify target groups for poverty alleviation programmes which can be implemented without much leakage.

Appendix 1

Monitoring Poverty

SUGGESTIONS FOR SURVEYS

The process of monitoring poverty should include not only the assessment of quantitative magnitude of the problem of poverty but also that of the policies, programmes and institutional mechanisms impacting the poor. With this broader scope in mind, poverty monitoring can be organized into the following broad topics.

1. Poverty Magnitudes

The National Sample Surveys of household consumer expenditure has the data base for calculating the MLS-based poverty measures. The quinquennial surveys (the latest being for 1993–4) take a much larger sample of 10 households per village or urban block compared to a 'thin' sample of 2 households in the annual surveys of consumer expenditure. The annual sample provides reliable estimates for the all-India rural and urban population. The quinquennial surveys provide the disaggregated estimates for the rural and urban population of major states. Within these, households are classified according to (i) social groups: Scheduled Castes, Scheduled Tribes and others, and (ii) socio-economic household types.

In the rural areas, the socio-economic household types cover the self-employed in agriculture, self-employed in non-agriculture, rural labour in agriculture, rural labour in non-agriculture and other (residual rural) households. Four household types have been distinguished for the urban population: self-employed, regular wage and salaried, casual labour and other (residual urban) households. Quinquennial surveys undertake household consumer expenditure and employment-unemployment surveys for an identical set of

A note contributed by Suresh Tendulkar.

sample households so that it is possible to trace the labour-market characteristics of the poor households. For calculating the HPI and CPM the data bases will be very different.

2. Impact of Macroeconomic Policies

Several macroeconomic policies of fiscal contraction as well as structural adjustment can have adverse consequences for the poor on a priori grounds. In this connection, three cautionary remarks are in order.

1. In so far as (i) fiscal contraction is warranted by unsustainable fiscal deficits and (ii) both macroeconomic stability and structural adjustment carry overriding priority for raising the long-term growth rate and (iii) imperative need for rapid economic growth is accepted for its instrumental role in making a lasting dent on persistent poverty, adverse consequences in the short-run can at best be minimized and not eliminated. The rational course of action is not to oppose macroeconomic policies and structural adjustment but to work out equitable cost-sharing arrangements and conflict-resolution mechanisms. Operationally, this would involve monitoring the units and sectors which are adversely affected by the macroeconomic policies and provide effective safety nets to the affected workers to alleviate immediate hardships and to facilitate the mobility of adversely affected segments into faster-growing sectors and areas.

2. Anticipated adverse consequences cannot be predicted for a given area or unit or sector on the basis of changes in aggregate budgetary allocations alone because (i) these allocations become effective with varying lags for different areas or units or sectors; and (ii) effectiveness of nominal monetary allocations differs in different (rural-urban) areas depending upon administrative and organizational capabilities.

3. It is important to recognize that variations in poverty had been taking place prior to reforms due to factors which had their own autonomous dynamics. In the post-reform period, all those factors are not influenced by reform-related policies either directly or indirectly. The observed poverty situation in the post-reform period is, therefore, a combined result of both (i) reform-related policies and (ii) other autonomous

factors affecting poverty but not influenced by the reform-related policies. Often, the observed accentuation of poverty in the post-reform period is blamed entirely on the reform-related policies without making an effort to assess the accentuating or offsetting impact of (ii) above.

3. Anti-poverty Programmes

There has been a proliferation of centrally-initiated anti-poverty programmes over the last ten years with changing administrative departments (with the re-organization of the departments and ministries) to look after them. Several states have their own targeted and general welfare programmes. Rural and urban programmes are under different administrative ministries.

The evaluation of these programmes can be undertaken by two alternative but complementary methods. One relates to the reach of the programme, i.e. what proportion of total rural/urban households or total population of the target group actually availed of the scheme under consideration. This can be assessed through a general large-scale sample survey with household frame covering all households in the population. This type of yes/no question was put to the sample households in the quinquennial surveys of consumer expenditure (1987–8 and 1993–4) with respect to public works programme and Integrated Rural Development Programme (IRDP).

The alternative complementary route is adopted by the concurrent evaluation surveys of Jawahar Rojgar Yojna (JRY) and IRDP wherein the sample is taken from the frame of beneficiary households whose listing is expected to be available with the authorities implementing the scheme. The objective is to assess how far programme guidelines have been followed in the field along with difficulties in following them, possible modifications for improving implementation and some impact evaluation of the programme under consideration.

The recent revamp of the concurrent evaluation surveys proposes to improve its design and methodology on the basis of past experience and decentralize the computer processing as well as the writing of report at the state or district level.

The anti-poverty programme can be examined at three distinct stages: design, implementation and monitoring. The role of alternative delivery mechanisms (block level bureaucracy, NGO, Panchayati Raj) in each of these stages in different areas require careful investigation.

4. Publicly Provided Services

Access to the publicly provided services such as primary school, primary health, drinking water, sanitation, etc. is important for monitoring poverty because (i) these services form part of the public provisioning component emphasized in the human development index, and (ii) access to these services, especially to the poor, complement private provisioning component, covered by the poverty measures based on (MLS).

In this connection, it is important to assess not just the *formal* access, in the sense of there being a physical presence of the facility within certain distance categories from the village or residence, but the *effective* access of various services provided publicly with specific reference to the intended target groups.

Effective access of a given facility for a given household can be defined as a situation where (i) a felt need (contingent or otherwise) arises for a given household, and (ii) an earmarked publicly provided service is used to satisfy the need. For ascertaining effective access, the capability approach to poverty developed and advocated by Amartya Sen can be fruitfully employed in a three stage procedure.

In the first stage, the village or urban block schedule may be developed to assess the formal area level presence and quantitative as well as qualitative supply characteristics of a given facility publicly provided. This can be regarded as *ex ante* capability through public provisioning.

In the second stage, two distinct segments need to be surveyed:

(i) Beneficiary survey to find the characteristics of those who actually availed of the facility over a given reference period and the share of the target segment among the beneficiaries. The frame for this purpose may be available from the records of the publicly provided institutional facility and a quick survey may have to be conducted to record the characteristics of the beneficiaries.

(ii) Household survey to assess the reach of the facility, i.e. the proportion of the total population households during a specified reference period that actually availed of the facility and the share of the target group or targeted segment among the beneficiaries. The reference period will have to take account of the frequency with which the publicly provided facility is needed by the intended beneficiaries.

In the third and the final stage, a sample survey of beneficiary households (identified in (i) or (ii) or both in stage two) may be undertaken to get the qualitative assessment of the service in ascertaining response to the following questions. How frequently did the need for facility arise over a specified long as well as short reference period? How frequently was the publicly provided facility used? Why was it not used when the need arose (in case it has not been availed of)? Whenever it was used, was it found to be qualitatively and in magnitude adequate and satisfactory? Did the facility suit the person specific-characteristics of the beneficiaries?

5. Diagnostic Surveys Public Action

Surveys can be and have been undertaken with a view to diagnosing the causes and designing public policy or public action at the local level. This requires microscopic as opposed to macro-level (areas suggested in 1 to 4) view of the problem at a given level of area disaggregation and for a given segment of the population. In this connection, it is necessary to understand the micro-level processes or causes leading to any given problem to be tackled and the possible change-agents. For this purpose, it is important to recognize the diversity of critical problems across areas as well as diversity of processes or causes leading to the same problem so that correct diagnosis becomes critical for policy or public action.

It would be useful to distinguish at least two sets of causes or processes, i.e. (i) those which are mainly universal and observed at all levels of the economic strata, and (ii) those which have their origin predominantly in the processes generating persistent MLS-based poverty. The point is that economic development may be expected to tackle the problems under (ii) but not under (i) where causes may be associated with culture, attitudes, beliefs, values and social norms. Changing these factors is a slow process requiring social movements as possible instruments. Legislation or carefully designed government policies can at best provide an enabling environment but not solutions. An illustration of (i) is widespread and high prevalence of female illiteracy cutting across economic strata in certain parts of India. On the other hand, sustained under-nutrition is most likely to be associated with a low living standard so that economic advancement can provide a long term solution without ruling out short term alleviation through nutrition-support programmes of various kinds.

It is also important to assess whether a dominant constraint operating on solving the problem lies on the supply or demand side. For example, low levels of enrolment and high rates of drop out for school-age girls may have their origin in the supply side factors (non-availability of schools in the vicinity or poor infrastructure of available schools) or demand side factors (including relevance and usefulness of syllabus as perceived by the parents or economic compulsions). Once we concede that centralized uniform solutions are unlikely to work in diverse socio-economic, cultural and geographical situations, microscopic surveys carried out across a broad spectrum of cross-section situations become critical for (local level) policy and public action.

The purpose of these studies is local level diagnosis of causes and processes and not to provide estimates of macro-level representative description of the problem as has been suggested in 1, 3 and 4 (For discussion, reference may be made to Tendulkar (1989) for combining large and small scale surveys and Tendulkar (1983) for the role of voluntary agencies).

6. Success Stories

In the context of economic as well as social policies, learning from success stories must not be taken to mean their blind replication in different and diverse situations. The idea is to highlight how the same seemingly intractable general problem in one area has been tackled successfully somewhere else. Most of the success stories bring out the important role of motivated local leadership often supplemented by an external change agent (mostly non-governmental organization) in devising area-specific institutional mechanisms which channel collective efforts towards successfully tackling the problem. They provide inspiration and motivation to populations faced with the same problem to overcome inertia and inaction and initiate the process of discussion, diagnosis, and action.

3

Human Development Profile
of Rural India

INTRODUCTION

In 1994, National Council of Applied Economic Research (NCAER) undertook a major survey comprising 33,230 households in rural India and a smaller sample of 2500 households in urban centres as part of a project on human development. This project was supported by UNDP, UNICEF and UNFPA, and was executed by the Planning Commission. The purpose of the survey was to estimate indicators relating to education, health and material well-being for different social groups.

Statistics of selected indicators, viz. level of income, distribution of income, poverty head count ratios (HCR) and a capability poverty measure are presented according to states and population groups. The all-India data are presented for fifteen states, namely Andhra Pradesh, Bihar, Gujarat, Haryana, Himachal Pradesh, Karnataka, Kerala, Maharashtra, Madhya Pradesh, Orissa, Punjab, Rajasthan, Tamil Nadu, Uttar Pradesh, West Bengal, and the whole of the North Eastern region taken together. The population groups are (i) average household income group (ii) poverty-line groups (iii) landholding size-classes and (iv) social groups. Finally, villages are sampled according to their level of development. The distribution of sample households, districts and villages is given in Table 3.1.

SURVEY CLASSIFICATIONS

Household Income Groups

Household incomes have been computed by adding all monetary receipts and imputed money incomes earned by all members of

TABLE 3.1

DISTRIBUTION OF SAMPLE DISTRICTS, VILLAGES AND HOUSEHOLDS
IN THE RURAL AREAS

Name of state	Total districts	Sample districts	Sample villages	Sample households
Andhra Pradesh	22	12	113	2100
Bihar	42	12	116	2155
Gujarat	19	10	88	1606
Haryana	16	11	90	1722
Himachal Pradesh	12	8	65	1225
Karnataka	20	15	135	2523
Kerala	14	8	75	1474
Maharashtra	30	16	151	2765
Madhya Pradesh	45	25	217	4162
Orissa	13	11	102	1971
Punjab	12	8	70	1303
Rajasthan	27	12	106	1984
Tamil Nadu	20	8	76	1456
Uttar Pradesh	63	23	217	4036
West Bengal	17	8	78	1515
N.E states	60	8	66	1233
All states	433	195	1765	33230

Source: NCAER (1994).

the households participating in various types of occupations and
enterprises. The information on returns from farming and wage
labour activities, trade, professions, regular jobs, and rents and
remittances was collected directly. The net agricultural income was
computed by estimating the gross cultivated area under various
crops, and by applying village-level norms of output per hectare
and the respective prevailing harvest prices at the village level.

Although per capita income was calculated, it was decided to
use household income for purposes of income classification. Five
household income categories have been created using the cut-offs
set by the standard income surveys of the NCAER. The class
intervals of annual household income are (i) upto Rs 20,000,

(ii) Rs 20,001 to Rs 40,000, (iii) Rs 40,001 to Rs 62,000, (iv) Rs 62,001 to Rs 86,000 and (v) above Rs 86,000. Fifty-eight per cent of all households fell in the less than Rs 20,000 category, followed by 27 per cent in the Rs 20,000 to Rs 40,000 category.

Poverty-line Groups

It is common practice to estimate the dimension of poverty on the basis of 'head-counts' using standard definitions. This method involves estimating a poverty line expressed in terms of the amount of money required to purchase goods necessary for obtaining the minimum required nutrition and a few minimum needs. After estimating such a poverty line, the population below the line has been further divided by using the mean income of the group below the poverty line. A similar division of those who are above the poverty line has been made. This exercise creates four groups identified as (i) lower segment of those below the poverty line (ii) upper segment of those below the poverty line (iii) lower segment of those above the poverty line and (iv) upper segment of those above the poverty line.

Classification According to Land Ownership

Land and agriculture remain the main sources of livelihood for a majority of the population of India. Therefore, landholding is an appropriate criterion for classification. The sample households have been grouped into (i) landless wage earners (ii) landless with other occupations (iii) marginal farmers (iv) small farmers (v) medium farmers and (vi) large farmers. Conventional land-size categorizations, viz. marginal, small, medium and large, are used to designate labels such as marginal, small, and so on. In this classification, the landless wage-earners are those who own no land at all but work at least part of the time as agricultural wage labourers. A dichotomy is thus introduced in terms of landownership, between all land-owners and all non-landowners.

Classification According to Social Groups

Social groups have been classified in terms of caste and religion. These groups are the Scheduled Tribes (STs), the Scheduled

Castes (SCs), and Other Hindus (who have been categorized under the social group based on caste). The other categorization is based on religious affiliation, which comprises Hindus, Muslims, Christians, and Other Minorities. Sikhs are shown as 'Other Minorities' in the Punjab. These groups are based on the caste and religion of the head of the household, as reported by him.

FINDINGS OF THE SURVEY

Levels of Total and Per Capita Household Income

The Net State Domestic Product (NSDP) normally contains many types of income which do not accrue at the level of the household. For example, profits from both public and private sector undertakings, though they are taken into account to compute domestic product, do not get entirely distributed among households. Similarly, value added due to mining activities, forest-based products and other natural resources gets directly accounted for in the National Accounts, while only a nominal proportion may get transferred to households through wage payment and activities relating to processing, storage and transport. Further, it is also a fact that household incomes, canvassed in surveys, are normally under-reported due to various practical considerations. Hence, directly measured levels of household income are expected to be lower than those derived from the NSDP estimates. Nonetheless, it is useful to compare the observed household income data from the household income survey with the available NSDP estimates. This could, however, be done only at the all-India level for reasons indicated later.

According to one point of view, consumer expenditure gives a better representation of well-being because consumption is believed to be influenced by past saving as well as prospects of future income. However, the objective of studying inequality in incomes or levels of living in a poor country is to display the disparities in the opportunities available to different sections of the population to earn their livelihood. Realized consumption often includes public expenditure on services such as health, education and nutrition, and thus reflect a higher level of well-being than income alone might indicate. Besides, at least in the short-term, it is possible that current consumption is maintained through liquidation of both movable and immovable assets, in which case data on direct income would seem more appropriate for analytical purposes. The NCAER Survey enables us to employ income data.

Interstate Variations in Levels and Distribution of Income

Data on interstate and intergroup variations in annual total household and per capita income are given in Table 3.2. Total and per capita household income donot take into account regional differences in the prices of essential commodities. However, the state-level poverty lines (Table 3.3) have been estimated, taking into account the differences in the state-level consumer prices.

In 1994, an average rural household in the country earned Rs 25,653 which corresponds to Rs 4485 per capita (Table 3.2). The states of Haryana and Punjab recorded the highest levels of household income at Rs 39,956 and Rs 37,418 respectively, which correspond to a per capita income of Rs 6368 and Rs 6380, respectively. It could be expected that the under-reporting of income would be higher in Punjab and Haryana. Other states whose total as well as per capita household income are above the all-India averages are Maharashtra (Rs 29,929 total household and Rs 5525 per capita), Gujarat (Rs 29,356 total household and Rs 5288 per capita) and Karnataka (Rs 27,372 total household and Rs 4769 per capita). Many states such as Orissa, West Bengal, Bihar, Madhya Pradesh and Himachal Pradesh have low household as well as low per capita incomes. Orissa recorded the least total household (Rs 17,208) and per capita (Rs 3028) incomes. It seems likely, however, that this survey has underestimated rural income in West Bengal which is shown to be even less than that in Bihar.

Although total household income in Kerala has been estimated at Rs 29,101, which is higher than the all - India average, the per capita income is considerably higher (Rs 5778) than the all-India average (Rs 4485). This reflects the small average household size in that state. The other states which have lower total household but higher per capita income than the national average are Tamil Nadu and Andhra Pradesh. On the contrary, Rajasthan and Uttar Pradesh have higher household income and lower per capita income than the national average, suggesting a relatively large household size. Except for West Bengal, all low-income states

TABLE 3.2
RURAL HOUSEHOLD INCOME PROFILE (1994) STATES

Region/State	Income (Rs per year) NCAER, 1994		Mean income (Rs per year) household income groups					
			upto Rs 20000			Rs 86000 and above		
	Per household	Per capita	Percent-age of households	Per household	Per capita	Percent-age of households	Per household	Per capita
North								
Haryana	39956	6368	33.5	12816	2378	8.1	103634	12671
Himachal Pradesh	23973	4168	53.6	11121	2165	1.4	86754	10594
Punjab	37418	6380	41.8	11702	2313	7.9	116695	15457
Upper Central								
Bihar	22459	3691	59.5	11366	2094	1.9	111199	11939
Uttar Pradesh	26733	4185	54.9	10701	1966	3.6	106852	11490
Lower Central								
Madhya Pradesh	25319	4166	59.2	11180	2181	3.4	108548	11980
Orissa	17208	3028	73.8	9451	1833	1.0	92179	10911
Rajasthan	27184	4229	55.5	11437	2089	3.7	106688	10672
*East***								
North Eastern Region	28160	5070	43.5	12527	2441	1.9	82286	12207
West Bengal	18113	3157	71.2	10947	2155	0.7	79482	8106

Region/State	Income (Rs per year) NCAER, 1994		Mean income (Rs per year) household income groups					
			upto Rs 20000			Rs 86000 and above		
	Per household	Per capita	Percentage of households	Per household	Per capita	Percentage of households	Per household	Per capita
West								
Gujarat	29356	5288	56.3	10869	2163	5.2	134449	19506
Maharashtra	29929	5525	56.3	11203	2389	5.7	123479	15811
South								
Andhra Pradesh	24776	5046	58.1	11322	2559	3.2	117052	20121
Karnataka	27372	4769	59.7	10168	1969	4.8	124399	17305
Kerala	29101	5778	49.7	12442	2840	4.3	110816	18339
Tamil Nadu	23271	5122	59.4	10458	2481	2.8	96874	15929
*Rural India**	25653	4485	57.6	11027	2192	3.4	110477	13778

Notes: a. * The all India Rural NSDP estimated indirectly based on CSO figure is Rs 5036.
b. ** The PCI estimate for Assam represents the North Eastern Region. The correlation coefficient between estimates of per capita income by NCAER and CSO estimates is 0.79. The corresponding rank correlation is 0.80.

Source: NCAER/HI Survey (1994).

TABLE 3.3
POVERTY ESTIMATES FOR RURAL INDIA

Region/State	Estimated poverty line* (Rs per capita per year)	Head count ratio (HCR)		Sen index of poverty	Gini ratio	Capability poverty measure (CPM)***	
		NCAER 1994	Expert group 1993–94			CPM1	CPM2
1	2	3	4	5	6	7	8
North							
Haryana	2818	27	28	0.11	0.37	46.8	38.3
Himachal Pradesh	2818	45	30	0.23	0.39	48.4	39.4
Punjab	2818	32	12	0.15	0.39	35.5	29.1
Upper Central							
Bihar	2535	42	58	0.21	0.39	65.6	56.9
Uttar Pradesh	2557	40	42	0.22	0.42	60.6	53.3
Lower Central							
Madhya Pradesh	2324	40	41	0.15	0.41	56.3	46.3
Orissa	2330	55	50	0.30	0.42	55.1	49.9
Rajasthan	2623	40	27	0.20	0.41	65.8	58.0
East							
North Eastern Region	2775	33	45**	0.12	0.34	40.4	36.4
West Bengal	2642	51	41	0.24	0.35	53.2	46.7

Region/State	Estimated poverty line* (Rs per capita per year)	Head count ratio (HCR)		Sen index of poverty	Gini ratio	Capability poverty measure (CPM)***	
		NCAER 1994	Expert group 1993–94			CPM1	CPM2
1	2	3	4	5	6	7	8
West							
Gujarat	2418	39	22	0.19	0.49	45.2	39.3
Maharashtra	2338	34	38	0.13	0.45	46.3	39.9
South							
Andhra Pradesh	1954	21	16	0.08	0.42	41.6	35.3
Karnataka	2241	33	29	0.18	0.49	47.5	38.7
Kerala	2922	30	26	0.13	0.40	12.0	10.7
Tamil Nadu	2370	34	33	0.16	0.43	29.6	23.7
Rural India	2444	39	37	0.18	0.43	52.3	45.0

Notes: a. * The poverty line for 1973–4, estimated by the planning commission, have been updates using consumer price index for agriculture labour (CPIAL) as inflator.

b. ** Represents Assa.

c. *** CPM1 has been computed using the 'stunting' concept wheras for the computation of CPM2 the 'wasting' concept has been made use of.

Sources: 1. Column (4): Planning Commission: Estimates of Poverty, Government of India, 11 March 1997.

2. NCAER/HI Survey (1994).

fall in the central region of the country and cover more than 50 per cent of India's population.

The households with an annual income of upto Rs 20,000 are 58 per cent of the total households in rural India, while only 3.4 per cent of all households belong to the richest category of Rs 86,000 and above. In Orissa and West Bengal 74 and 71 per cent of rural households respectively, fall in the annual household income category of upto Rs 20,000. Haryana and Punjab have lower proportions of households in this income category. The scenario is exactly the opposite for the richer income class. Haryana and Punjab have about 8 per cent of rural households in this income class, whereas Orissa and West Bengal have only about 1 per cent of their households in this class.

Differences in Levels and Distribution of Income among Population Groups

Table 3.4 presents the household and per capita incomes according to the following population groups: household income groups, poverty line groups, landholding categories, social groups, and village development groups.

The mean household incomes for the five income classes are Rs 11,027, Rs 28,141, Rs 49,072, Rs 72,178 and Rs 1,47,855 respectively. The corresponding per capita incomes are Rs 2192, Rs 4506, Rs 7132, Rs 9309 and Rs 17,865. The household income of the upper most size-class is about 12.4 times higher than the lowest group's income. In the case of per capita income, it is seven times larger. The Gini ratio, which presents relative dispersion within the group, is relatively low only for the highest income category.

The mean levels of household income for the four poverty-line groups are Rs 6950, Rs 12,379, Rs 22,138, and Rs 58,100, respectively. Households grouped under the lower segment below the poverty line (about 16 per cent of the households) have an average per capita income of only Rs 1095 per year (24 per cent of mean income), followed by Rs 2026 per year (45 per cent of mean income) for those in the upper segment below the poverty line (18.8 per cent of all households). Per capita per day availability of incomes, Rs 3 and Rs 5.5 respectively, is too low even to satisfy the survey calorie requirements during the year 1994. The Gini ratios are extremely low for all the four poverty-based categories,

TABLE 3.4

RURAL HOUSEHOLD INCOME PROFILE, POPULATION GROUPS (1994)

Population group	Percentage distribution of households	Mean income (Rs per year)		Head count ratio	Sen Index of poverty	Gini ratio	Capability poverty measure (CPM)	
		Per household	Per capita				CPM1	CPM2
Household income groups								
Upto 20,000	57.6	11027	2192	69	0.34	0.23	56.3	48.5
20,001 to 40,000	26.8	28141	4506	13	0.03	0.25	50.1	43.5
40,001 to 62,000	8.9	49072	7132	2	–	0.20	51.4	43.8
62,001 to 86,000	3.3	72178	9309	–	–	0.21	44.1	37.1
Above 86,000	3.4	147855	17865	–	–	0.07	37.4	31.2
Poverty-line groups								
Lower segment below	15.9	6950	1095	100	0.63	0.16	58.2	50.7
Upper segment below	18.8	12379	2026	100	0.22	0.07	56.3	49.2
Lower segment above	43.7	22138	3931	–	–	0.12	50.9	43.6
Upper segment above	21.6	58100	11396	–	–	0.17	42.3	35.1

Table 3.4 (continued)

Table 3.4 (continued)

Population group	Percentage distribution of households	Mean income (Rs per year)		Head count ratio	Sen Index of poverty	Gini ratio	Capability poverty measure (CPM)	
		Per household	Per capita				CPM1	CPM2
Landholding groups								
Landless wage-earners	19.4	11313	2308	68	0.35	0.30	56.4	47.4
Marginal	31.4	19586	3502	45	0.21	0.39	53.8	46.5
Small	18.1	29377	4803	27	0.11	0.36	52.3	45.5
Medium	8.8	44695	6516	16	0.07	0.37	51.7	44.3
Large	5.0	85969	10930	11	0.05	0.27	48.0	42.5
Landless others	17.2	21574	4111	37	0.16	0.36	47.7	42.8
Social groups								
Caste								
Scheduled Tribes	11.3	19556	3504	51	0.24	0.42	60.0	57.4
Scheduled Castes	23.7	17465	3237	50	0.24	0.32	67.9	50.6
Other Hindus	65.0	29786	5113	32	0.15	0.45	49.3	42.0
Religion								
Hindus	85.5	25713	4514	39	0.15	0.43	–	–
Muslims	9.2	22807	3678	43	0.19	0.40	56.1	48.6

Population group	Percentage distribution of households	Mean income (Rs per year)		Head count ratio	Sen Index of poverty	Gini ratio	Capability poverty measure (CPM)	
		Per household	Per capita				CPM1	CPM2
Religion								
Christians	2.4	28860	5920	27	0.12	0.39	26.3	20.6
Ohter Minorities	2.9	30330	5427	34	0.17	0.42	47.0	40.1
Adult literacy group								
Non literate	29.7	15271	3138	45	0.17	0.28	67.5	59.1
Female literate	3.1	19060	3987	43	0.21	0.42	35.9	30.1
Male literate	32.2	24367	4137	39	0.19	0.41	63.0	55.4
Both literate	35.1	36187	5683	27	0.12	0.42	34.9	28.6
Village development groups								
Low	29.0	24149	4045	43	0.21	0.42	60.8	53.8
Medium	39.4	25173	4369	38	0.18	0.41	52.8	48.2
High	31.6	27628	5079	33	0.15	0.45	42.0	34.7
All groups	100.0	25653	4485	39	0.18	0.43	52.4	45.1

Notes: a. CPM1 is based on 'stunting' and CPM2 on 'wasting'.
b. The sign – indicates that the data is either not available or not applicable.

Source: NCAER/HI Survey (1994).

showing a high degree of homogeneity in levels of income within these groups.

Twenty-two per cent of the households classified in the upper segment above the poverty line have a per capita income of Rs 11,396, which is 2.5 times the national average and 10.4 times the per capita income of those belonging to the lower segment below the poverty line. Data show that per capita income increases considerably with the size of the landholding. For example, landless wage earners have an average per capita income of Rs 2308 per annum, which is only 52 per cent of the all-India average of Rs 4485. For marginal farmers the corresponding figure is 78 per cent; while it is 107 per cent for small farmers, 145 per cent for the medium farmers, and 244 per cent for large farmers. Thus, in India, rural incomes are clearly a function of the size of the landholding. The Gini ratios for all these categories are moderate.

The NCAER Report (1994) lists (i) Agriculture (ii) Salaried, Professional and Self Employed (iii) Wage Earners (iv) All Others under Occupational Groups in its classification of population groups. The levels of income are high for the salaried, professional and trader classes who constitute about 13 per cent of all rural households (data not presented). Their per capita income is 31 per cent higher than the average for all groups, and their income is 2.4 times that of the wage-earners category. Wage-earners have recorded a per capita income of 45 per cent lower than the average for all groups. The wage-earners' income is only Rs 2450 per capita per year (Rs 6.70 per day per person) which is about 58 per cent lower than that for the salaried, professionals and traders, and 55 per cent less than that for the farmers. Wage-earners are a more homogeneous group in terms of income, as reflected by the Gini ratios.

While the household income increases consistently with the size of household (data not presented), the per capita income in fact falls. This phenomenon is indicative of the differences in the composition of households in terms of age and sex as well as in terms of the number of earning members. It is, therefore, desirable to undertake age standardized estimates to substantiate most of the above comparisons. However, household size is closely associated with the life-cycle characteristics which cause changes in both the size and composition of households and in turn affect the levels of income. Per capita income is about 30 per cent lower for large households (eight and above members) than for households with four or fewer persons.

The analysis of the distribution of income by social groups shows that both the total household income and per capita income are the least for the SCs followed by STs. Scheduled Castes have an average household income of Rs 19,556 and per capita income of Rs 3504 which is only about 68 per cent of the mean household income for all groups and 72 per cent of the mean per capita income. Scheduled Caste household income is only 59 per cent and per capita income is only 63 per cent of the corresponding levels of income of Other Hindus. Similarly, the STs have about 66 per cent of the household and 69 per cent of the per capita income of Other Hindus. On the whole, however, Other Hindus have a total household income of Rs 29,786 and per capita income of Rs 5113 per annum which is 14 per cent higher than the average for all groups.

Among the religious categories, Christians recorded the highest level of household income of Rs 28,860 per annum followed by the Hindus with Rs 25,713 and Muslims with Rs 22,807. The per capita income differences between the religious groups are pronounced due to vast differences in their family sizes. Per capita incomes were estimated at Rs 5920 for Christians, Rs 4514 for Hindus and Rs 3678 for Muslims.

As expected, the levels of both household and per capita income increase according to the level of village development. For example, developed villages have 25 per cent higher per capita income than the less developed villages. The share of income from non-agricultural sources is found to be higher in the developed villages

Levels of Poverty and Intensity of Poverty

A HCR is computed to measure the extent of poverty. This is the percentage of population which earns a certain level of income or has consumption expenditure below what is considered to be the poverty line. The HCR has been generally estimated on the basis of household expenditure data collected by the National Sample Survey Organization (NSSO) through nationally representative sample surveys. Household income has rarely been used to compute the HCR mainly because of the dearth of income data collected at regular intervals. The National Council of Applied Economic Research, however, has collected data on incomes from nationally representative sample surveys.

Interstate Variations in the Head Count Ratio

Poverty lines presented in Table 3.3 have been calculated by updating the Planning Commission's computation using the consumer price index for agriculture labour (CPIAL) to take into account state-level differences in prices and rates of inflation.

In rural India, the poverty line is high in Kerala, Punjab, Haryana, Himachal Pradesh, and in the North Eastern states. This suggests that a higher level of prices prevail in those states. Andhra Pradesh, Karnataka, Maharashtra, Madhya Pradesh and Orissa have a lower poverty line. Based on this poverty line, the HCR for rural India was estimated to be 39 per cent in 1994. The highest percentage of poor is found in Orissa (55 per cent), followed by West Bengal (51 per cent), Himachal Pradesh (45 per cent), Bihar (42 per cent), Uttar Pradesh, Madhya Pradesh and Rajasthan (40 per cent each). Lower proportions of poor are found in Andhra Pradesh, Haryana, Kerala, Punjab, Karnataka, Tamil Nadu and Maharashtra.

The comparison between the HCR calculated by NCAER and by the Expert Group, for the year 1993–4, show similar levels of incidence of poverty in the states of Haryana, Uttar Pradesh, Madhya Pradesh, Orissa, Maharashtra and Tamil Nadu. However, there is a significant discrepancy in the levels of HCR for the state of Punjab; 32 per cent according to the NCAER estimates, and 12 per cent according to the Expert Group's estimates. This may be partly due to the relatively higher under-reporting of household income in the Punjab. The NCAER computations seem to have also underestimated the HCR in Bihar.

The mean per capita income of those below the poverty line is Rs 1591 per annum, which is only 35 per cent of the overall per capita income of Rs 4485 for rural India. This income is around one-quarter of the respective per capita incomes in Punjab, Karnataka, Maharashtra and Gujarat, and over 40 per cent of per capita incomes in Orissa, Kerala and Madhya Pradesh. The depth or intensity of poverty as measured by the Sen Index is high in the states which have higher HCRs and Gini ratios. The states of Haryana, Maharashtra, Andhra Pradesh and Punjab have a lower Sen Index than the national average. Similarly, the states of Orissa, Uttar Pradesh, Kerala and Rajasthan have a Sen Index higher than the national average, indicating a wider disparity of income among the poor.

A simple distribution of households according to poverty groups suggests that Orissa and West Bengal have almost one quarter of their rural households in the lower segment below the poverty line. Andhra Pradesh has the least proportion of households in this category. This is probably because of the lower level of consumer price index reported for Andhra Pradesh. However, it is apparent that even in Haryana and Punjab over 10 per cent and 14 per cent of households, respectively, live in abject poverty.

Income Differences among Population Groups

The poverty estimates according to the classification by population groups (Table 3.4) show that the HCR declines substantially as landholding size increases. The HCR, which is 68 per cent for the landless wage earners decreases to 45 for marginal, 27 for small, 16 for medium and to only 11 for large farmers.

Both the incidence and intensity of poverty are higher among the STs and SCs than among Other Hindus. The HCR is about 50 among the STs and the SCs, compared with only 32 among Other Hindus. The Sen Index is as high as 0.24 among the STs and SCs compared to only 0.15 among Other Hindus. The HCR is 43 per cent among Muslims, compared with only 27 among Christians, and 39 among Hindus. The Sen Index is low only for Christians.

However, the highest intensity of poverty is among the households classified as the lower segment below the poverty line, with a Sen Index of 0.63.

CAPABILITY POVERTY MEASURE

The capability poverty measure (CPM), introduced by the UNDP in 1996, is a multi-dimensional measure of human deprivation, which indicates the percentage of people who lack basic, or minimally essential, human capabilities. This index is a simple average of three basic deprivation indicators, namely (i) percentage of children who are undernourished (ii) percentage of women who have undergone non-institutional deliveries, and (iii) female il-literacy rate. Since undernutrition is often measured using both the stunting and wasting concepts, we computed CPM1 using the incidence of stunting (−3 standard deviation) of children aged 0–4 years of age and CPM2 using the incidence of wasting (−2 standard deviation) of children aged 0–4 years of age.

The CPM based on stunting (CPM1) is 7 percentage points larger than the CPM based on the wasting concept (Table 3.3). The comparison between the HCR (39 per cent) and the CPM1 (52.4 per cent) both at the all-India level, shows the relatively limited role the direct income measure has in assessing the state of human development, as well as the glaring difference between these two measures. While enhancing levels of income is normally the objective of national planning and macroeconomic restructur-ing, an improvement in human development is possible only through adequate investments and the provision of efficient ser-vices in priority social sectors such as mass education, public and primary health care, and child nutrition.

Except in the case of Kerala, and to some extent Tamil Nadu, the CPM1 presents a picture which is more negative than the income-poverty parameter. While the HCR is 42 and 40 per cent in Bihar and Uttar Pradesh respectively, the corresponding CPM1 is 66 and 61 per cent. The CPM1 is as high as 36 per cent in Punjab, and around 46 per cent in the developed states of Haryana, Gujarat and Maharashtra.

An interesting feature of the HCRs and the CPM1s is their distribution according to income and poverty classes (Table 3.4). While the HCR drops sharply from 69 to 13 per cent, and then to 2 per cent, respectively, for the first three income groups, CPM1 falls only from 56 to 50.1 and 51.4 per cent. Thus, the HCR falls a lot more than the CPM1 when we move down income classes as well as the poverty-line groups. This again strengthens the conviction that a rise in income alone cannot be the sole means of improving human development.

There are noteworthy differences both in the HCRs and in CPM1 according to social groups identified in terms of caste and religion. The CPM1 is as high as 60 per cent among the STs, 67 per cent among the SCs, and 56 per cent among the Muslims. One also notices a clear fall in the CPM1 measure according to the levels of village development.

CONCLUSION

A large proportion of India's population still survives on scarce resources. The level of income-poverty was estimated to have been 39 per cent in rural India during 1994. While there are interstate differences, the level of absolute deprivation in general is considerable. Also, relative differences in deprivation among various population groups continue to exist. This has been substantiated by presenting levels and differences in household and per capita income, and by estimating the HCRs using the Planning Commission Expert Group methodology.

The second dimension discussed in this chapter points to a large gap between income-poverty and capability poverty. It is instructive to note that the programmes and policies aiming at reducing income-poverty do not necessarily guarantee a reduction in capability poverty. It is important to note that besides substantial increase in public and private sector investment in vital social sectors, there is a need for mobilizing communities and social institutions to eradicate income and capability poverty.

4

Food Security and the Poor

INTRODUCTION

The concept of food security has undergone considerable modification in recent years. Food availability and stability in food production were considered good measures of food security till the 1970s, and the achievement of self-sufficiency was accorded a high priority in the food policies of developing countries. Although some countries have been successful in achieving self-sufficiency by increasing food production and improving their capacity to cope with fluctuations in food production, they have not been able to solve the problem of chronic household food insecurity. This has led to a change in approach, with prominence now being given to the food energy intake of vulnerable groups.

It has now become common practice to estimate the number of food insecure households by comparing their calorie intake with stipulated norms. However, the widely accepted norms of levels of food required for overcoming undernutrition have been questioned. Nutritionists argue that energy intake is a poor measure of nutritional status because the latter depends not only on nutrient intake but also on non-nutrient food attributes, privately and publicly provided inputs and health status (Martorell and Ho 1984). It has been suggested, that the assessment of malnutrition should be based on output measures rather than input measures. Output indicators are in fact more closely related to health and functional capacity than input measures (Martorell and Ho 1984).

In policy design, a distinction is made between households that are chronically food insecure and those that are transitorily food insecure (those who are temporarily subject to hunger during the off-season, or in drought and inflationary years). While the problem of chronic food insecurity is primarily associated with poverty, transitory food insecurity is associated with the risks related to either access to, or availability of food. The strategy to overcome chronic food insecurity includes short-term intervention to raise the purchasing power of the poor through endowment of land and non-land assets with the help of programmes which generate employments. Long-term growth-mediated interventions to improve food availability and raise incomes (agricultural production programmes, infrastructure, human resource development, etc.) are also included. Policies such as price stabilization, easy credit, crop insurance and temporary employment creation are utilized for stabilizing the consumption of the transitorily food insecure groups.

India is one of the few countries that has experimented with a broad spectrum of programmes for improving food security. It has already made substantial progress in terms of overcoming transient food insecurity through public procurement and distribution of foodgrains, employment programmes, etc. However, despite a significant reduction in the incidence of poverty (from 55 per cent in 1973–4 to 36 per cent in 1993–4), chronic food insecurity persists with a large proportion of the population still below the poverty line.

Here a review of the trends in food and nutrition deprivation in India is presented, using a wide range of input and output measures, including per capita consumption of food, per capita food energy intake, and the extent of malnutrition based on anthropometric measures.[1] The main focus is on household food and nutrition deprivation.

FOOD PRODUCTION

Over the years, India has made rapid progress in the production of food (Table 4.1). India achieved near self-sufficiency in the availability of foodgrains by the mid-1970s. The annual growth rate of food production (including non-cereal food) increased from 2.1 per cent during the 1960s to 3.0 per cent in the 1970s and further to 3.8 per cent during the 1980s.[2] Although from 1960 to

---

[1] This chapter draws from Rao and Radhakrishna (1997).

[2] The growth rates of food and agricultural production in various sub-periods are similar since food accounts for a major portion of the agricultural output (see Table 4.1).

1980, food production barely kept pace with population growth rates, in the 1980s, per capita food production increased at 1.6 per cent per annum, a satisfactory rate. The 1980s have seen some diversification in food production, reflected in the impressive growth of the output of oilseeds and livestock products, in conformity with the growth pattern of domestic demand.

TABLE 4.1
ANNUAL COMPOUND GROWTH RATES
FOR FOOD AND AGRICULTURAL PRODUCTION

Period	Food production (per cent per annum)		Agricultural production (per cent per annum)	
	Aggregate	Per capita	Aggregate	Per capita
1961–3 – 1971–3	2.11	–0.21	2.03	–0.18
1971–3 – 1981–3	3.00	0.84	3.20	0.90
1981–3 – 1991–3	3.77	1.62	3.82	1.76
1961–3 – 1991–3	2.96	0.75	3.01	0.82

	Food availability (per cent per annum)		
	K.cal P.cap/day	Protein Gr. P.cap/day	Fat Gr. P.cap/day
1961–3 – 1971–3	–0.14	–0.44	–0.52
1971–3 – 1981–3	0.51	0.44	1.45
1981–3 – 1990–2	1.05	0.81	2.08
1961–3 – 1990–2	0.45	0.25	0.96

Source: Food and Agriculture Organization, State of Food and Agriculture, various issues; cited in Radhakrishna (1997).

The trend rate of growth of foodgrain production improved from 2.3 per cent during the 1970s to 2.8 per cent in the 1980s (Sawant and Achuthan 1995). The first half of the 1990s saw a slowing down in the growth of foodgrain production with a trend growth rate lower than the historical growth rate of the last four decades. Ironically, despite the slow growth of foodgrain production, supply has outstripped its effective market demand, and a rapid increase in the stock of foodgrains held by the government took place. Disposal of stocks became a cause of concern in 1995–6, a period during which the world stocks were declining.

The relative price of foodgrains, which showed a decline during the 1970s and 1980s, registered a rise during the first half of the 1990s (Figure 1, Table 4.2). The food-price elasticity estimates show that an increase in cereal price significantly reduced the calorie intake because for the poor, the food (calorie) price elasticity is numerically large (Table 4.3). The upward trend in the real price of foodgrains in the early 1990s also coincides with a slowdown in the downward trend in poverty.

The last decade has seen significant progress in meeting the food energy needs of the population. The per capita availability

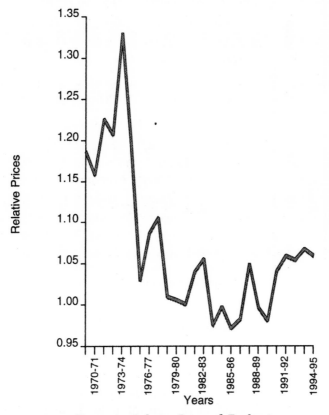

FIGURE 1. *Relative Prices of Foodgrains*

TABLE 4.2
ANNUAL INFLATION RATES IN CONSUMER PRICES

Year	Rural					Urban				
	Cereals	Non-cereal food	All food	Non-food	All commodities	Cereals	Non-cereal food	All food	Non-food	All commodities
1970–71	-1.3	8.7	3.2	4.4	3.6	-0.5	9.5	5.7	4.7	5.3
1971–72	2.4	-1.9	0.4	4.5	1.9	1.8	-1.3	-0.2	4.4	1.7
1972–73	13.3	11.2	12.3	4.4	9.4	11.1	9.4	10.0	3.5	7.3
1973–74	17.3	23.9	20.3	9.3	16.4	13.9	21.9	19.0	8.5	14.8
1974–75	40.4	17.7	29.8	20.3	26.6	44.1	20.9	29.1	20.0	25.6
1975–76	-8.9	-1.9	-5.9	6.5	-1.9	-7.6	-1.7	-4.0	7.7	0.2
1976–77	-11.1	0.0	-6.2	4.9	-2.3	-9.7	1.7	-2.6	3.6	-0.2
1977–78	4.4	17.7	10.7	1.9	7.4	3.4	16.1	11.6	2.1	7.8
1978–79	-2.1	-3.8	-2.9	2.5	-1.0	-1.4	-4.8	-3.7	3.5	-0.9
1979–80	9.5	4.6	7.0	9.3	7.9	9.9	5.6	7.0	9.6	8.1
1980–81	14.1	11.7	12.9	7.4	10.9	12.0	9.3	10.2	7.8	9.2
1981–82	11.4	10.0	10.7	9.8	10.4	10.2	10.8	10.6	10.1	10.4
1982–83	9.2	6.3	7.8	3.9	6.4	11.3	8.0	9.1	4.3	7.2
1983–84	9.7	17.7	13.5	5.6	10.7	9.0	18.5	15.1	5.5	11.4
1984–85	-5.0	5.4	0.1	5.4	1.8	-4.9	5.1	1.7	6.3	3.4

Year	Rural					Urban				
	Cereals	Non-cereal food	All food	Non-food	All commodities	Cereals	Non-cereal food	All food	Non-food	All commodities
1985-86	6.3	1.5	3.8	4.5	4.1	5.6	0.9	2.4	4.7	3.3
1986-87	5.4	13.1	9.3	5.1	7.8	5.6	13.2	10.8	4.6	8.4
1987-88	7.9	11.5	9.8	5.0	8.2	8.0	10.7	9.9	6.1	8.5
1988-89	12.1	5.0	8.3	8.1	8.2	12.4	3.5	6.2	8.6	7.1
1989-90	3.5	7.4	5.5	8.5	6.5	2.5	10.9	8.2	7.2	7.8
1990-91	6.1	14.8	10.6	9.5	10.3	8.3	14.5	12.6	8.0	10.9
1991-92	24.3	18.0	20.9	11.1	17.7	21.5	14.1	16.3	10.0	14.0
1992-93	14.2	5.9	9.8	8.1	9.3	13.9	7.0	9.1	10.5	9.6
1993-94	3.8	5.0	4.4	6.9	5.2	7.0	6.1	6.4	7.7	6.8
1994-95	12.7	9.5	11.1	11.6	11.2	10.5	8.2	8.9	11.4	9.8
1995-96	7.1	13.5	10.4	8.9	9.9	5.2	12.1	9.8	8.3	9.3
1996-97	11.9	7.2	9.5	5.3	8.2	13.6	6.7	8.9	6.0	7.9
1970-71 to 1979	6.7	8.3	7.5	7.2	7.4	6.7	8.4	7.8	7.0	7.5
1980-81 to 1989	6.4	8.6	7.5	5.5	6.8	6.3	8.6	7.8	5.9	7.1
1990-91 to 1996	10.7	9.5	10.1	8.5	9.6	10.6	8.9	9.4	8.7	9.2
1970-71 to 1996	7.0	8.2	7.6	6.7	7.3	7.0	8.2	7.8	6.8	7.4

Source: Centre for Economic & Social Studies (CESS) Project on Food Demand; cited in Radhakrishna (1997).

TABLE 4.3
FOOD, CALORIE AND PROTEIN ELASTICITIES IN 1993–94

Expenditure group	Elasticities with respect to prices of					Elasticities with respect to prices of				
	Cereals	Non-cereal food	All food	Non-food	Total Expend.	Cereals	Non-cereal food	All food	Non-food	Total Expend.
	Rural					Urban				
Food										
Very poor	−0.493	0.396	−0.889	−0.121	1.01	−0.313	−0.446	−0.759	−0.14	0.9
Moderately poor	−0.409	−0.461	−0.87	−0.53	0.923	−0.166	−0.504	−0.67	0.092	0.578
Non-poor lower	−0.297	−0.489	−0.786	−0.039	0.824	−0.104	−0.401	−0.505	0.018	0.487
Non-poor high	−0.135	−0.487	−0.622	0.083	0.54	−0.059	−0.405	−0.463	−0.024	0.488
All groups	−0.253	−0.475	−0.728	0.01	0.719	−0.1	−0.417	−0.517	−0.013	0.531
Calories										
Very poor	−0.612	−0.234	−0.846	−0.115	0.961	−0.318	−0.28	−0.598	−0.111	0.708
Moderately poor	−0.496	−0.216	−0.712	−0.043	0.755	−0.121	−0.258	−0.379	0.052	0.327
Non-poor lower	−0.321	−0.231	−0.522	−0.027	−0.579	−0.088	−0.269	−0.356	−0.012	−0.344
Non-poor high	−0.160	−0.245	−0.405	0.054	0.351	−0.059	−0.267	−0.326	−0.017	0.343
All groups	−0.317	−0.235	−0.552	−0.007	0.559	−0.101	−0.268	−0.369	−0.012	0.381

Expenditure group	Rural					Urban				
	Elasticities with respect to prices of					Elasticities with respect to prices of				
	Cereals	Non-cereal food	All food	Non-food	Total expend.	Cereals	Non-cereal food	All food	Non-food	Total expend.
Protein										
Very poor	-0.623	-0.221	-0.844	-0.115	0.959	-0.318	-0.254	-0.572	-0.106	0.678
Moderately poor	-0.504	-0.191	-0.694	-0.042	0.736	-0.121	-0.243	-0.363	0.050	0.313
Non-poor lower	-0.324	-0.198	-0.521	-0.026	0.547	-0.091	-0.272	-0.363	0.013	0.350
Non-poor high	-0.164	-0.198	-0.361	0.048	0.313	-0.063	-0.283	-0.346	-0.018	0.364
All groups	-0.325	-0.200	-0.524	-0.009	0.534	-0.105	-0.272	-0.378	-0.013	0.390

Source: Centre for Economic & Social Studies (CESS), Project on Food Demand; cited in Radhakrishna (1997).

of daily food energy, which remained stagnant between 1960 and 1980, increased from 2080 cal in 1979–81 to 2330 cal in 1990–2 (FAO 1996). The current availability of food energy, if evenly distributed, is just enough to meet the food needs (about 2200 cal/person/day) of the total population. Given the inequalities in food energy intake to raise the calorie intake level of the bottom 30 per cent (about 1600 cal in 1993–4) to 2200 cal, per capita daily availability of calories at the national level would have to increase to 2800 cal. This is within reach, even if the growth rate experienced in the 1980s, which was lower than the agricultural growth rate (4–4.5 per cent per annum) targeted during the Ninth Plan (1997–2002), is sustained.

FOOD AND NUTRIENT INTAKE

Cereal Consumption

Consumption data from the National Sample Survey (NSS) reveal that per capita consumption of cereals has been declining since the early 1970s (Figures 2.1 and 2.2; Tables 4.4A and 4.4B). Between 1970–1 and 1993–4, the per capita cereal consumption declined by 0.55 per cent per annum in the rural areas and by 0.27 per cent per annum in the urban areas. The average all-India rural per capita consumption fell from 15.25 kg per capita/month in 1977–8 to 13.40 kg in 1993–4, while urban cereal consumption fell from 11.62 to 10.60 kg during the same period.

The declining trend is visible across all the states with the exception of Kerala, West Bengal and Orissa. The decline is very prominent in Punjab and Haryana (Tables 4.4A and 4.4B). The absolute fall in consumption of about 4 kg per capita per month in rural areas of Punjab and Haryana and about 2 kg in the urban areas occurred mainly due to a reduced consumption of coarse cereals. What is striking is the low per capita intake of cereals in the prosperous state of Punjab (11 kg in rural areas and 9 kg in urban areas in 1993–4) and the high intake in the backward state of Orissa (16 kg in rural areas and 13.40 kg in urban areas). Diversification of the food basket in Punjab in favour of non-cereal food (particularly milk and milk products), meat, eggs, fish, vegetables and fruits, etc. could be a part of the reason for the low per capita intake of cereals there. The point that is being made

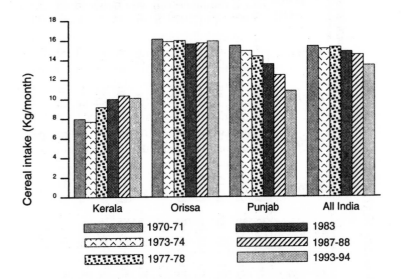

FIGURE 2.1 *Per Capita Cereal Intake in Rural Areas:*
Selected States and All-India

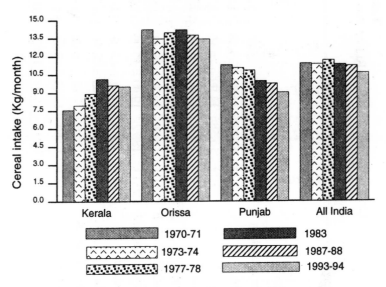

FIGURE 2.2 *Per Capita Cereal Intake in Urban Areas:*
Selected States and All-India

TABLE 4.4A

CEREAL CONSUMPTION IN RURAL AREAS OF VARIOUS STATES DURING 1970-94

kg/month/person

States	1970-71	1972-73	1973-74	1977-78	1983	1986-87	1987-88	1989-90	1990-91	1991-92	1993-94	Trend growth
Andhra Pradesh	16.05	15.25	15.80	15.85	15.37	13.99	14.35	14.31	13.62	13.60	13.30	-0.76
Assam	15.70	14.81	15.33	14.38	14.23	13.24	14.23	13.93	13.68	13.20	13.20	-0.64
Bihar	16.39	15.58	14.99	16.16	15.77	15.25	15.39	15.14	16.45	15.00	14.30	-0.23
Gujarat	15.00	13.32	13.87	13.44	12.56	11.05	12.00	12.22	11.75	11.10	10.70	-1.17
Haryana	18.13	17.57	16.56	15.22	14.54	14.84	15.02	13.74	14.15	10.20	12.90	-1.55
Himachal Pradesh	17.64	18.06	16.30	15.47	16.06	14.32	16.06	Na	Na	Na	Na	-0.84
Jammu & Kashmir	20.14	18.72	19.09	17.99	17.59	17.82	17.26	Na	Na	Na	Na	-0.70
Karnataka	15.71	15.63	15.61	15.01	15.03	13.16	13.75	12.11	11.62	12.30	13.20	-1.20
Kerala	7.99	7.97	7.69	9.18	10.01	10.28	10.36	9.75	10.73	10.00	10.10	1.29
Madhya Pradesh	16.51	17.28	17.12	16.08	15.83	15.14	15.39	14.60	15.22	14.30	14.20	-0.76
Maharashtra	12.83	12.60	13.45	13.52	13.79	11.84	13.03	11.89	11.48	11.70	11.40	-0.58
Orissa	16.12	15.22	15.88	15.97	15.61	16.02	15.72	16.52	15.98	17.10	15.90	0.16

States	1970-71	1972-73	1973-74	1977-78	1983	1986-87	1987-88	1989-90	1990-91	1991-92	1993-94	Trend growth
Punjab	15.46	15.38	14.89	14.35	13.52	11.86	12.41	12.29	11.69	12.00	10.80	-1.44
Rajasthan	17.91	18.17	18.76	18.18	17.19	16.69	16.62	15.54	15.75	14.90	14.90	-0.92
Tamil Nadu	13.95	14.53	14.72	13.85	13.05	12.27	12.24	12.43	12.20	11.60	11.70	-0.98
Uttar Pradesh	16.32	16.83	16.24	16.57	15.17	15.48	15.32	14.77	14.79	13.70	13.90	-0.74
West Bengal	13.35	13.64	12.97	14.74	14.28	15.41	15.12	15.44	15.06	14.20	15.00	0.56
All India	15.35	15.26	15.09	15.25	14.80	14.28	14.47	14.00	14.06	13.50	13.40	-0.55
Coefficient of variation*	15.7	16.1	16.0	13.2	11.5	13.8	11.9	12.8	13.5	14.6	13.0	

Note: a. * Excluding Himachal Pradesh & Jammu and Kashmir
b. Na: Not available
Source: Cited in Radhakrishna (1997).

TABLE 4.4B
CEREAL CONSUMPTION IN URBAN AREAS OF VARIOUS STATES DURING 1970–94

kg/month/person

States	1970-71	1972-73	1973-74	1977-78	1983	1986-87	1987-88	1989-90	1990-91	1991-92	1993-94	Trend growth
Andhra Pradesh	13.31	12.68	13.07	12,83	11.95	11.37	11.70	11.74	11.70	11.60	11.30	-0.60
Assam	12.91	12.55	12.31	13.44	12.78	11.89	12.39	12.34	12.08	11.50	12.10	-0.18
Bihar	13.68	13.49	13.22	14.06	13.44	12.90	13.37	13.50	12.85	13.70	12.80	-0.17
Gujarat	10.35	10.77	10.71	10.17	9.61	8.81	9.44	9.48	9.55	8.90	9.00	-0.77
Haryana	11.69	11.86	12.23	12.24	11.59	10.61	10.98	10.24	10.11	9.90	10.50	-0.83
Himachal Pradesh	11.30	11.97	12.57	11.62	11.79	11.44	13.28	Na	Na	Na	Na	0.26
Jammu & Kashmir	14.62	14.16	14.31	13.16	13.80	14.62	14.09	Na	Na	Na	Na	-0.04
Karnataka	11.91	11.32	11.24	12.68	11.69	10.37	11.06	10.71	10.40	10.40	10.90	-0.52
Kerala	7.55	8.17	7.93	8.91	10.12	9.55	9.60	9.88	9.60	9.70	9.50	1.03
Madhya Pradesh	12.88	12.88	12.53	12.61	12.32	11.70	11.89	11.63	11.54	11.50	11.30	-0.57
Maharashtra	9.75	8.95	9.24	9.92	9.95	9.23	10.18	10.18	9.79	9.40	9.40	0.14
Orissa	14.22	13.77	13.42	13.96	14.19	13.98	13.74	14.39	13.93	13.40	13.40	0.08

States	1970-71	1972-73	1973-74	1977-78	1983	1986-87	1987-88	1989-90	1990-91	1991-92	1993-94	Trend growth
Punjab	11.25	10.71	11.03	10.80	9.94	10.25	9.74	9.40	9.06	8.90	9.00	-0.98
Rajasthan	13.03	13.21	12.97	12.55	12.95	13.32	12.73	11.76	12.03	11.60	11.50	-0.48
Tamil Nadu	10.63	11.12	11.39	11.05	10.39	9.93	10.14	10.26	10.14	10.00	10.40	-0.49
Uttar Pradesh	11.79	12.24	12.48	12.27	11.66	11.77	11.63	11.33	11.14	11.40	11.10	-0.40
West Bengal	10.88	10.53	10.92	11.92	11.80	12.75	11.71	12.12	11.78	11.30	11.60	0.40
All India	11.36	11.24	11.32	11.62	11.30	10.94	11.19	11.04	10.87	10.70	10.60	-0.27
Coefficient of Variation*	14.3	13.5	12.8	12.1	11.6	13.5	11.5	12.4	12.1	12.9	11.7	

Note: a. * Excluding Himachal Pradesh & Jammu and Kashmir
b. Na: Not available
Source: Cited in Radhakrishna (1997).

here is that cereal-price induced inflation would tend to hurt the poor in the backward regions the most.

Food Consumption

Although estimates of the consumption of food items and nutrients for India for 1972–3 and 1993–4 based on NSS data indicate that per capita cereal intake declined, per capita total expenditure in real terms increased by 1.2 and 1.3 per cent per annum in rural and urban areas respectively over the same period (Table 4.5). However, the fall in cereal consumption was offset by an increase in the consumption of non-cereal food. Per capita food expenditure increased at 0.49 per cent per annum in rural areas and 0.51 per cent per annum in urban areas. However, these increases were not commensurate with the increase in per capita total expenditure.

Despite this moderate increase in food expenditure, the nutrient intake did not improve between 1972–3 and 1993–4. During this period, per capita calorie intake declined at 0.25 per cent in rural areas and 0.08 per cent in urban areas (Table 4.6). The stagnancy or marginal decrease in the food energy intake, despite improvement in incomes, was due to the fall in the consumption of cereals, which are the cheapest source of calories.

There are substantial interstate variations in the per capita food energy intake (Figures 3.1 and 3.2, Table 4.7). While the average intake of calories was very low in Kerala and Tamil Nadu, it was high in Madhya Pradesh and Karnataka. Nevertheless, there does not seem to be a strong positive correlation between calorie intake and the per capita State Domestic Product (SDP) of the states. For the lowest 30 per cent of the population, there has been hardly any perceptible improvement in the cereal and nutrient intake in the rural as well as urban areas (Figures 4.1(a, b), 4.2(a, b), 4.3(a, b), 4.4(a, b); Tables 4.5 and 4.6). The improvement in the economic access to food made possible by income growth has not resulted in a higher consumption of cereals.[3]

The saturation in cereal consumption would not be a major

[3] The per capita cereal consumption of the poor remained the same despite a significant improvement in their real per capita expenditure and a decline in the relative cereal prices. This counter-intuitive result could be attributed to changes in consumer preferences (Radhakrishna 1991; Radhakrishna and Ravi 1992; Suryanarayana 1995; Meenakshi 1996).

TABLE 4.5
COMPOUND ANNUAL GROWTH RATES (CAGR) OF PER CAPITA CEREAL, FOOD AND TOTAL CONSUMPTION EXPENDITURE

Expenditure groups	Cereals (Kg/month)					Food (Rs 0.0/Month)					Total expenditure (Rs 0.0/Month)				
	1972-78	1977-83	1983-88	1988-94	1972-94	1972-78	1977-83	1983-88	1988-94	1972-94	1972-78	1977-83	1983-88	1988-94	1972-94
Rural															
Lowest 30%	0.6	-0.3	0.4	-0.8	-0.1	0.4	2.0	0.3	1.0	0.9	1.7	2.0	1.4	1.1	1.5
Middle 40%	0.0	-1.0	-0.4	-1.3	-0.7	0.1	1.4	-0.3	0.8	0.6	0.9	2.6	-0.1	1.1	1.2
Top 30%	-0.7	-1.1	-1.5	-2.0	-1.4	-0.5	1.4	-0.1	0.0	0.2	3.5	0.0	0.0	0.7	1.0
All	-0.1	-0.9	-0.6	-1.4	-0.8	-0.1	1.5	-0.1	0.5	0.5	2.4	1.1	0.2	0.9	1.2
Urban															
Lowest 30%	0.1	-0.7	1.2	-0.3	0.0	-0.3	2.2	-1.5	1.5	0.6	1.1	2.3	-0.3	1.7	1.3
Middle 40%	0.7	-0.6	-0.4	-1.0	-0.4	-0.3	1.6	-1.0	1.3	0.5	1.1	1.9	0.3	1.6	1.3
Top 30%	1.1	-0.4	-1.5	-1.2	-0.5	-0.6	1.5	-0.3	1.0	0.5	0.9	1.9	0.8	1.6	1.3
All	0.7	-0.6	-0.3	-0.9	-0.3	-0.4	1.7	-0.8	1.2	0.5	1.0	2.0	0.4	1.6	1.3

Note: Class specific price deflators have been used for estimating real expenditure.
Source: Cited in Radhakrishna (1997).

TABLE 4.6
AVERAGE PER CAPITA CALORIE AND
PROTEIN INTAKE IN INDIA AND CAGRs

Expenditure groups	Calories (Cal/Day)				Protein (Mg/Day)			
	1972–73	1977–78	1983	1993–94	1972–73	1977–78	1983	1993–94
Rural								
Lowest 30%	1504	1630	1620	1678	42.56	46.37	46.92	46.55
Middle 40%	2170	2296	2144	2119	60.55	66.70	60.95	58.89
Top 30%	3161	3190	2929	2672	85.69	97.40	81.47	75.60
All	2268	2364	2222	2152	62.70	69.81	62.90	60.20
Urban								
Lowest 30%	1579	1701	1627	1682	44.6	48.7	45.6	46.8
Middle 40%	2154	2438	2148	2111	58.0	74.1	58.8	58.3
Top 30%	2572	2979	2506	2405	67.1	93.5	67.6	66.2
All	2107	2379	2099	2071	56.7	72.3	57.5	57.2

COMPOUND ANNUAL GROWTH RATES (CAGR)

Expenditure groups	Calories				Protein			
	1972–8	1978–83	1983–94	1972–94	1972–8	1978–83	1983–94	1972–94
Rural								
Lowest 30%	1.6	–0.1	0.3	0.5	1.7	0.2	–0.1	0.4
Middle 40%	1.1	–1.2	–0.1	–0.1	1.9	–1.6	–0.3	–0.1
Top 30%	0.2	–1.5	–0.9	–0.8	2.6	–3.2	–0.7	–0.6
All	0.8	–1.1	–0.3	–0.2	2.2	–1.9	–0.4	–0.2
Urban								
Lowest 30%	1.5	–0.8	0.3	0.3	1.8	–1.2	0.3	0.2
Middle 40%	2.5	–2.3	–0.2	–0.1	5.0	–4.1	–0.1	0.0
Top 30%	3.0	–3.1	–0.4	–0.3	6.9	–5.7	–0.2	–0.1
All	2.5	–2.2	–0.1	–0.1	5.0	–4.1	–0.1	0.0

Source: Cited in Radhakrishna (1997).

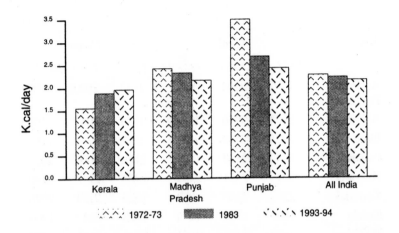

FIGURE 3.1 *Calorie Consumption in Rural Areas:*
Selected States and All-India

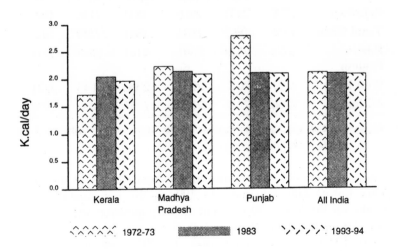

FIGURE 3.2 *Calorie Consumption in Urban Areas:*
Selected States and All-India

TABLE 4.7
PER CAPITA CALORIE INTAKE IN SELECTED STATES

Cal/Day

States	Rural			Urban		
	1972–73	*1983*	*1993–94*	*1972–73*	*1983*	*1993–94*
Andhra Pradesh	2103	2204	2052	2143	2009	1992
Assam	2074	2056	1983	2135	2043	2108
Bihar	2225	2189	2115	2167	2131	2188
Gujarat	2142	2113	1994	2172	2000	2027
Haryana	3215	2554	2491	2404	2242	2140
Karnataka	2202	2260	2073	1925	2124	2026
Kerala	1559	1884	1965	1723	2049	1966
Madhya Pradesh	2423	2323	2164	2229	2137	2082
Maharashtra	1895	2144	1939	1971	2028	1989
Orissa	1995	2103	2199	2276	2219	2261
Punjab	3493	2677	2418	2783	2100	2089
Rajasthan	2730	2433	2470	1841	2140	1922
Tamil Nadu	1955	1861	1884	1841	2140	1922
Uttar Pradesh	2575	2399	2307	2161	2043	2114
West Bengal	1921	2027	2211	2080	2048	2131
All India	2266	2221	2153	2107	2089	2071

Source: National Sample Survey (NSS) Report No. 405; cited in Radhakrishna (1997).

cause for concern if the food energy intake levels of the poor were nutritionally adequate. In 1993–4, the per capita calorie intake for the lowest 30 per cent of the population was 1678 cal per day in the rural areas and 1682 cal per day in the urban areas. The per capita protein intake in 1993–4 was 46 grams per day in the rural areas and 47 grams per day in the urban areas (Table 4.5). Thus, the lowest 30 per cent of the population fails to enjoy an adequate diet that would provide them with the

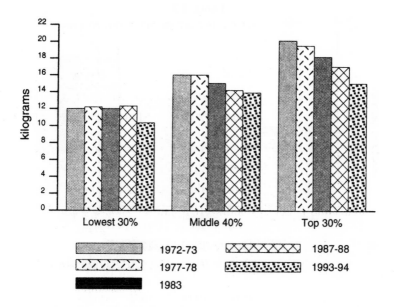

FIGURE 4.1a *Per Capita Monthly Cereal Consumption (Rural)*

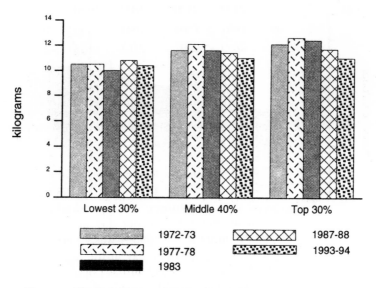

FIGURE 4.1b *Per Capita Monthly Cereal Consumption (Urban)*

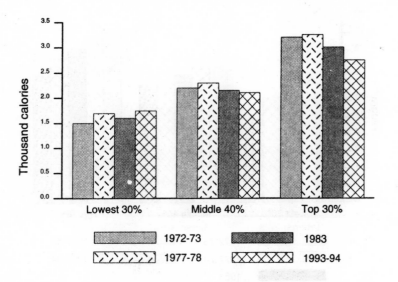

FIGURE 4.2a *Per Capita Daily Calorie Consumption (Rural)*

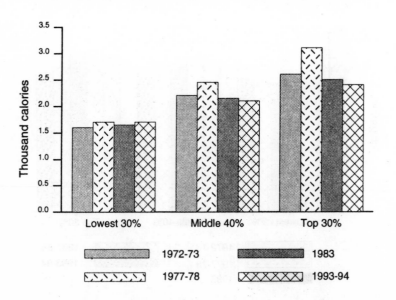

FIGURE 4.2b *Per Capita Daily Calorie Consumption (Urban)*

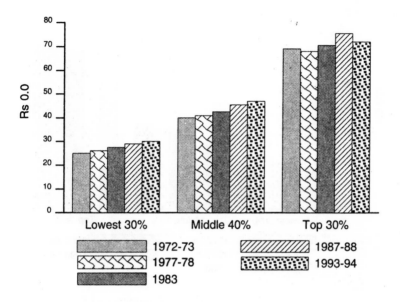

FIGURE 4.3a *Per Capita Monthly Food Expenditure (Rural)*

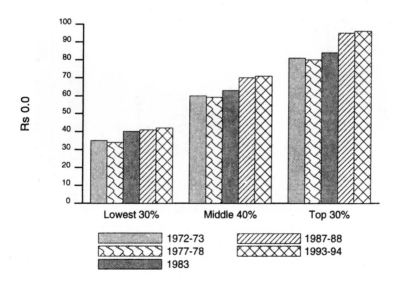

FIGURE 4.3b *Per Capita Monthly Food Expenditure (Urban)*

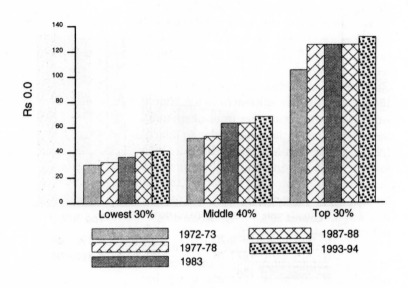

FIGURE 4.4a *Per Capita Monthly Total Expenditure (Rural)*

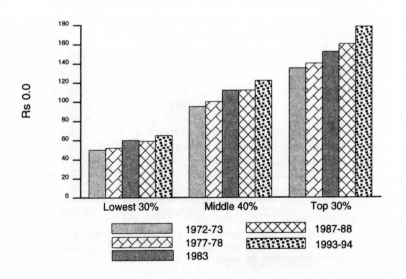

FIGURE 4.4b *Per Capita Monthly Total Expenditure (Urban)*

required food energy, such deficiency having adverse effects on their health and nutritional status.[4]

The poor have also seen a substantial diversification in their consumption basket in favour of non-cereal items, particularly non-food items.[5] The change in the composition of their diet has tended to increase the cost of calories to them (Radhakrishna and Ravi 1992). A question of topical interest is: are poor households buying diets that are efficient from a nutritional perspective? Studies suggest that the poor suffer from micro-nutrient (Vitamin A, Ribo-flavin and Niacin) deficiencies due to a lack of variety in their diet (National Nutrition Monitoring Bureau (NNMB) Reports). It therefore becomes important to analyse the implications of changes in dietary preferences on the nutritional and health status of the poor. So long as the diversification of the consumption basket improves nutritional status, even though it may not add calories, it should not be a cause for concern.

At the moment, the picture that emerges is one of stagnancy in the per capita consumption of cereals. The apparent cause of national self-sufficiency in cereals is the slow growth of aggregate cereal demand (about 2 per cent per annum in aggregate terms and negative in per capita terms). This can be attributed to changes in consumer preferences, so that there has been no noticeable improvement in the per capita intake of calories and proteins. Therefore, despite the decline in income-poverty between 1972–3 and 1992–3, food poverty (i.e. the proportion of households consuming less than the norm) might not have declined.

NUTRITIONAL STATUS

Data provided by the NNMB for a sample of seven states reveal that the percentage of children suffering from severe malnutrition in rural areas declined from 15.0 in 1975–9 to 8.7 in 1988–90 and

[4] There is considerable disagreement about the minimum calorie consumption per consumer unit per diem. Sukhatme (1982) and Minhas (1991b) have questioned the sanctity of the calorie norms widely used by nutritionists and consider them to be exaggerated. However, the calorie intake of the poorest 30 per cent was lower than the norms suggested by Sukhatme.

[5] The share of cereals in the marginal budgets of the very poor in rural areas declined from 53 per cent in 1964–77 to 39 per cent in 1977–86 and from 39 to 29 per cent in urban areas during the same period (Radhakrishna and Ravi 1990).

further to 7.5 in 1994. If moderate and severely malnourished children are considered together, the percentage declined from 62.5 in 1975–9 to 52.5 in 1988–90 and further to 50.9 in 1994.[6] The decline in the percentage of severely malnourished children is very visible across all NNMB sample states except Orissa. The decline is very striking in Kerala and Tamil Nadu. It is evident that inspite of some improvements in nutritional status, nearly half the children in rural areas suffer from malnutrition.[7]

National Nutritional Monitoring Bureau data also indicate that 46 per cent of the rural adult population suffered from chronic energy deficiency in 1994, bringing the extent of malnutrition among adults closer to that among children (51 per cent). The regional patterns of adult malnutrition are similar to those among children (NNMB). Chronic energy deficiency was found to be lower in Kerala (33 per cent) and Tamil Nadu (37 per cent) and higher in Gujarat, Maharashtra and Madhya Pradesh (above 50 per cent).

There are substantial interstate variations in the malnutrition levels of children under five years.[8] In 1994, the percentage of moderately and severely malnourished children varied between 34 per cent in Kerala and 57 per cent in Gujarat. Middle-income states such as Kerala, Tamil Nadu and Andhra Pradesh performed better than high-income states like Gujarat and Maharashtra in terms of the nutritional status of children. Not surprisingly, poorer states such as Madhya Pradesh and Orissa performed the worst. It is worth noting that despite low food energy intake, Kerala and Tamil Nadu could perform better. The National Family Health Survey (NFHS) data also reveal more or less similar patterns as the NNMB data[9] (Table 4.8).

[6] Based on Standard Deviation Criterion, i.e. children with weight/height less than 2 SD of the NCHS median value, are treated as malnourished, 63 per cent of the children were underweight in 1994.

[7] Children belonging to poor communities, suffering from malnutrition, do not achieve full genetic growth potential and are also exposed to greater risk of child mortality. Pelletier *et al.* (1995) identify malnutrition as a major cause of child deaths in developing countries. Their results reveal that malnutrition, by virtue of its synergistic relationship with infectious diseases has a powerful impact on child mortality in India.

[8] The interstate variations in malnutrition of children under five years are more or less similar to those in infant mortality rates (Radhakrishna and Narayana 1993).

[9] While all the NNMB repeat surveys revealed poor status records for rural Gujarat, the NFHS revealed better performance. This needs further examination.

TABLE 4.8

NFHS ESTIMATES OF MALNUTRITION AMONG CHILDREN UNDER AGE FOUR (1–4 YEARS) IN 1993

	Weight-for-age Percentage below 2SD (underweight)			Height-for-age Percentage below 2SD (stunted)			Weight-for-height Percentage below 2SD (wasted)		
	Rural	Urban	Total	Rural	Urban	Total	Rural	Urban	Total
Andhra Pradesh	52.1	40.2	49.1	Na	Na	Na	Na	Na	Na
Assam	51.8	37.3	50.4	53.5	39.6	52.2	11.4	5.6	10.8
Bihar	64.1	53.8	62.6	61.8	55.2	60.9	22.7	16.3	21.8
Gujarat	45.8	40.5	44.1	44.6	41.6	43.6	20.3	16.1	18.9
Haryana	39.4	33.0	37.9	48.0	42.4	46.7	5.7	6.4	5.9
Himachal Pradesh	48.3	30.2	47.0	Na	Na	Na	Na	Na	Na
Jammu & Kashmir	Na	Na	44.5	Na	Na	40.8	Na	Na	14.8
Karnataka	Na	Na	54.3	Na	Na	47.6	Na	Na	17.4
Kerala	30.6	22.9	28.5	29.6	21.5	27.4	11.5	12.0	11.6
Madhya Pradesh	59.4	50.1	57.4	Na	Na	Na	Na	Na	Na
Maharashtra	57.5	45.5	52.6	50.8	39.1	46.0	21.5	18.3	20.2
Orissa	Na	Na	53.3	Na	Na	48.2	Na	Na	21.3
Punjab	47.4	40.0	45.9	40.4	38.4	40.0	21.4	14.3	19.9
Rajasthan	41.1	43.9	41.6	43.0	43.5	43.1	17.7	29.1	19.5

Table 4.8 (continued)

Table 4.8 (continued)

	Weight-for-age Percentage below 2SD (underweight)			Height-for-age Percentage below 2SD (stunted)			Weight-for-height Percentage below 2SD (wasted)		
	Rural	Urban	Total	Rural	Urban	Total	Rural	Urban	Total
Tamil Nadu	52.1	37.3	46.6	Na	Na	Na	Na	Na	Na
Uttar Pradesh	Na	Na	49.8	Na	Na	49.2	Na	Na	16.2
West Bengal	Na	Na	56.8	Na	Na	43.2	Na	Na	11.9
North-East									
Arunachal Pradesh	40.3	36.2*	39.7	52.7	61.7*	53.9	10.6	14.9*	11.2
Manipur	31.6	25.9	30.1	34.9	29.6	33.6	8.3	10.2	8.8
Nagaland	30.5	19.7	28.7	32.7	31.0	32.4	14.1	5.6	12.7
Tripura	53.0	31.6	48.8	49.1	33.3	46.0	19.7	8.8	17.5
Meghalaya	47.2	37.5	45.5	55.5	29.7	50.8	20.1	14.1	18.9
Mizoram	34.5	22.0	28.1	54.0	29.1	41.3	2.3	2.2	2.2
All India	55.9	45.2	53.4	54.1	44.8	52.0	18.0	15.8	17.5

Notes: a. * Based on 25–49 cases.
b.   Children below 2 standard deviation from the International Reference Population median are treated as suffering from malnutrition.
c.   Na: Not available.
Source: National Family Health Survey 1992–3 (1995); cited in Radhakrishna (1997).

Interstate comparisons reveal weak correlations between nutritional status and per capita SDP, as well as between nutritional status and per capita calorie consumption. Differences in education, health, availability of safe drinking water, and environmental sanitation could lead to the interstate mismatch between food intake and nutritional status. Improved nutritional status at a comparatively lower level of consumption of food energy as observed in Kerala and Tamil Nadu could be due to better health care and nutritional interventions.[10]

Does all this imply that calorie intake matters little? Empirical evidence tends to suggest a positive association between calorie intake and nutritional status. However, the strength of the relationship is likely to be affected by health and environmental factors. Thus, the question of what constitutes a desirable diet from a nutritional perspective still remains to be settled.

THE PUBLIC DISTRIBUTION SYSTEM

The Public Distribution System (PDS), a producer price support-cum-consumer subsidy programme, was evolved in the wake of the foodgrain shortages of the 1960s. Till the late 1970s, its main emphasis was on price stabilization and it was confined to urban areas in the food deficit states. In the early 1980s, the welfare dimension of the PDS gained importance and its coverage was extended to the rural areas in some states and to areas with a high incidence of poverty. Public Distribution System supplies have increased rapidly since the mid-1960s; the average annual supply increased from 6.5 million tonnes during 1961-5 to 18.4 million tonnes during 1990-2. In 1993-4, the food subsidy cost accounted for 0.7 per cent of GDP. In the wake of economic reform, the PDS is perceived to be the main safety net to protect sections of the poor who might be adversely affected from potential short-run, price-induced adverse effects of economic reforms.

The recent increases in procurement prices and the consequent upward revisions in the central issue prices have had an adverse impact on the efficacy of the PDS. Between 1990-1 and 1995-6,

[10] Kerala and Tamil Nadu have better health care, educational facilities and PDS coverage. Here, the per child public expenditure on nutrition as well as per capita public expenditure on social sectors has been high for the past few decades.

the minimum support price has been raised by 69 per cent for wheat and 44 per cent for rice. On the other hand, large increases in the issue prices caused a decline in the offtake of cereals from the PDS (from 19.3 million tonnes in 1991–2 to 15.0 million tonnes in 1994–5). This led to buffer stocks reaching uneconomic levels, far exceeding the norms suggested by the Technical Group constituted by the government.[11] In 1994–5, the carrying costs of buffer stocks amounted to 36 per cent of the central food subsidy of Rs 51,000 million (Radhakrishna et al. 1996). The economic costs of withholding foodgrains from the market could be high, as it would lead to an increase in the open market price of foodgrains. This in turn would hurt the poor most as not all the poor are reached by the PDS, and even those who are covered, depend on the open market for a major portion of their foodgrain requirements.

Despite the upward trend in the central food subsidy, consumer cereal subsidy (Food Corporation of India (FCI) economic cost minus its sales realization) declined from Rs 32,238 million in 1992–3 to Rs 23,507 million in 1994–5. What is more disquieting is the decline in the proportion of subsidies allocated to poverty alleviation programmes (PDS, Revised Public Distribution System, ITDP, Jawahar Rozgar Yojana and Employment Assurance Scheme). These received Rs 16,238 million in 1994–5, i.e. about 30 per cent of the central food subsidy (Radhakrishna et al. 1996). The effective share of the food subsidy going to the poor would be much less than this 30 per cent, since the non-poor too avail of a proportion of the PDS supplies.

PDS and Food Access for the Poor

It is important to ask whether the poor have benefited from the increased tempo of PDS operations and how efficient it is in distributing food to them. Inter-regional biases in the distribution of PDS supplies have been brought out by many empirical studies.

11 While foodgrain stocks reached uneconomic levels during 1993–6, they have fallen below the required stocks in late 1996 and early 1997. The decline could be partly attributed to shortcomings in food management. Without perceiving the expected decline in foodgrain production, foodgrains were exported when the international prices were low and domestic prices were on an upward trend.

States with high incidence of poverty such as Bihar, Orissa and Madhya Pradesh are seen to receive a lower share of PDS supplies (Figure 5). With a few exceptions, the PDS remained an untargeted programme (Radhakrishna *et al.* 1996).

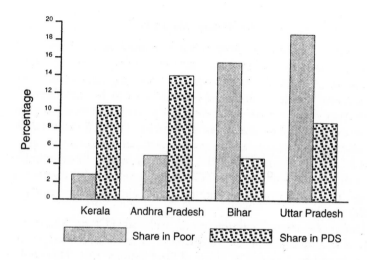

FIGURE 5. *Share of Selected States in Poverty and PDS Cereal Offtake in 1993-4*

Furthermore, in some states, the PDS seems to suffer from an urban bias. In Jammu and Kashmir, Karnataka, Maharashtra and West Bengal, the per capita purchases from PDS and their share in the market purchases of cereals were higher in the urban areas. Among these states, the urban bias was the most extreme in Jammu and Kashmir and West Bengal. On the whole, however, the major issues associated with the malfunctioning of the PDS can be associated with the universal character of its entitlement and regional mistargeting rather than its urban bias (Radhakrishna *et al.* 1996).

The fiscal crunch being faced by the state governments could be one reason for the PDS not functioning well in the poorer states. In such a scenario, the prospect of these states providing safety nets to the poor by delving into their own resources seems bleak. The proposed new scheme of providing 10 kg/month at half the issue price to poor households may help to improve access to food, provided it is implemented effectively and the delivery systems in the poorer states function efficiently and without leakages.

Reforming the PDS

The Public Distribution System has remained an expensive and largely untargeted programme and its poverty reducing effects are weak. Against the backdrop of a changing agricultural and institutional scenario, structural reforms need to be introduced.[12] A strategy could consist in phasing out government controls over grain markets and procurement operations. The FCI should then be allowed to compete in the market, without budgetary support and free from controls, with the added advantage of economies of scale. In its new role, the FCI could stabilize prices within a range, provide a minimum support price, and maintain strategic buffer stocks.

Under the altered circumstances, with the FCI no longer involved in procurement and distribution of subsidized foodgrains, there would be a saving in terms of food subsidy cost. This could be distributed among the state governments and Panchayati Raj Institutions using poverty incidence as the criterion. The Panchayati Raj Institutions should be entrusted with the responsibility of identifying the poor based on household-specific characteristics. The Panchayati Raj Institutions and the state governments should be free to buy foodgrains from the FCI or the open market to meet their PDS requirements. Making use of the central subsidy, they could then distribute the foodgrains to the poor at a price lower than the purchase price. In the very poor states, where administrative structures and local institutions are weak, schemes which tie food distribution to wage employment programmes, nutrition programmes, and welfare programmes for old and disabled persons should be given high priority.

The need to focus on food security for the very poor and to prevent food distress caused by less-than-adequate access to foodgrains, can be envisaged to persist in the years to come.

12 For arguments in favour of the reforms and other details, see Radhakrishna et al. (1996).

Even if during the Ninth Plan period the GDP grows at a rate of 6–7 per cent, the projections reveal that in the year 2000 about 256 million people will be poor, and about half of them very poor. Provided that food transfers can be made without leakages, about 3 million tonnes of cereals would be required to meet chronic cereal deficiency (taking the all-India average as the norm) in the year 2000, and 1 million in the year 2010. In the case of the poor nearer the poverty line, policies promoting broad-based growth are required to help them reach subsistence levels. If the poverty-reducing effects of high growth are supplemented with well-targeted, cost-effective food distribution and/or employment programmes, the problem of chronic cereal deficiency can be overcome to a large extent in the next decade. However, it can be argued that even if cereal needs are met, malnutrition may persist due to other forms of deprivation.

Food Demand

Food demand is projected to increase at 4.44 per cent per annum between the years 2000 and 2010. This level is close to the targeted agricultural growth rate in the Ninth Plan. This projection is based on the assumption that (i) private consumption will grow at more than 5 per cent between 1994 and 2000 and 6 per cent between 2000 and 2020 (ii) the rural–urban distribution of population and rural-urban differences in per capita expenditure will follow past trends (iii) inequality of expenditure distribution will remain constant at the 1993–4 levels in the rural and urban areas. The projected annual rate of increase in household demand is different for different food items: it is more than 5 per cent for milk and milk products, 4–5 per cent for meat, egg and fish, sugar and jaggery, and edible oils, and less than 3 per cent for cereals. These differential growth rates imply substantial diversification in the food basket in favour of non-cereal food, particularly milk, meat, etc. The household demand for cereals will slow down in the future, and will eventually level off at about the rate of growth of population, which itself is likely to decline.

On the whole, non-cereal household demand can be expected to have a maximum growth rate of 4.5 per cent, while the growth rate of national demand (household and non-household) for cereals can be expected to be 2.8 per cent during 2000–10 and

2.5 per cent during 2010–20. It is pertinent to note that household cereal demand has been projected assuming that the historical downward trend in per capita consumption of cereals due to changes in taste will be arrested, and that food demand will depend only on population, per capita income, level of urbanization, and income inequalities. Hence, the estimated growth rate of 2.8 per cent for cereal demand is likely to be on the higher side.

On the supply side, the above pattern of domestic food demand requires a substantial diversification of agricultural and allied sectors. To match the growing food demand, food production would have to grow at a rate of 4.4 per cent, well above the growth rate of 3.4 per cent achieved during the 1970s and the 1980s. The objective of National Food Security requires that the deceleration in the growth rate of foodgrain and agricultural production experienced during the first half of the 1990s and the weaknesses of the PDS are overcome. It is also necessary to solve the long-term problem of sustaining a growth rate of at least 2.8 per cent in cereal production during 2000–10 and 2.5 per cent during 2010–50.

Conclusion

Improvements in food consumption are a necessary but not sufficient condition for overcoming the problem of malnutrition in India. Besides inadequate food consumption, other causes of malnutrition are high incidence of gastro-intestinal and respiratory infections and behavioural factors such as faulty breastfeeding and weaning practices, etc. These lead to low absorption of nutrients from the food consumed. Economic growth, left to itself, may not have any dramatic impact on nutritional status in the near future, although it does provide greater opportunities for public intervention. However, effective and efficient food and environmental interventions are needed to free the poor from food and nutritional insecurity.

5

Current National Policies, Strategies and Programmes with an Impact on Poverty

INTRODUCTION

Poverty alleviation has been a part of the Indian development strategy from the very beginning, with direct poverty alleviation programmes introduced from the early 1970s. In India, a four-pronged strategy has been pursued to reduce poverty. This includes strategies that promote (i) economic growth and overall development (ii) human development with emphasis on health, education and minimum needs (iii) directly targeted programmes for poverty eradication through employment generation, training and building up asset endowments of the poor; and (iv) a targeted Public Distribution System (PDS) to protect the poor from inflationary pressures and provide them with access to essential foods at affordable prices. In what follows, the last two strategies are studied in depth, with specific focus on the implementation and impact of anti-poverty programmes associated with them.

In India, direct state intervention for poverty alleviation has taken place mainly in the rural areas. Here, the Integrated Rural Development Programme (IRDP) has been the major self-employment programme, with Training for Rural Youth for Self-Employment (TRYSEM) and Development of Women and Children in Rural Areas (DWCRA) as its sub-schemes. In addition, a scheme for the supply of improved tool-kits was also introduced to supplement the IRDP. To provide employment in the agricultural lean seasons and thus generate supplementary wage incomes, public works programmes — the Jawahar Rozgar Yojana (JRY) and the Employment Assurance Scheme (EAS) — are in operation. To streamline the existing PDS, a Targeted Public Distribution System (TPDS) was introduced in 1997. Under this scheme, special cards are issued to families below the poverty line and essential articles under the PDS sold to them at specially subsidized prices.

The centre's allocation towards anti-poverty programmes in rural areas amounted to Rs 1095 million in the Seventh Five Year Plan (1985–6 to 1989–90) and stepped up to Rs 3000 million in the Eighth Five Year Plan (1992–3 to 1996–7) (Table 5.1). The central and the state governments share the expenditure on anti-poverty programmes on a 50:50 basis. Under the self-employment programmes, this ratio increases to 80:20 for the wage-employment programmes.

To alleviate urban poverty, the Nehru Rozgar Yojana (NRY) was introduced in 1989 on a limited scale with a small allocation. This programme continued during the Eighth Plan period (1992–3 to 1996–7). The Prime Minister's Integrated Urban Poverty Eradication Programme (PMIUPEP) was also introduced in Class II towns and urban agglomerations, but again on a limited scale. Under these programmes self- and wage-employment opportunities were created in urban areas.

SELF-EMPLOYMENT PROGRAMMES
FOR POVERTY ALLEVIATION

Integrated Rural Development Programme

Initiated in 1978–9 to cover 2300 selected blocks, the Integrated Rural Development Programme (IRDP) was extended to the entire country in the Sixth Plan period (1980–1 to 1984–5). The objective of the IRDP has been to enable poor families in rural areas, with an annual income of Rs 11,000 or less, to cross the poverty line. Financial assistance is given in the form of subsidies by the government and term credit advanced by financial institutions. The pattern of subsidy is 25 per cent for small farmers, 33.33 per cent for marginal farmers, agricultural labourers and rural artisans, and 50 per cent for the Scheduled Castes and Scheduled Tribes (SCs and STs) and the physically handicapped. Within the target group, there is an ensured coverage of 50 per cent for SCs and STs, 40 per cent for women and 3 per cent for the physically handicapped.

TABLE 5.1

STATEMENT SHOWING OUTLAYS AND EXPENDITURE
FROM FIRST FIVE YEAR PLAN ONWARDS ON RURAL DEVELOPMENT PROGRAMMES

Rs Crore

Plan period	CD and Panchayats		IRDP and Related Programmes		Rural Development Programmes	
	Outlay	Expnd	Outlay	Expnd	Outlay	Expnd
First Plan (1951–56)	79.03	46.02	–	–	–	–
Second Plan (1956–61)	218.73	206.61	–	–	–	–
Third Plan (1961–66)	322.47	288.50	–	–	–	–
Annual Plan (1966–69)	99.00	99.40	–	–	–	–
Fourth Plan (1969–74)	115.50	115.20	195.27*	133.80*	–	–
Fifth Plan (1974–79)	127.45	173.41	596.83**	461.00**	–	–
Annual Plan (1979–80)	58.65	–	NA	817.72**	–	–
Sixth Plan (1980–85)	345.03	481.53	4397.70#	4598.95#	–	–
Seventh Plan (1985–90)	–	–	–	–	6179.21	10955.96
Eighth Plan (1992–97)	–	–	–	–	30000	31291.11

Notes: a.   *   Includes provision for SFDA, MFAL, DPAP and DDP
       b.   **   Includes provision for SFDA, MFAL, DPAP, DDP and IRDP and Food for Work Programme
       c.   #   Includes provision for IRDP, NREP, RLEGP, DDP, DPAP and other Programmes
       d.   Eighth Plan outlay at 1996–7 prices is Rs 44,562 on Ninth Plan outlay communicated earlier by number was Rs 40,000 crore. Final Ninth Plan outlay not known yet.

Source: Cited in Meenakshisundaram (1997).

Since its inception, Rs 280,477 million has been invested in this programme and about 51 million families have been covered. Of the total number of families assisted under the programme, 44.75 per cent were SCs and STs and 27.07 per cent were women. Table 5.2 sums up the performance of the IRDP during the Eighth Plan period.

TABLE 5.2

PERFORMANCE OF IRDP DURING THE EIGHTH FIVE YEAR PLAN

(in million)

Year	Financial allocation	Expenditure	Families covered
1992–3	6622.2	6930.8	2.069
1993–4	10934.3	9566.5	2.539
1994–5	10982.2	10083.2	2.215
1995–6+	10972.1	10771.6	2.089
1996–7+	10972.1	11394.9	1.912
Total	50482.9	48747.0	10.824

Note: + Provisional
Source: Documents of the Ministry of Rural Areas and Employment and Planning Commission; cited in Meenakshisundaram (1997).

In absolute terms, IRDP assets generated an incremental income of more than Rs 2000 each for 56.58 per cent of the assisted families. They generated an incremental income of Rs 1000 to Rs 2000 in 9.35 per cent of the cases, and less than Rs 1000 in 4.81 per cent of the cases. However, in about 29.26 per cent of the cases, the IRDP assets generated no income.

While the IRDP has been successful in providing incremental income to the poor, in most cases this income has not been adequate to enable the poor families assisted to cross the poverty line on a sustained basis. The major constraint in the implementation of the IRDP has been sub-critical investments which have adversely affected the incremental capital output ratio and consequently undermined the viability of the projects. The last concurrent evaluation of the programme, completed in 1993, revealed that only 14.81 per cent of the assisted families could cross the poverty line.

On the basis of the recommendations of a high-powered committee constituted by the Reserve Bank of India in 1993, the government took a few steps to enhance the efficacy of the programme. These consisted in:

Targeting the levels of investment per family at progressively higher levels each year
Enhancing the ceiling limit of collateral-free loans to a uniform limit of Rs 50,000 with a view to easing constraints faced by the poor while taking loans from the banks
Decentralization of sanctioning powers for infrastructural projects.

These interventions have had an impact on the average level of assistance provided by the programme, which rose from Rs 7889 per family in 1992–3 to Rs 15,036 in 1996–7.

Inadequate development of infrastructure and market facilities and absence of forward and backward linkages continue to be the key areas of concern under the IRDP. In addition, banks are unable to meet the full credit requirements of IRDP beneficiaries because of poor recovery of IRDP loans, lack of adequate rural banking infrastructure in certain areas, and the precarious financial position of the Regional Rural Banks and Cooperative Banks.

Training of Rural Youth for Self-employment

The Training of Rural Youth for Self-employment (TRYSEM) is a facilitating component of the IRDP. It aims at providing technical and basic managerial skills to the rural youth below the poverty line, enabling them to take up income-generating activities. During the Eighth Plan period, 1.528 million youth were trained under TRYSEM (34.16 per cent were self-employed and 15.05 per cent wage-employed). Efforts have been made to strengthen this programme by increasing the stipend, emphasizing professional training through established and recognized institutes (like the Industrial Training Institutes (ITIs), Community Polytechnics, Krishi Vigyan Kendras, etc.) and setting up production groups from TRYSEM trainees for the undertaking of ancillary activities. Despite these efforts, TRYSEM continues to be a weak link in the overall strategy for self-employment in rural areas, largely because of its poor convergence with IRDP.

The concurrent evaluation of IRDP during 1992–3 revealed that only 3.88 per cent of the IRDP beneficiaries received training under TRYSEM. It was also observed that the candidates who had undertaken training in TRYSEM only wanted stipendary benefits and did not utilize the knowledge gained under the programme to further their self-employment prospects.

Development of Women and Children in Rural Areas

Started in 1982 on a pilot basis, the upliftment of rural women belonging to families below the poverty line has been the focus of the Development of Women and Children in Rural Areas (DWCRA). The programme focuses on the empowerment of women and improvements in their socio-economic status. This is aimed to be achieved through awareness-building and the creation of income-generating opportunities for them on a sustained basis. The main strategy adopted has been to facilitate the access of poor women to employment, skill training, credit and other support services.

To improve the welfare and quality of life of the family as well as the community, it was envisaged that the DWCRA, 'women's groups', would form the focus for the convergence of other services like family welfare, health care, nutrition, education, child care, safe drinking water, sanitation, etc. From the inception of the scheme till 1996–7, 187,918 women's groups have been formed and 3.04 million rural women have benefitted from the expenditure of about Rs 2500 million.

In the implementation of DWCRA, the states of Andhra Pradesh, Kerala, Tripura and Gujarat have performed very well, while other states have lagged behind. Several successful groups have been formed, particularly in Andhra Pradesh, facilitating the empowerment of women in decision-making. The success of this programme in Andhra Pradesh is generally attributable to adult female literacy and the active involvement of non-governmental organizations (NGOs). In the states where DWCRA has not performed well, some reasons have been identified for the poor performance of the scheme. They include improper selection of groups, lack of homogeneity among group members, selection of traditional non-viable economic activities which generally yield low income, poor linkages in the supply of raw material and

marketing, lack of institutional financial support, inadequate training, poor access to upgraded technological inputs, and the inability
of trained, motivated staff to organize efficient women's groups in
the rural areas.

Supply of Improved Tool-kits to Rural Artisans

Launched in July 1992, this scheme supplied a kit of improved
handtools to a variety of craftspersons within a financial ceiling of
Rs 2000. Under the scheme the artisans had to bear only 10 per cent
of the cost, while the government provided the rest as a subsidy.
Rural artisans were also trained under TRYSEM, for which an age
relaxation was provided. Since the inception of the scheme until
1996–7, 610,000 tool-kits have been distributed to rural artisans at
an expenditure of Rs 1162 million. The scheme has been well-
received by rural artisans who are involved in blacksmith work,
carpentry, stonecraft, leatherwork, pottery, cane and bamboo work.
The limited evaluation studies conducted on this scheme also affirm
a positive impact of this scheme on rural artisans.

Future Strategy

Unlike wage employment programmes which tend to be relief-
oriented, the creation of self-employment opportunities through
the provision of assets can make the poor economically viable.
In practice, however, schemes for self-employment have operated
like programmes distributing doles, and made meagre contributions to reducing poverty or adding to growth (Rao 1987). Studies
on the implementation of self-employment programmes have
pointed out two major weaknesses – very little interaction with
the beneficiaries at the grassroots, and lack of concern for responding to real market demand.

Despite all its shortcomings, the IRDP continues to be the major
self-employment programme for poverty alleviation in the Ninth
Plan. The focus is now on pursuing an integrated approach by
subsuming the TRYSEM and Improved Tool-kits to Rural Artisans
schemes into the main programme. Now, IRDP will be specifically
targeted at those beneficiaries who have the requisite skills and
knowledge, an easier access to credit, and a better absorption
capacity to derive greater benefits from the investments made.

The average level of investment per family would be targeted at enhanced levels in the range of Rs 25,000 to Rs 50,000, depending upon the income gap between the beneficiary family and the estimated poverty line.

WAGE EMPLOYMENT PROGRAMMES FOR POVERTY ALLEVIATION

Jawahar Rozgar Yojana

Low productivity and unemployment are the factors largely responsible for rural poverty. It therefore becomes imperative to improve productivity and increase employment in rural areas. While an employment-oriented growth strategy can achieve this goal in the medium and long run, in the short run, supplementary employment has to be provided to the needy, especially in the agricultural lean season. To meet this specific requirement, two wage employment programmes — the National Rural Employment Programme (NREP) and the Rural Landless Employment Guarantee Programme (RLEGP) — were put into operation during the first four years of the Seventh Plan (1985–6 to 1989–90).

From 1 April 1989, the NREP and the RLEGP were merged into a single rural employment programme called the Jawahar Rozgar Yojana (JRY) which continued to be in operation throughout the Eighth Plan. Two main sub-schemes under the JRY include the Indira Awas Yojana (IAY), a massive housing programme, and the Million Wells Scheme (MWS). The latter is aimed at providing open irrigation wells free of cost to poor, small and marginal SC/ST farmers and bonded labourers.

The main objective of the JRY has been the generation of additional gainful employment through the creation of rural economic infrastructure, and community and social assets. As compared to earlier rural works programmes, a distinguishing feature of the JRY is that it is self-targeting. The employment offered by it is in fact at the statutory minimum wage for unskilled labour, which is usually lower than the prevailing market wage-rates. It is therefore assumed that only those willing to do manual work for the offered wage would seek employment on these public works. The programme thus provides a means of livelihood to those who are at critical levels of subsistence.

From its inception, till 1996–7, the states have utilized Rs 251,903 million under the JRY, generating employment of 6585 million mandays. Of the total employment generated, the share of SCs/STs was 3659.5 million mandays (55.57 per cent) and that of women 1681.40 million mandays (25.53 per cent). Besides generating supplementary employment of the casual labour kind, the JRY also contributed to the development of rural infrastructure through the creation of medium irrigation works, soil conservation works, land development, drinking water wells, rural roads, construction of school buildings, Panchayat offices, women's club buildings, housing and sanitation, and social forestry. In fact, assistance for the construction of classrooms under Operation Blackboard was specially provided under the JRY. The performance under JRY during the Eighth Plan period is presented in Table 5.3.

TABLE 5.3

PERFORMANCE OF JRY

DURING THE EIGHTH FIVE YEAR PLAN

(in million)

Year	Allocation (Centre+states)	Expenditure	Mandays generated
1992–3	31690.5	27095.9	782.10
1993–4	40594.2	38787.1	1025.84
1994–5	43769.2	42683.3	951.71
1995–6+	48487.0	44594.9	894.72
1996–7+	22367.9	21569.3	381.91
	186908.8	174730.5	4036.28

+ Provisional

Source: Documents of the Ministry of Rural Areas and Employment and Planning Commission; cited in Meenakshisundaram (1997).

A concurrent evaluation of the JRY conducted during 1993–4 revealed that nearly 82.16 per cent of the available funds were spent on community development projects, with the construction of rural link roads receiving the highest priority. The evaluation report also brought out certain inadequacies in the programme. It showed that 57.44 per cent of the elected Panchayat heads did not have any training for the implementation of JRY works.

Shortage of funds led to 49.47 per cent of the works not being completed on time. The share of women in the employment generated was poor and there were differentials in the wages paid to male and female workers. Locally-available material had not been adequately used in a large number of JRY works leading to cost overruns. Annual action plans were not discussed at the Gram Sabha meetings thus reducing the role of the community in the implementation of the works.

Based on the evaluation reports on wage programmes, a comprehensive restructuring was undertaken on 1 January 1996. The IAY and the MWS, the two main sub-schemes under the JRY, were made independent schemes both serving the cause of people below the poverty line. The second stream of JRY was merged with the EAS as part of this restructuring.

Employment Assurance Scheme

The Employment Assurance Scheme (EAS) was launched on 2 October 1993, in 1778 identified backward blocks, and universalized to cover all the rural blocks in 1997. Its main objective was to provide assured employment for 100 days of unskilled manual work, at the statutory minimum wages, to the rural poor in the age-group 18–60 years, especially during the agricultural lean season. The village Panchayats were the agency involved in the registration of persons seeking employment as well as in coordinating and monitoring the works. The scheme continued to be demand-driven and therefore no fixed allocations were made for the districts/blocks. Since its inception, 25.90 million persons have been registered for employment under the scheme.

The EAS has not been evaluated till date. However, a report of the Comptroller and Auditor General (CAG) on a review of EAS, during 1995–6, has highlighted certain shortcomings in the implementation of the programme. These include lack of proper planning and effective control in the execution of works, non-adherence to sectoral norms prescribed for execution of works, irregular diversion of funds by the states to other activities unconnected with EAS, poor maintenance of the assets created under the EAS, etc. The report brings out that on an average, only 18 and 16 days of employment per person were provided during 1994–5 and 1995–6 respectively. It also reveals that in Bihar,

CURRENT NATIONAL POLICIES

Madhya Pradesh and Uttar Pradesh, some works were either left incomplete or abandoned midway either for want of funds and/or non-availability of labour.

Future Strategy

In the Ninth Plan period, the thrust of government policy will continue to be on assuring at least 100 days of wage employment per person, per year. The EAS, coupled with the JRY, will be the channels through which funds will be allotted to the village Panchayats to generate employment and to maintain the assets thus created. Asset creation and poverty alleviation will be made compatible through a detailed planning exercise by involving the Panchayati Raj Institutions. This will contribute significantly towards reducing the administrative costs involved in delivery.

AREA DEVELOPMENT PROGRAMMES

To minimize the adverse effects of drought on the productivity of land, water and human resources and to control desertification and restore the ecological balance, the government is implementing four area based programmes. These are the Drought Prone Area Programmes (DPAP), launched in the Fourth Plan period (1969–70 to 1973–4), the Desert Development Programme (DDP), launched in the Fifth Plan period (1974–5 to 1978–9), the Western Ghats Development Programme (WGDP), and the Hill Area Development Programme (HADP).

The programme strategy in the DPAP and DDP is based on enhancing core sector activities such as afforestation, pasture development, soil and moisture conservation and water resources development. The scale of funding in both these programmes is roughly around Rs 2 million to Rs 2.5 million per 500 square kilometres of area covered under the programme. The WGDP and the HADP are being implemented with a view to improving the ecology and environment of the Western Ghat region and certain identified hill areas in the country. Afforestation gets the highest priority under both these schemes, followed by rural communication. Funds are allotted directly to the states concerned.

The creation of assets is incidental to providing employment under the Wage Employment Programmes, while the provision of employment becomes incidental under the Area Development Programmes (ADPs) which are essentially directed towards safeguarding and improving the environment and drought and desert proofing. Evaluation studies on the ADPs reveal that low levels of investment in widely disbursed areas, implementation of schemes without proper feasibility studies, diversion of funds for administrative expenditure, etc. have weakened the focus in these programmes. In the Ninth Five Year Plan period the ADPs will be therefore implemented on a watershed basis by the local communities, under the supervision of the Panchayats. This would ensure their integration with the other poverty alleviation programmes at both the planning and implementation levels.

LAND REFORMS AND POVERTY

Land is likely to remain the main source of livelihood for a large proportion of the rural population at least for several decades to come. Land management will continue to have crucial importance in the organization of the rural economy. Land reform is a programme of high socio-economic and political content. Such a programme has important implications for the structure of power in a society and, therefore, its implementation necessarily needs strong political will and responsive administration. It entails siphoning off the most important asset, i.e. land, from the most powerful sections of rural society, viz. the landlords, and distributing it among the landless and the poor.

Post-independence India saw several land reforms being enacted to abolish intermediaries, abolish or regulate tenancy, impose ceilings on landholdings, redistribute surplus land among the landless and semi-landless poor, and to prevent the alienation of tribal land by non-tribals. However, due to poor implementation of the land reforms, a substantial proportion of the total land still remains concentrated in a few hands. The vast majority of rural households constitute landless or semi-landless marginal farmers who are poor and indebted. Concealed tenancy exists and tribal alienation is a common problem.

Land reforms are not like other social reforms. Land reforms, if implemented radically and properly, could change the social composition and alter the class relations in a society. A responsive administration can play an important role in the implementation of land reforms. Lack of political will and the lukewarm attitude of the bureaucracy combined with an absence of organized pressure from below are the causes for the existence of small acreage of ceiling surplus land even in the large states of Uttar Pradesh, Madhya Pradesh, Rajasthan, Tamil Nadu and Maharashtra.

Poverty and Agrarian Reform: Some Case Studies

West Bengal and Kerala are universally acclaimed for successfully implementing land reforms, in particular tenancy reforms. The Left Government in West Bengal organized special drives to record the rights of tenants under the Operation Barga programme (1977). Making the beneficiaries aware of their rights was an important aspect of this campaign. Kerala, on the other hand, is the only state in India which successfully implemented the radical tenancy reform of land to the tiller, started in 1970, within the federal democratic set-up. Implicit in this policy of 'land to the tiller' was a ceiling on land ownership. The implementation of the core of the reforms, which was the abolition of landlordism, was quite successful (Herring 1983).

The reform programmes of these two states are criticized on the ground that these are not of a fundamental nature. The West Bengal programme has been criticized on the ground that it perpetuates the institution of tenancy. The Kerala model is criticized because in conferring ownership rights on tenants, no distinction was made between those who only supervised cultivation and those who contributed their labour. Therefore, the benefits of reform could also be reaped by the upper strata of tenants who used hired labour to operate their holdings.

Despite the somewhat limited nature of reforms in these two states, they were implemented quite successfully. One would therefore expect these states to have experienced human development and a reduction in poverty. To study the status of human development in these states, four variables, viz. birth rate, death rate, infant mortality rate and literacy rate, were considered. This data was compared to the information recorded in their respective neighbouring states, namely Tamil Nadu and Bihar. It was found that on all four grounds, the states of Kerala and West Bengal have done better, lending credence to the notion that land reforms contribute to human development and a reduction in poverty.

Over the last two decades, the experience of Kerala shows that land reforms contribute significantly to the socio-economic transition of the state. The beneficiaries received a boost in their dignity with the conferment of ownership rights to land. West Bengal also saw large changes in rural society as a consequence of the land reforms, which was followed by the pro-poor Panchayati Raj system.

Liberalization and the Land Question

The last five decades have witnessed a remarkable change in India's agrarian structure, in the sense that all large intermediaries have been abolished and land ownership rights have been conferred on a large army of erstwhile tenants. However, the basic character of the agrarian economy — a high concentration of land in the hands of a few landholders, and a growing number of marginal and sub-marginal farmers — remains unchanged. Also, the fragmentation of landholdings continues on a large scale. Only the states of Punjab, Haryana, Uttar Pradesh and parts of Maharashtra have enforced compulsory consolidation of holdings.

In the wake of economic liberalization, ceiling laws have been modified by several states to exempt orchards, fish ponds, etc. Despite agricultural tenancy being abolished in most states, concealed tenancy continues to exist on a large scale. There is now a move to open up tenancy to encourage private investment in agriculture and the upward mobility of various sections of the rural population. All these developments have made it necessary to reconsider the land question, particularly from the point of view of the access of poor people to land, the land rights of women, and the efficiency of land use and management.

Given such a backdrop one may ask whether a rationale exists for the further redistribution of land, and if so, how can it be achieved, given the limited success such efforts have had so far. In the present changing economic environment, can we really think of the emergence of small, albeit viable family farms, as the main form of farm organization through appropriate technological, institutional and policy changes? Alternatively, can we accept the reality of a growing capitalist pattern of agrarian society in which landholdings may get further concentrated in a few hands, while the majority of small and marginal farmers would be slowly converted into landless labourers?

In the wake of economic liberalization, several state governments are considering whether ceilings could be relaxed upwards in order to enable the private sector to participate in commercial farming. The Sub-group on Land Reform, Land-Use and Land Management of the Planning Commission has expressed the view that such a relaxation will not be helpful, primarily because non-farm employment opportunities are not yet available in adequate measure to a vast majority of the rural poor. Also, the amount of ceiling surplus land distributed was much lower than the estimated surplus area. In several states, notably Uttar Pradesh, Madhya Pradesh, Andhra Pradesh, Maharashtra, Rajasthan and Bihar, the absolute amount of surplus land distributed was much lower than that distributed even in a smaller state like West Bengal.

The Sub-group has said that through greater political and administrative commitment, at least the land already declared surplus should reach the intended beneficiaries. Institutional and legal rigidities have led to a large gap between land declared surplus and land actually distributed. According to the latest information, the net surplus available for redistribution is about 100,000 acres in the whole country, of which, 70 per cent is located in the two states of Madhya Pradesh (49 per cent) and Assam (30 per cent). In most other states, there is practically no surplus area left for redistribution unless surplus area taken out of the purview of revenue courts or area declared unfit for cultivation is reclaimed and put into the distributable pool. The Sub-group has strongly emphasized the need for a special drive to detect all *benami* and *farzi* transactions of land besides removing the legal hurdles in the distribution of land already declared surplus.

It has been found that the ceiling surplus land that has been redistributed among the poor is generally of poor quality. It is essential to make a provision for land improvement at the time of redistribution. Proper implementation of the central scheme of financial assistance to land reform beneficiaries for land improvement would help improve the quality of land assigned to them. This would also discourage reselling of the land allotted to a large extent.

In a majority of states, agricultural tenancy is banned, except for certain categories of disabled people. But concealed tenancy is present almost everywhere. The blanket ban on tenancy does not seem to have benefited either the rich or the poor. As suggested by the Sub-group, agricultural tenancy should be opened up, at least within the ceiling limits. This would enhance poor people's access to land and also activize the land lease market for rural growth. Several studies have indicated that in relatively backward areas, marginal farmers and landless labourers earn a substantial part of their income through leased in land. The important aspect in this regard is that the land rights of small farmers who lease out land should be protected. This will become possible only when there is a proper system of land records for which the involvement of Panchayat Institutions and local-level functionaries should be sought.

Access to Common Property Resources/Forest Land

In rural areas, every village has common lands and other common property resources. In some states, certain portions of these lands have been allotted to the rural poor under land distribution programmes, viz. in the 'Free Patta Scheme'. This scheme aimed at promoting productive utilization of marginal lands for poverty alleviation, and gave preference to the landless poor. However, experience has shown that such schemes have not been very effective. Nevertheless, instances of successful joint forest management by people, forest departments and co-operatives to improve the socio-economic conditions of the landless poor are not lacking. Several research findings show that excessive use, encroachment, and lack of care of the common property resources by the rich have led to erosion and degradation of these resources in recent years. As a consequence, the access of poor people to grazing land, fuel-wood, fodder, etc. has considerably diminished. Awareness needs to be created at the village and Panchayat level for the protection and proper management of these resources.

Access of Women to Land

The existing landownership pattern in India is male-oriented except in some isolated pockets where the matrilineal system is in operation. The land reform measures undertaken so far have not focused on safeguarding the interests of women, either as owners or as co-cultivators of land. Ceiling laws are also unequal in most states. In the context of poverty alleviation, gender-sensitivity with regard to the access to land becomes all the more compelling. In most parts of the country, women constitute a disproportionately large part of the poor. Rural women are more dependent on agriculture for their livelihood than men. Hence, measures to provide land assets to poor women should have a direct effect on poverty.

A large proportion of rural households are female headed and it has been estimated that about 20 per cent of them are among the poorest. Land redistribution in favour of such households should have a direct impact on poverty. A significant proportion of farms are managed by women in the absence of male heads, who have migrated to towns in search of employment. Enhancing women's land rights will improve welfare and efficiency in production by improving their access to credit, etc. Even in male-headed households, the intra-household distribution of basic necessities such as food and health-care is unequal. Hence, there can be poor women in non-poor households. It is also found that where women control incomes directly, family needs are better taken care of. Hence, women's direct access to land assets will alleviate poverty for women in particular and for the households in general.

Policy Directions in Land Reform

The task of agrarian reform does not end with the implementation of ceilings on landholdings or with the conferment of ownership or occupancy rights on tenants. To consolidate gains from land reform, an efficient utilization of land is very important. In the predominantly poor states, which are densely populated, and also add to the agricultural population at a faster pace, there has been a steep decline in the per capita and per worker area. Thus, even to maintain the present standards of living, productive efficiency would need to rise to compensate for the decreases in the net sown area. For an efficient use of land, the beneficiaries of land reforms will have to be provided with supporting facilities. They could also be brought together for group activities such as horticulture, floriculture, etc.

The demands for relaxing land reform laws has been a stronger phenomenon in the post-New Economic Policy (NEP). But there is every need to go on with land reforms, because land reforms are very likely to contribute to human development and reductions in poverty. They also empower the poor and therefore ensure that the poverty alleviation programmes and the benefits thereof reach them. Besides these, the development model which usefully served the non-poor states, particularly Punjab, need not suit the poor states as in the latter it need not lead to sustainable development and could damage the ecosystem, leading to problems of equity.

LEGAL ENABLING FRAMEWORK

The Directive Principles of State Policy enshrined in Part IV of the Constitution of India lay down the principles fundamental to the governance of the country. Article 41 makes it obligatory for the state to make 'effective provision for securing the right to work, to education and to public assistance in cases of unemployment, old age, sickness and disablement and in other cases of undeserved want' however, within the limits of its economic capacity and development. Article 42 directs the state to make provisions for securing just and humane conditions of work and maternity relief.

Subsequent Articles make it clear that the state

shall endeavour to secure, by suitable legislation or economic organization or in any other way, to all workers, agricultural, industrial or otherwise, work, a living wage, conditions of work ensuring a decent standard of living and full enjoyment of leisure and social and cultural opportunities. In particular, the state shall endeavour to protect and improve the environment and to safeguard the forests and wild life of the country.

Thus, poverty reduction and ensuring better livelihood to the poor with environmental safeguards have been among the basic tenets of governance in India.

The National Social Assistance Programme (NSAP) came into effect from 15 August 1995, specially to fulfil the commitments made under Articles 41 and 42 of the Constitution. This programme has three components: (i) National Old Age Pension Scheme (NOAPS); (ii) National Family Benefit Scheme (NFBS); and (iii) National Maternity Benefit Scheme (NMBS), all of which are targeted at people below the poverty line.

Under the NOAPS, an old age pension of Rs 75 per month is provided per beneficiary aged 65 and above. The NFBS provides a lumpsum family benefit to the bereaved household in case of the death of the primary breadwinner, in the 18–64 age group. Under the NMBS there is a provision of Rs 300 per pregnancy, for pre-natal and post-natal maternity care, for the first two children, for women above the age of 19 years and belonging to poor households. Amongst these three programmes, the NOAPS has performed relatively well. Lack of awareness and poor community involvement are cited as the main reasons for the poor performance of the NMBS and the NFBS programmes. As these programmes have been in operation for only two years, no evaluation of these has been conducted so far.

URBAN POVERTY ALLEVIATION

Migration from rural areas is seen as the main cause for urban growth as well as urban poverty, making urban poverty alleviation an important element of urban policy in India. The Nehru Rozgar Yojana (NRY) and the Prime Minister's Integrated Urban Poverty Eradication Programme (PMIUPEP) are two urban poverty alleviation programmes in addition to a centrally-sponsored scheme to provide Urban Basic Services for the Poor (UBSP).

Launched in October 1989, the NRY consists of three sub-schemes: (i) a Scheme for Development of Urban Micro Enterprises (ii) a Scheme for Urban Wage Employment and (iii) a Scheme for Housing and Shelter Upgradation.

Under these schemes, the main task of identifying, earmarking and coordinating relevant sectoral inputs is the responsibility of the states and local bodies, while the central government indicates its overall contribution. In the Eighth Plan period, Rs 4980.4 million was spent on these schemes, generating urban employment to the tune of 69.07 million mandays, and setting up over 0.9 million micro enterprises in the urban areas of the country.

There has been no concurrent evaluation of the performance of the urban poverty alleviation programmes. A close look at the performance of these programmes during the Eighth Five Year Plan reveals that the priority attached to the alleviation of urban poverty under these programmes is quite low, despite the fact that the magnitude of the problem is quite large. One reason for this could be the perception that urban poverty is basically a transfer of rural poverty into urban areas and therefore, urban poverty can be minimized by dealing with rural poverty appropriately.

Also, poverty alleviation programmes in the urban areas are highly fragmented, with overlapping objectives and strategies. The

integration of these programmes with sectoral and area development has not taken place effectively. It needs to be noted that in
the planning and implementation of these programmes the role
played by voluntary organizations, community-based organizations, and local bodies remained peripheral. For better implementation of urban poverty alleviation programmes, effective targeting
of the urban poor combined with a bottom-up approach, and an
active involvement of the local bodies and NGOs is needed.

DELIVERY SYSTEMS

Evaluation studies have consistently shown that many development programmes with laudable objectives have failed to deliver
results because of inadequacies in design and implementation.
Available channels for efficient delivery of development benefits
include NGOs, the Panchayat Raj Institutions (who now have
constitutional responsibility to plan and implement poverty alleviation programmes), central and state governments (who also have
the constitutional mandate to eradicate poverty), and the beneficiaries themselves. A combination of all the four channels would
be the best option for an effective implementation of poverty
alleviation programmes. We discuss below the experience gained
and problems encountered in the implementation of poverty
alleviation programmes through different delivery mechanisms.

PARTICIPATORY APPROACHES

Besides designing and implementing anti-poverty programmes
through the state and local governments, the government and
various NGOs have been encouraging the implementation of
programmes which involve participatory approaches for the benefit of the poor. Participatory approaches involve the people in the
implementation of programmes designed for their own upliftment.
Implementation of watershed development programmes, which
have been taken up on a large scale under the DPAP and DDP,
depend entirely on the participation of the beneficiaries. These
programmes are designed and executed by a watershed development team which includes women and backward community
members and the funds for these programmes are channelized
through the village Panchayats.

The Pani Panchayat Model in Maharashtra is an ideal example of community participation in the implementation of an effective poverty alleviation programme. Pani Panchayat Lift Irrigation Schemes are undertaken by a group of farmers, water being allocated on the basis of the number of family members and not as a proportion of landholdings, so that water rights are not attached to land rights. Cropping patterns are restricted to seasonal crops with low water requirements. Water is acknowledged as a common property resource and all members of the village community, including the landless, have the right to its use. The beneficiaries of the Lift Irrigation Scheme are responsible for planning, administering, implementing and managing the scheme and for distributing the water to the members in an equitable manner.

On the same principle of community participation, Community Lift Irrigation Projects in Purandhar and other neighbouring blocks in Maharashtra have brought about 3000 acres of land under irrigation, covering 10,000 people from 1500 families. The total capital investment for this irrigation project has been Rs 70 million, of which the beneficiaries have contributed Rs 1.5 million, the remaining being met by loans and subsidies from various financial institutions.

NON GOVERNMENT ORGANIZATIONS

Non government organizations play an important role in the efficient and cost-effective provisioning of services, in mobilizing communities and groups and thereby providing effective channels of communication between the government and the people, and in the implementation of programmes requiring innovative/experimental approaches.

The government, because of its command over and access to much greater resources and working under a broader institutional framework, has the potential for designing and implementing suitable programmes to reach much wider sections of the poor. Non government organizations on the other hand, have several advantages over government organizations in the provision of assistance to the rural poor, and this aspect needs to be given due recognition. Their close contact with the poor, willingness to spend more time on various experiments (as they are not under any

pressure to disburse funds to meet a fixed target, unlike government officials) and their ready acceptability by society, give them
an edge over the government. While NGOs may have the capacity
to access the poor better, governments are still required to initiate
suitable changes to enable sustained expansion of the economy.

The Council for Advancement of People's Action and Rural
Technology (CAPART) is an example of government support to
NGOs. It was created specifically to channel funds from the
government to the NGOs for the implementation of direct poverty
alleviation programmes. It has so far supported over 5000 projects,
both small and large, and the sanction process for projects under
CAPART has been decentralized.

Despite acknowledged efforts by the government to involve
voluntary agencies in the implementation of its development
programmes, the existing relationship between the government
and NGOs is, to say the least, unsatisfactory. The government is
apprehensive about the political motivations, financial impro-
prieties, and lack of suitable accountability mechanisms in the
functioning of NGOs. The NGOs on their part are dissatisfied
with the rigidity in government norms and criteria which inhibit
any innovation, the inflexible framework in which they have to
function, delays in the release of grants and the huge gap between
project appraisal and the disbursement of funds, red tape, poor
monitoring mechanisms adopted by the government, and delays
in the redressal of grievances and problems faced by NGOs during
the implementation of their projects. The need of the hour is a
narrowing down of the gulf that exists between the government
and the voluntary organizations so that their synergy can be
exploited for the upliftment of the deprived.

Although on the face of it, the central and state governments
share the concern for ensuring a responsive, accountable, transparent, decentralized and people-friendly administration at all
levels, yet there is considerable frustration and dissatisfaction
among the people, especially the weaker sections of society, about
the apathy, irresponsiveness and lack of accountability of public
servants. The Government of India convened a conference of the
chief ministers of the states in May 1997, to evolve a concrete
action plan to gear the government machinery to provide a
responsive, transparent and clean administration to the people,
especially the poor. The action plan arrived at proposes to make

the administration accountable and citizen-friendly, ensure transparency and the right to information, and take measures to cleanse and motivate the bureaucracy. The adoption and implementation of this action plan would, however, require strong political will and a reiteration from the central, state and local governments of their commitment to provide an accountable and responsive administration.

While the NGOs and Panchayati Raj Institutions can also effectively implement poverty alleviation programmes, the very size of the country and the magnitude of its problems require a people-friendly bureaucracy. Motivating and training the bureaucracy to perform better in the quest for poverty alleviation will contribute substantially to the success of poverty eradication programmes in India. The need to restore a sense of idealism and a spirit of dedication among the bureaucrats will therefore remain the real challenge for quite some years to come.

COMMITMENTS MADE AND FOLLOW-UP TO UN CONVENTIONS

India has actively participated in all UN Conferences and initiated the inclusion of commitments on education, health and culture at the Copenhagen Social Development Summit.

Poverty: In consonance with the programme of action of the Social Development Summit, India has established goals and targets for poverty reduction. The action programme also called for higher priority to be assigned to basic social services and access to productive assets and economic opportunities. India's twin goals of growth with equity and human development heed this call.

Women: India, unlike many other countries, adopted the Platform for Action of the Beijing Conference (1994) without reservations. Ratification of the Convention for the Elimination of all forms of Discrimination Against Women is a step forward towards gender equality.

Basic education: The pledge to provide free and compulsory education to children up to the age of fourteen by the year 2000 was reaffirmed by India at the Jomtien Conference (1990) on Education for All. India ratified the Convention on the

Rights of the Child and reflected it in the National Policy on Education (1992).

Environment: Following the Rio Earth Summit (1992), India ratified the Convention on Biodiversity and Climate Change. Agenda 21 must animate the national environment action plan.

Population: The adoption of the Programme of Action of the International Conference on Population and Development (1994), commits India to ensure universal access to a full range of safe and reliable family planning and reproductive health services, by the year 2015, and to reduce, by the year 2000, maternal mortality rates to one half of the 1990 levels.

Children: India endorsed 27 child survival and development goals at the World Summit for Children (1990), to be achieved by the year 2000.

Human rights: The Vienna Human Rights Conference (1993), reaffirmed that all human rights are universal, indivisible and interdependent; and that democracy, development and fundamental freedoms are mutually reinforcing. India's Constitution subscribes to this philosophy. But there are gaps between the law in the books and law in action. The National Human Rights Commission and other civil society actors are striving to close these gaps.

Habitations: Poor, disadvantaged and vulnerable groups were not forgotten at the Habitat II City Summit, Istanbul, 1996. Shelter for the homeless in rural areas is one of seven basic services in the common programme adopted in India in the same year.

Food and nutrition: It constitutes the first line of defence to safeguard human security. The great strides made since the 'green revolution' enabled food production to overtake population growth. India now needs an 'evergreen revolution' to safeguard health and nutrition. The call from the Rome Food Summit (1996) has been heard (UNDP 1997).

CONCLUSION

The anti-poverty strategy in India relies chiefly on government programmes to create assets, and employment and make basic goods and services available to the poor. Despite their inherent weaknesses, the anti-poverty programmes implemented in India have played an important role in reducing both under-employment and poverty. Not only do the statistical estimates indicate the reduction, but field studies in areas affected by drought and scarcity conditions also provide convincing evidence of the beneficial impact of anti-poverty programmes (Tendulkar 1993; Acharya 1989). While there may not be any need to evolve new programmes to meet the situation arising out of the current process of globalization, it would, however, be necessary to identify measures that need to be taken to ensure that the existing anti-poverty programmes are sharply focused and suitably altered to meet the requirements of the poor.

There is a general feeling that only a very small percentage of funds allotted by the government for the implementation of anti-poverty programmes reaches the poor. There are three main reasons for this: (i) a multiplicity of programmes, which needs to be reduced by amalgamating similar programmes, making implementation and monitoring simple and cost-effective (ii) ineffective monitoring and evaluation strategies adopted because of deficiencies in the machinery for concurrent evaluation (e.g. lack of manpower and technical competence), particularly at the grass roots level and (iii) lack of will to take punitive action against inefficiency and corruption.

One possible remedy to ensure better utilization of funds meant for the poor is to ensure people's participation by actively involving the Panchayati Raj Institutions in the planning and implementation of development programmes. Under the Constitution (73rd Amendment Act), every state in the country now has a legally constituted Panchayati Raj Institution set-up whose key functions include implementation of anti-poverty programmes. This has to be carried out now, both in letter and in spirit, by devolving appropriate resources from the state and central levels to the Panchayati Raj Institutions. A strong monitoring system, consisting of inspections through the official machinery and vigilance through responsible non-official committees at Panchayat levels would, however, be necessary to help the local bodies in discharging their responsibilities efficiently.

The time is now opportune to aim at eradicating poverty in India by the end of the century. In the Ninth Five Year Plan, it is proposed to tackle the issue in a two-pronged manner. The first approach would be to involve the poor themselves in the task of poverty eradication. This can be achieved by building organizations of the poor to enable them to save and invest effectively, organize their production activities, market their products and have access to credit and inputs. It would aim at empowering the poor to assert their right to resources (including credit), with particular emphasis on the empowerment of women, and the creation of a network of support organizations (NGOs, banks for the poor, cooperatives, thrift groups, etc.).

The second approach would be to clearly define and implement a development strategy which is conducive to the elimination of poverty. Such a development strategy would require land reforms at the forefront, a strengthening and diversification of the agricultural sector, and improvements in rural infrastructure. Programmes would need to be designed to provide employment security to the poor. In the short run they would get cash security in the form of wages, and gain sustainable employment in the long run. Food security would also be an integral part of such a development strategy which would ensure adequate availability of food to the poor at affordable prices. A human development orientation to the strategy is imperative. Special emphasis has to be given to nutrition, health, education, shelter and self-employment, to promote the status of women and the rights of children in society.

Alongside the steps taken to effectively implement poverty alleviation programmes, the Government of India also proposes to evolve a national population policy, which is to be the bedrock of all its development activities. The proposed policy aims at achieving the replacement level of fertility for the nation by the year AD 2010. Efforts to stabilize the population, provide people with basic minimum services as well as employment through better implementation of anti-poverty programmes, and a more efficient system of public distribution of food will hopefully assist the rural poor in crossing the poverty line in the not too distant future.

6

Dimensions and Measures
of Human Poverty

INTRODUCTION

Income-poverty, defined as a basic minimum calorie intake, captures a limited perspective of what poverty really connotes. Human poverty is more than income-poverty – it is the denial of choices and opportunities for living a tolerable life (UNDP 1997a). Human deprivation has several forms which include poor survival chances, unjust employment of children, child prostitution, bonded labour, hunger, environmental pollution, domestic violence, and social exclusion, which arise out of caste and gender discrimination and are not related to income in a predictable manner. To capture all the facets of poverty, a multi-dimensional, people-centred concept is required which takes into account along with income and consumption, other aspects of human life.

According to Drèze and Sen (1989: 183), it is possible to distinguish between two contrasting approaches to poverty alleviation. One approach is to promote economic growth. This would not only enable the population to take advantage of the potentialities released by greater general affluence but would also provide an improved basis for public support. This is called the strategy of 'growth-mediated security'. The alternative approach, called 'support-led security', consists of resorting to direct public support in fields such as employment provision, income redistribution, health care, education, and social assistance so that destitution may be removed without waiting for an improvement in the general level of affluence. While this distinction is important as it reflects ' . . . an important strategic aspect of public action', several interconnections between the two routes also have to be recognized in order to avoid a 'false, total dichotomy' (Drèze and Sen 1989: 187).

Anand and Ravallion (1993) carry the analysis forward and provide further insights by identifying three routes that link human development and aggregate affluence. These are (i) capability expansion through economic growth (ii) capability expansion through poverty reduction, and (iii) capability expansion through social services. Drèze and Sen maintain that, the first route belongs to the category of 'growth-led security', whereas the other two could be considered as distinct components of 'support-led' security. The distinction between these two components within support-led security is necessary as one is aimed at raising the income levels of individuals, whereas the other is intended to raise capabilities in terms of education and health which may or may not get translated into higher incomes.

Non-income indicators such as education, health, and nutrition, also need to be given emphasis when studying human deprivation. A glance at some human development indicators reveal that female literacy varied from 20.44 per cent in Rajasthan to 86.17 per cent in Kerala in 1991 (GOI 1997). The Sample Registration System's estimates for 1995 indicate that infant mortality varied from 103 in Orissa to 16 in Kerala (Office of Registrar General 1997). If the focus is narrowed to the level of the district, the inter- and intra-state disparities in human deprivation turn out to be even starker. For example, female literacy in rural areas varied from 4.20 per cent in Barmer (Rajasthan) to 93.97 per cent in Kottayam (Kerala) (National Institute of Adult Education, 1993).

On the issue of hunger, the National Sample Survey (NSS) provides information on the distribution of households based on the availability of two square meals a day. In 1983, the proportion of rural households able to have two square meals a day was 81 per cent, it rose to 88 per cent in 1991, and by the end of 1993, it was 93 per cent (Parikh 1997). Post-reform years have therefore seen a reduction in the percentage of hungry people.

Five states, viz. Bihar, Madhya Pradesh, Orissa, Rajasthan and Uttar Pradesh, have very low levels of human development. They also have low per capita incomes. However, indicators of well-being are not necessarily strongly correlated with income indicators. Punjab and Haryana for example, have high per capita incomes but do not have correspondingly high literacy rates, and their female-to-male ratios are relatively on the lower side. To understand the various facets of poverty better, it is essential to consider non-income related aspects such as health, education, qualitative changes in the conditions of the poor, and the size and state of vulnerable groups such as child labour, widows, rural artisans, and the disabled.

REDEFINING POVERTY

One of the early recommendations to widen the definition of poverty from the more common calorie-based income criterion came from the Expert Group on Poverty which was constituted by the Planning Commission to 'look into the methodology for the estimation of poverty at national and state levels and also to go into the question of redefining poverty line if necessary' (Planning Commission 1993: 2). The report states, 'While quantifying poverty, it is desirable that we not only consider the calorie needs of an individual but also give due weightage to the basic needs of shelter and health and other needs like education and transport, which would help him\her in living a "normal" and "effective" existence' (emphasis as in the original) (ibid.: 31).

Specifically, the Expert Group recommended the inclusion of (i) the dominant characteristics of the poor population in terms of their distribution by region, social group and family characteristics (ii) nutritional status including anthropometric measurements and activity patterns by age, sex and socio-economic categories (iii) health status including mortality, morbidity, access to and use of health services and costs (iv) educational status comprising school enrolment, reach, cost and quality of public education services, and (v) living environment including density of settlements, living space per head, type of houses, access to amenities, safe drinking water and sanitation. These recommendations have not been translated into relevant empirical exercises that redefine poverty in keeping with the broader approach, either by the Planning Commission or by other scholars.

More recently, interest in redefining poverty has been triggered off by the initiative undertaken by the United Nations Development Programme (UNDP) in devising two new measures of human deprivation, viz. the Capability Poverty Measure (CPM) in 1996, and a Human Poverty Index (HPI) in the 1997 report. Commenting on the inadequacy of the income measure of poverty, the

1995 report states, ' . . . "income-poverty" is only part of the picture. Just as human development encompasses aspects of life much broader than income, so poverty should be seen as having many dimensions' (UNDP 1996: 27). While the reports draw attention to human deprivation to complement income measures of poverty, their focus is on the percentage of poor who lack the basic or minimal capabilities (1996) as well as access to minimal facilities (1997) rather than on the average attainment of minimum capabilities by individuals.

The CPM is a composite index which considers the lack of three basic capabilities. The capability to be well-nourished and healthy, represented by the proportion of children under five who are underweight; the capability for healthy reproduction, represented by the proportion of births unattended by trained health personnel; and the capability to be educated and knowledgeable, represented by female illiteracy. These three deprivations have equal weights. It is evident that the index captures deprivations suffered by women and children.

The HPI extends the concept of CPM to other dimensions. Three indicators are included: (i) survival deprivation represented by people not expected to survive to age 40 (ii) deprivation in education and knowledge represented by the adult illiteracy rate and (iii) deprivation in economic provisioning which is a combined index of the indicators of population without access to safe water, health services and of undernourished children below age 5.

A common shortcoming of the CPM as well as the HPI is that they do not distinguish between outcome and process indicators, and deprivations based on the individual, household, community and region. An additional shortcoming arises from the differing dimensions of the indicators used for calculating the indices.

Despite its limitations, the HPI may be considered to be a useful first attempt at including education and health deprivations in the measurement of poverty.

HUMAN POVERTY INDEX

The HPI visualized by UNDP comprises three types of deprivations, deprivation in health, knowledge and provisioning from both public as well as private sources. The three indicators have been given equal weight.

Following the UNDP's methodology an attempt has been made to calculate the HPI for Indian states.[1] The following is the procedure for computing HPI.

Deprivation in longevity has been represented by the percentage of people not expected to survive upto age 40 (P_1), and deprivation in knowledge by the percentage of people who are illiterate (P_2). The deprivation in a decent living standard in terms of overall economic provisioning is represented by a composite (P_3) of three variables, i.e. the percentage of people without access to safe water (P_{31}), the percentage of people without access to health services (P_{32}) and the percentage of moderately and severely undernourished children (P_{33}).

The composite variable P_3, is constructed by taking a simple average of the three variables P_{31}, P_{32} and P_{33}.

The formula for calculating the HPI is given by

$$HPI = [(P_1^3 + P_2^3 + P_3^3) - 3]^{1\backslash 3}$$

Calculating the Human Poverty Index

The indicators used to measure the three main dimensions of deprivation included in the HPI for the Indian states are given in Table 6.1. Health deprivation has been measured in terms of the probability of dying before age 40. The life tables reported in the Sample Registration System's (SRS's) Analytical Studies Report No. 1 of 1996 is used for the purpose of deriving the values of this indicator.

Deprivation in knowledge is a composite indicator of the two variables, adult illiteracy, and percentage of children in the age group 6–14 years not attending school, with the former having a weight of two-thirds and the latter one-third. The data for illiteracy rates are obtained from the population Census of 1991, while the data for the latter variable is taken from the National Family Health Survey (NFHS) conducted by the International Institute for Population Sciences (IIPS) in 1992–3.

Deprivation in provisioning is in two parts, public and private. Deprivation in public provisioning is represented by the following

---

[1] The indicators used to construct the HPI were agreed upon at the workshop organized by UNDP (24–26 November 1997), at Kandy to discuss the South Asia Poverty Monitor.

TABLE 6.1
DEPRIVATION INDICATORS USED IN THE CONSTRUCTION OF HUMAN POVERTY INDEX FOR INDIAN STATES

States	Health (probability) of dying before 40)	Illiteracy	Children (age 6–14) not attending school	Knowledge	Children not fully immunized	Deliveries outside institutions	No access to health services	No access to safe water	Not living in electrified houses	No access to safe water and electricity	Children under 4 undernourished (wt for age)*	Provisioning
	1989–3	1991	1992–3		1992–3	1992–3		1992–3	1992–3		1992–3	
(1)	(2)	(3)	(4)	(5)†	(6)	(7)	(8)#	(9)	(10)	(11)‡	(12)	(13)§
1. Andhra Pradesh	14.88	55.91	36.7	49.51	17.5	67.2	42.35	36.6	37.8	37.20	49.1	42.88
2. Assam	21.81	47.11	29.9	41.37	43.6	88.9	66.25	56.8	79.6	68.20	50.4	61.62
3. Bihar	19.48	61.52	48.7	57.25	53.5	87.9	70.70	36.4	83.4	59.90	62.6	64.40
4. Gujarat	16.75	38.71	24.3	33.91	18.9	64.4	41.65	24.9	23.4	24.15	50.1	38.63
5. Haryana	15.37	44.15	18.7	35.67	17.5	83.3	50.40	27.0	15.0	21.00	37.9	36.43
6. Karnataka	15.68	43.96	29.5	39.14	15.2	62.5	38.85	24.4	36.0	30.20	54.3	41.12
7. Kerala	5.14	10.11	5.2	8.47	11.4	12.2	11.80	79.0	39.7	59.35	28.5	33.22
8. Madhya Pradesh	25.34	55.80	37.7	49.77	34.4	84.1	59.25	44.2	37.6	40.90	57.4	52.52
9. Maharashtra	12.27	35.13	18.5	29.59	7.5	56.1	31.80	21.5	26.4	23.95	54.2	36.65
10. Orissa	22.33	50.91	30.4	44.08	28.0	85.9	56.95	49.1	72.2	60.65	53.3	56.97
11. Punjab	13.87	41.19	19.2	33.86	17.5	75.2	46.35	1.4	8.0	4.70	45.9	32.32
12. Rajasthan	19.88	61.45	41.2	54.70	48.5	88.4	68.45	42.7	48.1	45.40	41.6	51.82
13. Tamil Nadu	13.45	37.24	17.6	30.69	3.3	36.6	19.95	25.4	36.2	30.80	48.2	32.98
14. Uttar Pradesh	22.24	58.40	38.7	51.83	43.3	88.8	66.05	25.7	68.1	46.90	59.0	57.32

(1) States	(2) Health (probability) of dying before 40) 1989–3	(3) Illiteracy 1991	(4) Children (age 6–14) not attending school 1992–3	(5)[†] Knowledge	(6) Children not fully immunized 1992–3	(7) Deliveries outside institutions 1992–3	(8)[#] No access to health services	(9) No access to safe water 1992–3	(10) Not living in electrified houses 1992–3	(11)[‡] No access to safe water and electricity 1992–3	(12) Children under 4 undernourished (wt for age)* 1992–3	(13)[§] Provisioning
15. West Bengal	14.82	42.30	32.3	38.97	22.4	68.5	45.45	15.1	67.1	41.10	56.8	47.78
India	17.99	47.79	32.5	42.69	30.0	74.5	52.25	31.8	49.1	40.45	53.4	48.70
Mean	16.89	45.59	28.57	39.92	25.50	70.00	47.75	34.01	45.24	39.63	49.95	45.78
Standard Deviation	4.91	12.73	10.98	11.95	15.08	21.25	16.99	18.09	22.83	17.07	8.52	10.63
Coefficient of Variation	29.09	27.92	38.42	29.94	59.13	30.35	35.58	53.18	50.46	43.09	17.05	23.23

Notes:
a. * Anthropometric indice weight for age, -2SD, also includes the children who are below-3 standard deviation
   units from the International Reference Population median.
b. † Column 5 is an arithmetic mean of columns 3 and 4. Weights attached are 2/3 for illiteracy and 1/3 for
   children not attending school.   c. # Column 8 is an arithmetic mean of columns 6 and 7.
d. ‡ Column 11 is an arithmetic mean of columns 9 and 10.
e. § Column 13 is an arithmetic mean of columns 8, 11 and 12.

Sources: 1. Column 2: Registrar General, 1996, SRS Based Abridged Life Tables 1989–93, SRS Analytical Studies Report
   No. 1, New Delhi (1996).
2. Column 3: Census of India, 1991, Final Population Totals: Brief Analysis of Primary Census Abstract,
   Series 1, Paper 2, Office of Registrar General, New Delhi (1992).
3. Columns 4, 6, 7, 9, 10 and 12: International Institute of Population Studies, National Family Health Survey
   1992–3 India, Bombay.

indicators: (i) percentage of population without access to health services (ii) percentage of population without access to safe water; and (iii) percentage of population not living in electrified houses. The percentage of population without access to health services is a composite indicator encompassing the variables (i) percentage of children not fully immunized and (ii) percentage of deliveries outside institutions, with both the variables being given equal weights. A similar procedure has been used to combine the variables, percentage of population without access to safe water, and not living in electrified houses.

Deprivation in private provisioning has been represented by the percentage of children under four years of age who are malnourished.[2] The final indicator on provisioning is an average of the percentage of population without access to health services, percentage of population without access to safe water and electricity, and percentage of children undernourished, with all the three dimensions being given equal weight.

The values of the HPI for the period 1991–3 are given in Table 6.2. The human poverty at the all-India level is 41 per cent,

TABLE 6.2

HUMAN POVERTY INDEX FOR INDIAN STATES, 1991–93

(per cent)

	States	*Health*	*Knowledge*	*Provision-ing*	*Human poverty index*
1.	Andhra Pradesh	14.88	49.51	42.88	40.78
2.	Assam	21.81	41.37	61.62	47.18
3.	Bihar	19.48	57.25	64.40	53.60
4.	Gujarat	16.75	33.91	38.63	32.33
5.	Haryana	15.37	35.67	36.43	31.90

[2] The suggested indicator was a percentage of children under five who were malnourished but the data available from the International Institute for Population Science, National Family Health Survey is for the age group 0–4. An alternative source could be the data supplied by the National Nutrition Monitoring Bureau. The data for 1988–90 from this source does not include all the fifteen major Indian states.

States	Health	Knowledge	Provision-ing	Human poverty index
6. Karnataka	15.68	39.14	41.12	35.42
7. Kerala	5.14	8.47	33.22	23.19
8. Madhya Pradesh	25.34	49.77	52.52	45.60
9. Maharashtra	12.27	29.59	36.65	29.49
10. Orissa	22.33	44.08	56.92	45.42
11. Punjab	13.87	33.86	32.32	29.27
12. Rajasthan	19.88	54.70	51.82	46.96
13. Tamil Nadu	13.45	30.69	32.98	28.19
14. Uttar Pradesh	22.24	51.83	57.32	48.32
15. West Bengal	14.82	38.97	47.78	38.52
India	17.99	42.69	48.70	40.49

Note: The Human Poverty Index has been computed using the methodology of the UNDP (1997).

Source: Prabhu and Kamdar (1997).

though it ranges between a low of 23 per cent (Kerala) to a high of 54 per cent (Bihar). Among the three dimensions, the highest deprivation at the all-India level as well as for fourteen individual states (the only exception being Punjab) is observed in the case of provisioning, with knowledge following closely. Health deprivation in terms of probability of dying before age 40 is found to be much lower. It is surprising that even in Kerala, as high a proportion as 33 per cent of the population is deprived in terms of provisioning. While a part of the perceived deprivation could be due to the definitions adopted for items such as 'safe water', this alone cannot be the sole explanation, and the result needs to be examined further.

Nine states recorded lower ranks on the HPI as compared to their SDP rankings. These included rich states such as Haryana and Punjab, Gujarat and Maharashtra as well as poorer states such as Rajasthan and Uttar Pradesh. Only four states, viz. Kerala, Madhya Pradesh, Orissa and Tamil Nadu, had higher ranks on HPI as compared to SDP. The states of Bihar and West Bengal had no difference in their rankings of HPI and SDP. The analysis clearly points to the fact that relatively better economic status does not ensure lower deprivation in terms of basic capabilities.

States have been ranked in Table 6.3, on the basis of HPI and SDP values.

TABLE 6.3
RANKING OF STATES ACCORDING TO HPI AND SDP

States	HPI value 1991–93	HPI rank	SDP per capita 1989–90 to 1991–92	Rank	Column 5 minus column 3
(1)	(2)	(3)	(4)	(5)	(6)
1. Andhra Pradesh	40.78	9	4779.3	7	–2
2. Assam	47.18	13	4065.7	10	–3
3. Bihar	53.60	15	2610.7	15	0
4. Gujarat	32.33	6	5725.0	4	–2
5. Haryana	31.90	5	7492.0	2	–3
6. Karnataka	35.42	7	4855.0	6	–1
7. Kerala	23.19	1	4352.7	9	8
8. Madhya Pradesh	45.60	11	3915.3	12	1
9. Maharashtra	29.49	4	7250.3	3	–1
10. Orissa	45.42	10	3400.7	14	4
11. Punjab	29.27	3	8679.7	1	–2
12. Rajasthan	46.96	12	3981.0	11	–1
13. Tamil Nadu	28.19	2	5108.0	5	3
14. Uttar Pradesh	48.32	14	3510.3	13	–1
15. West Bengal	38.52	8	4681.3	8	0

Notes: a. The state with the lowest HPI value has been ranked one as the HPI is a deprivation measure.

  b. Column (4) is computed from GOI (1996).

Source: Prabhu (1997).

7

Expenditure for Human Development and Public Provisioning for Poverty Alleviation

INTRODUCTION

It is now well recognized that economic growth cannot be relied upon exclusively to attain higher levels of human development. There is also a need to judiciously combine capability enhancement through poverty reduction and social services with direct state intervention. The multitude of poverty alleviation programmes implemented in the country since the 1970s have had only limited success in achieving their objectives. The public provision of education, health and nutrition have been important elements of India's Five Year Plans though they have always remained peripheral in nature and never occupied centre-stage till the Eighth Plan.

The Indian states offer a very rich and interesting arena for the study of the relative importance of the routes linking economic and human development. No single state has in fact been able to achieve a balance between 'growth-mediated' and 'security-led' development strategies.

This chapter makes an attempt to include education, health and nutritional deprivations in the definition of poverty, and to delineate the main features pertaining to financing of poverty alleviation programmes as well as social-sector services. Changes in absolute and relative levels of government expenditure on rural development and social services are illustrated and an attempt is made to understand the trends in growth rate of real per capita social-services expenditure between 1974-5 and 1995-6. The effectiveness of expenditures incurred in terms of human development outcomes, and the relative importance of economic growth and public provisioning in capability enhancement of Indian states are considered.

GOVERNMENT FINANCING OF RURAL DEVELOPMENT AND SOCIAL SERVICES

Rural development programmes designed to provide both non-land based assets and employment have been an integral part of India's Five Year Plans. Expenditure on rural development has been 6 per cent of total revenue expenditure on an average (when data for 25 states are considered). Some states such as Andhra Pradesh, Bihar, Maharashtra, Orissa and West Bengal have however recorded higher shares, ranging between 6 and 9 per cent. In the 1990s, allocations to the rural employment component of rural development expenditure have increased, particularly in Bihar, Madhya Pradesh and Orissa, where they constitute 6–8 per cent of revenue expenditure.

Total public expenditure on social sectors by central and state governments constitutes 6.4 per cent of GDP on an average. Allocations to education account for 3.3 per cent of GDP, while allocations to health account for 1.45 per cent. Housing, labour, social security and welfare account for the rest (Tulasidhar 1997). The intention of the government to accord greater priority to social expenditure has been reiterated periodically. However, utilization of earmarked funds has been unsatisfactory. During 1992–5, the average utilization rate for all the states was a little over 44 per cent of the Eighth Plan outlay (60 per cent was the best performance). More recently, out of Rs 14,000 million allocated by the central government for midday meals in the 1996–7 budget, states were able to utilize only Rs 8000 million (GOI 1998). An important reason for this shortfall is inadequate capacity in state governments to implement programmes sponsored by the centre.

Economic reforms accord priority to reducing the fiscal deficit, but deficits have not been cut significantly. The increase in government borrowing at market rates has resulted in a steep escalation of the interest burden. Interest payments will continue to claim a substantial part of the central government's revenue receipts in the foreseeable future. Although the central government allocations to the social sector have been slightly increased, the combined total of central and state government expenditure has been adversely affected. There is a growing risk that the twin objectives of sustaining long-term growth and overcoming human deprivation may be defeated because social-sector resource requirements remain unfulfilled (UNDP 1997b: 18).

The current composition of central government health expenditure shows a welcome shift away from tertiary health care towards communicable diseases which control family welfare schemes, nutrition schemes, and the Integrated Child Development Services (ICDS) programmes. Similarly, elementary education has been accorded greater priority relative to secondary and higher education. However, as the quality of schooling depends on the quality of higher education provided to teachers, and because shortfalls in skill levels relative to requirements must be addressed through post-school education, it is not desirable to promote school education at the expense of higher education. More resources will have to be found to improve quality in all educational institutions.

There is a wide variation in the levels of per capita social expenditure among states (Prabhu 1997b). There has also been a sharp deceleration in the rate of growth of state per capita social expenditure between 1985–92. Per capita expenditure on maternal and public health in low-income states is about one-third of that in high-income states. Differences in levels of spending were more pronounced with respect to the expenditure on disease-control programmes, which are partly financed by the central government. Real per capita health-related expenditure, was highest in Rajasthan (mainly on water supply and sanitation), Punjab and Tamil Nadu. It was lowest in Bihar, Uttar Pradesh and Andhra Pradesh. In 1990–1, public health as a proportion of total state expenditure varied from 5 per cent in Rajasthan to 28 per cent in Maharashtra. Per capita expenditure on education was higher in Punjab, Kerala and Maharashtra, compared to low per capita expenditure in Madhya Pradesh, Bihar and Uttar Pradesh. These patterns indicate that the relationships between needs and resources are lopsided and unbalanced.

EDUCATION AND HEALTH: ACCESS, COST AND QUALITY

Education and health services in India face three fundamental problems: lack of easy access for the needy, high costs, and poor quality. These afflict primary education, where public provisioning is predominant, as much as health services, where private-sector provisioning is more prominent (UNDP 1997b: 19).

Field studies conducted in selected states have uncovered several inefficiencies in primary schooling. High levels of teacher absenteeism mean that little teaching takes place in a large number of schools, especially in the rural areas. Even when teachers attend to duties with more regularity, teaching quality is a major problem. The learning environment in many schools is not congenial to creative teacher–pupil interaction. Learning levels of children, measured by achievement tests, are disappointing.

Overall costs of schooling are relatively high, even though the fee element is insignificant in government primary schools. Recent estimates show that a family, on average, has to spend anywhere between Rs 317 (in government schools) and Rs 742 (in private schools) per year per child aged 6–14 years (NCAER 1996). Even those families which send their children to government schools find that education imposes a large financial burden. Compounding this burden are certain socio-cultural norms and the intra-household division of labour which affect schooling. Girls in rural areas invariably replace or supplement adult women's labour. In remote tribal and hill economies, the non-availability of fuel, fodder and water directly increases the workload of children, especially girls. Such economic and socio-cultural factors have dampened the motivation of parents to keep them in school long enough to acquire even the minimum levels of basic skills. Many families may not even enrol their children because of such reasons.

The demand for education depends upon the mobilization of those communities which have never had experience with schooling, and getting them to appreciate its long-term value. It also depends on tangible improvements in the quality of education and ease of access. Both the supply of and demand for education must be increased in order to overcome the extent of human poverty in India. There is considerable scope for realizing efficiency gains, provided substantial investments are made in management and training capacities.

Educationally-backward states must be accorded priority in the allocation of resources, including technical assistance, to improve their capacity to utilize additional resources to come up to the level of educationally-advanced states like Kerala. Substantial additional resources must be mobilized for education from national and external sources. The government's aspiration to increase the allocation to education from the current 3.9 per cent of GDP to 6 per cent of GDP by the year 2002 shows a recognition of the importance of this sector. But translating this aspiration into reality will mean increasing by 415 per cent of the total Eighth Plan allocation for education during the Ninth Plan period (UNDP 1997b).

Government expenditure on direct nutrition programmes assume importance for India's poor. The main nutritional problems in India are identified as: inadequate nutritional entitlements, lack of women's control over resources, and the malnutrition-infection complex (Gillespie and McNeill 1992). For a country burdened with a large problem of under-nutrition, the expenditure incurred on direct nutrition programmes is negligible, constituting less than 1 per cent of GNP in 1990–1. Among the states, higher amounts of total revenue expenditure were allocated to this sector in Gujarat (2 per cent), Karnataka (2 per cent) and Tamil Nadu (5 per cent).

India spends about 7 per cent of its GDP on health. This is relatively high for developing countries. Expenditure on health accounts for 75 per cent of total household expenditure. This high proportion of household expenditure indicates a relatively high disease burden and poor quality of services provided in public health-care centres. Aggregate expenditure statistics mask the fact that over 65 per cent of beds are in government hospitals. The government is also the principal source of preventive and promotive health care. Poor health outcomes relative to the amounts spent on it show that both public and private health facilities are sub-standard. Some indicators that substantiate this claim are the following:

Only one out of three deliveries is attended to by a trained birth attendant.
Only one out of four deliveries takes place in institutions.
Less than a third of children receive ORS or RHS as treatment for diarrhoea.
Thirty-five per cent of children who are 12–23 months are fully immunized (UNDP 1997b).

Private household expenditure is predominant in curative primary care, which accounts for about 46 per cent of total health expenditure. Secondary and tertiary (hospital) care accounts for 27 per cent of the total. Although direct treatment costs in public hospitals are largely subsidized, households have to bear substantial costs for the purchase of medicines (owing to shortages in public dispensaries), food, and transport. A recent study estimated that for the poorest tenth of the population, these costs amounted to between 10 per cent (in Kerala) and 230 per cent (in Uttar Pradesh, Punjab, Rajasthan, and Bihar) of annual per capita consumption expenditure (Krishnan 1996). The top 10 per cent of the population, however, bore a relatively lighter burden, as the average cost of treatment was between 5 and 40 per cent of the annual per capita consumption expenditure of that class.

Financial protection against illness is available to only the small number of people in the organized sector through such schemes as Employees State Insurance Scheme and the Central Government Health Insurance Scheme. The medical insurance plan of the General Insurance Corporation covers a very small proportion of the population. As a result, curative health can be very expensive relative to household budgets. The present situation in the health sector is serious. Anti-poverty programmes have failed to take into account the strong nexus between health and poverty. For those trapped in the prison of poverty, the crisis in the health sector spells calamity.

Social sector allocations are almost all absorbed by staffing costs. Little remains for capital investment and the maintenance of essential infrastructure. The bulk of public expenditure for health is appropriated for recurrent costs, with 62 per cent spent on salaries. Maintenance costs account for about 20 per cent, capital investments in building and machinery for about 7 per cent, and transfers to local bodies for 11 per cent (average of 14 major states in 1985–90, NIPFP, 1993; World Bank 1995: 22). In the case of education, the share of salaries was 84 per cent in 1987–8 with the proportion increasing to over 90 per cent for elementary education. The share of teaching materials, libraries, etc. constituted a very low proportion (7 per cent) of elementary education expenditure (Tilak 1995). The increase in the education expenditure since the 1980s has been attributed to a sharp increase in teachers' emoluments which have grown at an 'extraordinary rate of 9 per cent per year in real terms' (Dréze and Sen 1995: 123).

The emphasis on higher-level facilities, normally located in urban areas, has meant sharp rural–urban disparities in the attainment of crucial human development indicators. While in the case of education at least the physical infrastructure exists (95 per cent of the habitations are reported to be provided with schools), in the health sector even the infrastructure provision is biased towards urban areas. Thus, in 1991, rural areas accounted for only 32 per cent of hospitals and 20 per cent of total hospital beds (Duggal *et al.* 1995). The utilization of primary health centres in rural areas is reflected in the percentage of illness episodes that are referred to them. In 1990, this varied from a low of 2 per cent in Madhya Pradesh to 21 per cent in Maharashtra (NCAER 1992).

Financial norms for the construction of public health facilities need revision to take inflation into account. State governments have been unable to meet physical targets out of allocated funds as they are based on outdated norms. Even though returns on investments in health care are sub-optimal, and need to be urgently improved, additional resources are required to meet the growing demand for services. The reasons for this growing demand include a demographic bulge in the number of aged persons, and rising morbidity on account of unhealthy living environments. The spread of HIV infection will cause a steep increase in the demand for health care, overwhelming health facilities that are already inadequate.

Health services are in need of major reforms. Existing facilities in the health sector are not being used by people because of low-quality, irregular attendance of medical staff, inadequate equipment, and poor maintenance and upkeep. Most private medical practitioners in rural areas are untrained and unqualified. Lack of decentralization has frequently led to a mismatch between local needs and the health services on offer, and to low accountability and higher inefficiency. A substantial proportion of the specialist posts in community health centres are vacant, rendering many of them useless as first referral units. At the same time, the ratio of qualified doctors to para-medical and nursing personnel is lopsided in India. There are severe imbalances in India between public and private health care; and within public health care between preventive and curative services; between primary, secondary and tertiary health care services; and between salary expenses and other recurrent expenditures (UNDP 1997b).

Indian states seem to differ in the emphasis accorded to rural development and what in popular nomenclature are termed social sectors. Even within the social sectors, which are usually taken to comprise education, health, and nutrition, the emphasis placed on the different components varies widely. The tendency to emphasize one or two components of social security with no comprehension of the synergistic relationship between the various aspects of such security is an important reason for the limited success achieved in human development indicators in most states. The examples of Maharashtra and Tamil Nadu prove this point convincingly.

Maharashtra has pioneered the Employment Guarantee Scheme (EGS) that provides employment to the able-bodied in rural areas for cash wages. However, the beneficial impact of this measure is limited by the fact that the state charges higher-than-warranted prices (23 per cent higher than the central issue price for wheat in 1994) for foodgrains issued through the Public Distribution System (PDS). The state also does not place much emphasis on social protective measures for the old and the destitute. Tamil Nadu, on the contrary, places overwhelming emphasis on protective social security measures such as pensions to the aged and needy and direct provision of food through the midday meal scheme and a variety of other similar programmes. The price charged by the government for rice, the main cereal consumed, is 35 per cent lower than the central issue price, indicating the priority given to this item in government policy. A curious fact is that while the state gives substantial importance to doles which impose a heavy financial burden on the government, it makes no concerted effort to promote productive employment, despite the prevalence of high rates of unemployment, particularly in rural areas (Prabhu 1997c). Such fragmented and short-sighted policies are pursued in most states so that the synergies accruing from even the limited expenditure incurred on the social sectors are not realized.

TRENDS IN GOVERNMENT EXPENDITURE ON RURAL DEVELOPMENT AND SOCIAL SERVICES

Union Government: The centre's role is important in setting priorities and providing leadership and guidance but the bulk of expenditure on social services as well as rural development is incurred by the state governments. Trends in the expenditure incurred by the centre and the states since 1980–1 on these two major heads are given in Table 7.1. The expenditure of the

TABLE 7.1

STATEWISE TRENDS IN REAL PER CAPITA EXPENDITURE ON
RURAL DEVELOPMENT AND EMPLOYMENT AND SOCIAL SERVICES

Amount in Rs

State	Rural Development and Employment					Social Services					Human Priority Expenditure				
	I	II	III	IV	V	I	II	III	IV	V	I	II	III	IV	V
1. Andhra Pradesh	7.06	19.56	28.41	26.96	28.59	70.75	112.40	137.32	120.81	121.80	32.21	59.25	78.43	68.91	70.30
2. Assam	2.87	6.80	11.23	13.17	12.77	65.24	94.87	125.97	127.11	146.18	31.87	50.68	77.25	82.62	89.63
3. Bihar	28.31	28.76	27.09	20.82	17.37	34.43	65.67	77.98	101.45	86.64	–	98.17	79.68	61.42	49.95*
4. Gujarat	8.39	23.15	25.16	29.71	24.44	84.54	123.04	168.66	176.07	181.16	46.32	71.80	103.93	110.09	106.09
5. Haryana	6.79	14.52	19.75	19.65	13.03	76.11	120.27	177.27	185.32	188.76	36.34	64.64	89.95	90.27	83.26
6. Karnataka	4.47	13.53	19.85	24.66	26.22	77.38	97.25	147.91	152.67	170.08	42.51	60.30	82.30	83.90	86.42
7. Kerala	5.09	13.79	14.96	18.79	15.74	122.94	131.86	164.40	190.55	195.20	61.58	66.82	80.96	102.13	87.53
8. Madhya Pradesh	4.84	14.22	16.79	22.35	23.43	65.31	82.68	109.09	118.84	123.03	34.04	52.53	69.86	77.67	79.40
9. Maharashtra	11.40	18.60	23.38	15.49	31.02	95.25	126.30	172.25	185.57	202.06	52.20	73.42	96.99	86.44	86.36
10. Orissa	6.72	13.83	20.09	25.91	25.15	74.46	99.20	116.03	120.56	136.53	36.28	48.72	75.07	80.48	83.24*

Table 7.1 (continued)

Table 7.1 (continued)

State	Rural Development and Employment					Social Services					Human Priority Expenditure				
	I	II	III	IV	V	I	II	III	IV	V	I	II	III	IV	V
11. Punjab	2.88	10.04	10.23	5.69	4.63	97.85	137.70	207.61	198.55	177.90	40.75	62.93	72.64	71.56	65.26
12. Rajasthan	9.39	14.30	30.78	24.88	21.46	78.74	93.78	124.13	156.30	162.61	46.77	59.48	93.42	103.20	99.10
13. Tamil Nadu	13.68	19.50	16.98	22.18	20.43	103.34	121.44	155.85	201.43	201.03	51.59	69.12	79.09	103.81	102.56
14. Uttar Pradesh	4.39	13.41	20.11	31.34	24.92	47.24	69.65	89.33	113.25	100.58	29.00	46.18	62.19	92.48	71.83*
15. West Bengal	4.48	7.27	15.00	21.57	20.78	79.44	109.36	121.12	156.28	147.91	27.99	38.74	51.72	68.05	62.64
Mean	8.05	15.42	19.99	21.54	20.67	78.20	105.70	139.66	153.65	156.10	37.96	61.52	79.57	85.54	67.90
Std. Dev	6.17	5.58	5.87	6.34	6.71	21.03	21.22	34.14	33.31	35.40	13.75	13.70	12.79	14.27	35.98
C.V	76.65	36.21	29.39	29.42	32.45	26.90	20.08	24.45	21.68	22.68	36.21	22.27	16.07	16.68	52.98

Notes:
a. I   indicates 1974–5 to 1978–9 – V Plan.
b. II   indicates 1980–1 to 1984–5 – VI Plan.
c. III   indicates 1985–6 to 1989–90 – VII Plan.
d. IV   indicates 1990–1 – Pre-adjustment year.
e. V   indicates 1991–2 to 1995–6 for Social Services and 1991–2 to 1993–4 for Rural Development and Human Priority Expenditure indicates post-adjustment period.
f. *   indicates 2 year averages.

Source: Cited in Prabhu (1997): Reserve Bank of India, Finances of State Governments NIPFDP data bank.

union government on social services and rural development taken together has been increasing. Particularly, since 1993–4, such expenditure continues to constitute less than 2 per cent of GDP in 1994–5.

Also interesting is the fact that the expenditure incurred by the states on these two heads declined from 7.35 per cent of GDP in 1989–90 to 6.92 per cent in 1994–5. The combined expenditure of the centre and the states also exhibits a declining trend in relative terms since 1989–90, and despite a slight improvement in the ratio since 1993–4, it continues to be lower than the share registered in 1980–1. However, partly due to a compression in total expenditures since 1991–2, the share of the two sectors in aggregate disbursements increased since 1993–4 from 25 per cent to over 26–27 per cent.

The structural adjustment programme initiated in mid-1991, led to expenditure compression in union government finances in the first two years, though the situation improved in subsequent years. There has been a step-up in the allocations to rural development, education and health at the level of the union government since 1992–3, though the emphasis has been on different items in different years. A detailed examination of the intra-sectoral allocations of the union government (Prabhu 1997c) indicates a shift in the pattern of expenditure towards primary-level facilities in education and health, in the urban areas, whereas in the rural development sector, the shift has been towards rural employment. Thus, while trends in the level and pattern of union government expenditure on rural development and social services have been encouraging, the impact of this favourable development is likely to be limited owing to a number of factors.

First, in the case of programmes for rural development, there exist a variety of heads under which programmes are undertaken. There is a bewildering variety of schemes initiated under each head, with each scheme adhering to different norms for the identification of beneficiaries, pattern of financing, provision of matching grants by states, etc. In some of the schemes, the allocations are so meagre that it has led to comments that the 'centre has been more interested in establishing its presence rather than in making a serious substantive contribution' (Guhan 1995: 1098).

Second, in the social-services sector, the allocations of the union government form a very small proportion of the total expenditure on the sector. Moreover, the programmes are implemented in the development of infrastructure provided by the states. The poor quality of this infrastructure has further been undermined by the deceleration in social-services expenditure since the mid-1980s (Prabhu and Chatterjee 1993). This combined with the low and declining share of materials and components in the expenditure on education and health is likely to have further undermined the quality of services rendered in government schools and primary health centres.

Third, the implementation of centrally sponsored programmes rests critically on the interest evinced by the state governments, which in many cases includes the provision of matching grants. The fiscal stringency experienced by several states implies that many state governments, particularly those of the poorer ones, may not be in a position to have access to the central allocations for social sector development. A glaring instance of well-meaning gestures by the union government being reined in by the states is evident in recent reports (*The Economic Times* 1997: 1), which indicate considerable shortfalls in union government allocations for the programme of the provision of basic needs. As against a provision of Rs 24,660 million that was to have been spent on this head during 1996–7, the actual expenditure till the end of February 1997 was only Rs 16,900 million, indicating a shortfall of Rs 9000 million. The main reason for this was the reported reluctance of states to manage the programme.

Finally, large centrally-sponsored programmes are also criticized on the score that they are designed and implemented uniformly in all the states without much importance being given either to the regional peculiarities or needs of the states. This is very clearly evident in the central allocations for disease control, which seldom have much correlation with either the disease pattern or the organizational structure in the states. The problem is compounded by excessive reliance on the target approach to the exclusion of broader issues facing these sectors. Moreover, the targets are most often inappropriate and are specified mainly in terms of expenditure to be incurred.

State Governments: Trends in levels of real per capita expenditure on rural development and employment, social services and human priority expenditures for the period 1974–5 to 1995–6, are given in

Table 7.1. Trends in the share of revenue expenditure on each of these heads are given in Table 7.2. The data are presented in terms of five year averages for the periods 1974–5 to 1978–9 (period I) which coincides with the Fifth Five Year Plan period, 1980–1 to 1984–5 (period II) coinciding with the Sixth Plan period, 1985–6 to 1989–90 (period III) which is the Seventh Plan period, 1990–1 as a single time point (period IV) which is the pre-adjustment year, and 1991–2 to 1995–6 (period V) which constitutes the post-adjustment period. In the case of rural development and employment and human priority expenditures, data were available only upto 1993–4 and hence data reported for period V comprise an average for three years only, viz. 1991–2 to 1993–4.

Human Priority Expenditures

Human priority expenditures have been defined to include expenditure on elementary education, primary health (comprising public health, rural health services and family welfare), water supply and sanitation, and nutrition. Rural development and employment comprise expenditure on budget heads for special rural development programmes, rural employment and other rural development programmes. Real per capita expenditures have been calculated using state specific deflators from Central Statistical Organization (CSO) data on state domestic product and mid-year population. All the data pertain to revenue expenditure, which constitutes over 95 per cent of total expenditure on these sectors. All data pertain to final accounts figures except for 1995–6, which are revised estimates. Data on social services and revenue expenditure are from the Reserve Bank of India's annual article on the finances of state governments, whereas those on rural development and employment and on items constituting human priority expenditure are from the data bank of the National Institute of Public Finance and Policy (NIPFP).

Over various plan periods there has been an increase in government expenditure on social services, rural development, as well as human priority expenditure. The coefficient of variation exhibited a declining trend till 1990–1 (the pre-structural adjustment year) in all the three items, while thereafter it has increased particularly in the real per capita human priority expenditure across states.

TABLE 7.2

STATEWISE TRENDS IN PERCENTAGE SHARE OF REVENUE EXPENDITURE ON RURAL DEVELOPMENT AND EMPLOYMENT AND SOCIAL SERVICES AND HUMAN PRIORITY EXPENDITURE IN TOTAL REVENUE EXPENDITURE

(Per cent)

State	Rural Development and Employment					Social Services					Human Priority Expenditure				
	I	II	III	IV	V	I	II	III	IV	V	I	II	III	IV	V
1. Andhra Pradesh	4.19	7.64	8.46	8.58	7.85	41.66	43.68	41.43	38.45	38.55	18.94	23.10	23.58	21.93	22.51
2. Assam	1.76	3.18	3.63	4.22	3.24	40.31	43.02	41.97	40.71	41.02	19.65	23.28	25.58	26.46	26.79
3. Bihar	5.82	9.43	10.78	11.40	9.51	41.01	43.79	40.18	39.35	35.32	27.27	30.76	32.34	33.63	29.42*
4. Gujarat	4.40	8.00	5.82	6.64	4.39	43.98	42.42	39.40	39.36	36.47	24.33	24.86	24.25	24.61	22.43
5. Haryana	2.89	4.13	3.92	3.55	1.52	31.37	34.38	35.78	33.44	25.95	15.12	18.54	17.85	16.29	14.40
6. Karnataka	2.18	5.05	5.33	6.26	5.21	37.51	35.06	40.64	38.75	38.03	20.60	21.98	22.40	21.30	20.07
7. Kerala	2.20	5.43	4.27	4.46	3.10	52.54	50.03	47.78	45.23	41.23	26.25	25.49	23.69	24.24	20.80
8. Madhya Pradesh	3.08	6.68	6.13	7.36	6.42	41.13	39.25	40.34	39.14	37.38	21.45	24.79	25.72	25.58	24.77
9. Maharashtra	4.21	5.23	4.66	2.95	5.00	35.06	34.94	35.96	35.38	36.43	19.20	20.42	19.89	16.48	19.72*
10. Orissa	3.49	6.48	7.06	8.26	6.34	38.75	46.04	41.27	38.45	38.93	18.87	22.72	26.68	25.66	25.31*

State	Rural Development and Employment					Social Services					Human Priority Expenditure				
	I	II	III	IV	V	I	II	III	IV	V	I	II	III	IV	V
11. Punjab	1.20	2.85	2.03	1.01	0.61	40.51	38.83	42.99	35.36	26.58	16.79	17.79	15.08	12.74	10.08
12. Rajasthan	5.13	6.17	9.41	6.73	4.45	40.01	41.24	38.34	42.27	37.39	24.24	26.14	28.82	27.91	24.71
13. Tamil Nadu	5.76	7.56	5.11	5.64	3.88	41.98	44.16	43.94	44.17	38.45	21.88	27.18	24.17	26.42	20.89
14. Uttar Pradesh	3.34	7.71	8.02	9.84	6.86	35.42	38.59	36.28	35.57	31.40	21.72	26.01	25.31	29.05	22.91*
15. West Bengal	2.79	3.49	5.83	6.63	5.51	44.73	48.53	43.67	44.76	40.16	16.97	18.57	20.08	20.90	19.18

Notes:
a.   I   indicates 1974–5 to 1978–9 – V Plan.
b.   II   indicates 1980–1 to 1984–5 – VI Plan.
c.   III   indicates 1985–6 to 1989–90 – VII Plan.
d.   IV   indicates 1990–1 – Pre-adjustment year.
e.   V   indicates 1991–2 to 1995–6 for Social Services and 1991–2 to 1993–4 for Rural Development and Human Priority
       Expenditure indicates post-adjustment period.
f.   *   indicates 2 year averages.

Source: Cited in Prabhu (1997): Reserve Bank of India, Finances of State Governments NIPFDP data bank.

In the period 1974–5 to 1978–9, the mean per capita expenditure on rural development and employment across fifteen major states was Rs 8, and only five states recorded levels of expenditure which were higher than this amount (Table 7.1). Bihar recorded the highest level of per capita expenditure (Rs 28), whereas Punjab recorded the lowest level (Rs 3). In the period 1991–2 to 1995–6, the mean per capita expenditure was Rs 21 and as many as ten states spent at levels which were either equal or higher than the mean. The highest expenditure per capita was incurred by Maharashtra (Rs 31), whereas the lowest was by Punjab (Rs 5). Maharashtra's emphasis on rural employment through the much acclaimed Employment Guarantee Scheme is well known. Punjab's agricultural progress evidently obviates the need for separate rural development programmes.

In the case of social services, the mean per capita spending increased substantially from Rs 78 in 1974–5 to 1978–9 to Rs 156 in the period 1991–2 to 1995–6. Kerala recorded the highest level (Rs 123) in the former period, whereas the lowest level (Rs 34) was recorded by Bihar. In the latter period, surprisingly, Maharashtra recorded the highest level (Rs 202) with Bihar continuing to register the lowest spending per capita (Rs 87).

While social services expenditures indicate the level of spending, the pattern of spending and its orientation towards basic-level facilities is indicated by human priority expenditures. In the Fifth Plan period, as against a mean human priority expenditure level of Rs 38, Kerala recorded the highest level of Rs 62 among the fourteen states for which data have been reported. The lowest level was recorded in Uttar Pradesh (Rs 29 per capita). In the post-adjustment period, Gujarat recorded the highest level of human priority expenditure (Rs 107) as against an average for fourteen states of Rs 80. Tamil Nadu obtains the second rank, with a per capita spending of Rs 103, even as Kerala's spending at Rs 68 is much lower than that recorded in other states.

It may be noted that in the post-adjustment years, state governments experienced fiscal compression. It may be argued that there could be a general compression of expenditures during such adjustment and therefore a perusal of the share of social-services expenditure in total revenue expenditure may be more meaningful (Table 7.2). While social-services expenditure has increased in real per capita terms, its share in total revenue expenditure has exhibited a decline between the Fifth Plan period and the post-adjustment period in most states. The share of revenue expenditure on social services in total revenue expenditure ranged between 31 (Haryana) and 53 per cent (Kerala), in the Fifth Plan period, whereas in the post-adjustment years, the range was between 26 (Haryana) and 41 per cent (Assam and Kerala). As compared to the Fifth Plan period, seven states report a decline in the share of social services expenditure in the post-adjustment years. The share of social services in 1991–6 is lower than that recorded in 1974–9. Whereas in earlier periods, over nine states spent over 40 per cent of revenue expenditure on social services, a level considered essential by the UNDP (1991), in the post-adjustment years, only four states exceeded this norm. In fact, all the states except Assam and Maharashtra have experienced a decline in the relative share of social services in the total revenue expenditure. The decline is observed in 1990–1 (the pre-adjustment year), though it is sharper in the post-adjustment period. The decline in relative expenditure on social services is sharpest in Haryana and in the high-income state of Punjab. In Haryana, the share of social services in the total expenditure declined from 36 per cent in the Seventh Plan period (1985–6 to 1989–90) to 33 per cent in the pre-adjustment year (1990–1) and further to 26 per cent in 1991–2 to 1995–96. In Punjab, the situation was similar with the share of social services in total revenue expenditure declining from 43 per cent in the Seventh Plan period to 35 per cent in 1990–1 and further to 27 per cent in the period 1991–2 to 1995–6.

The decline in the share of social services is partially compensated by the rise in the share of rural development, which ranged from 1 to 10 per cent of revenue expenditures in the post-adjustment period as compared to the range of 1 to 6 per cent in the Fifth Plan period. An analysis of the share of human priority expenditure in the total revenue expenditure indicates ratios that are less than half of those recorded for social services in most states, pointing to the fact that less than 50 per cent of expenditure on social services is on basic-level services.

For the rural development expenditure and human priority expenditure heads, comparison of ratios for the Fifth Plan period and the post-adjustment period is not possible as the figure for the former is a five-year average, for the latter, the average is for three years. To provide a more consistent picture, the following analysis focuses on the pre-adjustment period (1988–9 to 1990–1) and the post-adjustment period (1991–2 to 1995–6).

Human Expenditure Ratios

The public expenditure ratio is the ratio of total revenue expenditure to State Domestic Product (SDP), social allocation ratio is the share of social services in revenue expenditure, social services and rural development expenditure ratio is the share of social services and rural development in total revenue expenditure, and human allocation ratio is the ratio of revenue expenditure on items of human priority.[1] Public expenditure ratio, social allocation ratio, social services and rural development expenditure ratio and human allocation ratio are analysed to gain a better understanding of the pattern of social-services expenditure incurred in Indian states over the period 1988–91 and 1991–4 (Table 7.3).

TABLE 7.3
STATEWISE HUMAN DEVELOPMENT EXPENDITURE RATIOS
1988–91 AND 1991–94

States	PER		SAR		SRR		HAR	
	1988–91	1991–94	1988–91	1991–94	1988–91	1991–94	1988–91	1991–94
Andhra Pradesh	18.39	17.34	39.31	37.10	47.23	46.26	22.06	22.51
Assam	21.65	21.90	41.23	42.03	44.80	45.85	25.37	26.79
Bihar	19.86	22.80	40.35	34.70	49.60	45.04	32.31	29.42*
Gujarat	17.13	18.68	38.77	33.93	44.56	38.64	23.89	22.43
Haryana	16.37	16.68	35.76	29.78	39.32	32.02	16.46	14.40
Karnataka	19.34	18.74	39.43	37.92	44.50	44.05	20.70	20.07
Kerala	22.43	21.85	46.28	40.92	50.16	44.65	24.12	20.80
Madhya Pradesh	18.22	19.59	39.99	37.21	46.36	44.50	25.40	24.77
Maharashtra	15.83	14.52	35.81	35.59	38.96	41.41	17.21	19.72*
Orissa	20.15	22.18	39.72	38.84	46.87	46.44	26.13	25.31*

[1] The public expenditure ratio and the social allocation ratio are similar to the ones suggested in UNDP, *Human Development Report*, 1991.

States	PER		SAR		SRR		HAR	
	1988–91	1991–94	1988–91	1991–94	1988–91	1991–94	1988–91	1991–94
Punjab	14.45	16.46	41.10	26.86	42.54	27.57	14.48	10.08
Rajasthan	19.44	22.17	40.81	37.93	47.84	42.03	28.02	24.71
Tamil Nadu	19.49	22.34	43.22	37.06	48.04	41.23	24.16	20.89
Uttar Pradesh	18.35	19.23	36.24	31.74	44.60	39.71	27.30	22.91*
West Bengal	14.93	14.68	43.57	40.31	49.81	46.71	20.36	19.18

Note:
  a. PER – Public Expenditure Ratio – Total revenue expenditure as % of SDP.
  b. SAR – Social Allocation Ratio – Rev. exp. on social services as % of total revenue expenditure.
  c. SRR – Social Services and Rural Development Ratio – Rev. exp. on social services and rural development as % of total revenue expenditure.
  d. HAR – Human Allocation Ratio – Rev. exp. on human priority items as % of total revenue expenditure.
  e. *   indicates 2 year average.
Source: Prabhu (1997), Computations based on data from RBI Bulletins and respective State Budget Document.

The social services and rural development expenditure ratio is included as an additional ratio, in keeping with the view that in any analysis of human development of Indian states, it is necessary to take into account the considerable rural development expenditures incurred. The human allocation ratio is a modification of the social priority ratio suggested in UNDP, *Human Development Report*, 1991. The social priority ratio is the ratio of social priority expenditures to social services expenditure, whereas the human allocation ratio is a ratio of human priority expenditures to total revenue expenditures. The human allocation ratio includes elementary education, primary health (comprising rural health services, public health and family welfare), water supply and sanitation, and nutrition.

The social allocation ratio decreased in all states except Assam during the adjustment period 1991–4, as compared to the pre-adjustment period 1988–91. What is surprising is that the decline was steepest in the high income states of Punjab (41 to 27 per cent) and Haryana (36 to 30 per cent). In 1988–91 as many as seven states had social allocation ratios above 40 per cent. These included Punjab, Tamil Nadu, West Bengal, Kerala, and Assam as well as the low-income states of Bihar and Rajasthan. In 1991–4 only Assam (a special category state), Kerala and West Bengal reported social allocation ratios over 40 per cent. Though the social allocation ratios continued to be higher than the norm (40 per cent), the decline registered was consistent.

The social services and rural development expenditure ratio also declined in all states (except Assam and Maharashtra) over the period 1991–4. The decline was particularly sharp in Punjab (43 to 28 per cent).

The public expenditure ratio, i.e. the proportion of total revenue expenditure to SDP declined in only five states, viz. Andhra Pradesh, Karnataka, Kerala, Maharashtra and West Bengal. In other states, including Haryana and Punjab, where the social allocation ratios had declined, there was an increase in the public expenditure ratio during the adjustment years though it was lower than the 25 per cent norm suggested by the UNDP (1991).

The human allocation ratio also indicates a decline in twelve out of fifteen states between 1988–91 and 1991–4. The states that reported an increase in the allocation were Assam, Andhra Pradesh (though only marginally) and Maharashtra. Bihar, despite a decline (from 32 to 29 per cent) continued to record the highest share of human priority expenditure in total revenue expenditure. Likewise, Punjab, which recorded a very low share of human priority expenditure in total revenue expenditure in 1988–91 experienced a further decline from 14 per cent to 10 per cent between the two time periods.

STATEWISE TRENDS IN GROWTH RATE OF REVENUE EXPENDITURE ON SOCIAL SERVICES

The decline in the relative share of social services in total revenue expenditure raises questions regarding trends in growth rates of social sector expenditures. Analysis conducted by Prabhu and Sarker (1997) indicates a deceleration in growth rates of social services expenditure in most states since the mid-1980s.

Computation of growth rates of social services expenditure between 1974–5 and 1995–6 using the kinked exponential model suggested by Boyce (1986) shows that the overall growth rate masks the deceleration in growth rates in the period starting between 1984–5 and 1988–9 in most states (Table 7.4). In four

states, the breakpoint in the series came earlier — 1981–2 in
Bihar, 1975–6 in Orissa, 1976–7 in Rajasthan and 1978–9 in West
Bengal. Two states reported a break in the series at later time
points — Uttar Pradesh reported a break-point in 1990–1 and
Kerala in 1992–3. There was a decline in growth rates in all
states except Kerala, Tamil Nadu and Rajasthan. In three states,
viz. Andhra Pradesh, Punjab and Uttar Pradesh, the growth rate
was negative. In Bihar, Haryana, Orissa and West Bengal the
deceleration was very sharp (a decline of more than 6 percentage
points).

TABLE 7.4

STATEWISE EXPONENTIAL GROWTH RATES IN REAL PER CAPITA
REVENUE EXPENDITURE ON SOCIAL SERVICES

States	Overall	Before break (per cent)	After the break (per cent)	Year of shift (per cent)	Nature of shift
Andhra Pradesh	3.45	8.36	−1.47	1984–85	Downward
Assam	4.82	6.29	2.27	1986–87	Downward
Bihar	9.25	12.28	2.39	1981–82	Downward
Gujarat	4.67	6.37	0.71	1987–88	Downward
Haryana	5.66	7.38	0.21	1988–89	Downward
Karnataka	5.00	5.84	2.33	1988–89	Downward
Kerala	2.85	2.32	12.85	1992–93	Upward
Madhya Pradesh	4.05	4.85	1.51	1988–89	Downward
Maharashtra	4.62	5.52	3.05	1986–87	Downward
Orissa	3.74	26.37	3.20	1975–76	Downward
Punjab	4.05	6.55	−3.91	1988–89	Downward
Rajasthan	4.44	−6.03	5.00	1976–77	Upward
Tamil Nadu	4.27	2.79	4.73	1980–81	Upward
Uttar Pradesh	4.70	5.74	−2.18	1990–91	Downward
West Bengal	3.81	9.04	3.02	1978–79	Downward

Source: Prabhu (1997).

The states of Rajasthan and Tamil Nadu provide a welcome contrast and report an acceleration in the growth rate since 1976–7 and 1980–1 respectively. Kerala's experience is unique, with the growth rate increasing from 2.32 to 12.85 per cent since 1992–3. The deceleration in growth rates in social services expenditure in a majority of states since the 1980s may have serious implications for human poverty and is a matter that requires immediate policy attention.

Effectiveness of Government Expenditures

The expenditure incurred on rural development and social sectors can get translated into better human development outcomes only if the allocated funds are effectively spent. The impact of the levels of expenditure incurred, as well as the trends in such expenditures, depends to a large extent on the efficacy with which they are translated into outcomes that reduce human poverty. It is useful to analyse available evidence on the efficacy of government expenditures incurred on select items, viz. rural employment, particularly the EGS in Maharashtra, social assistance schemes, nutrition programmes, education, and health.

Rural Employment: Employment Guarantee Scheme

One of the distressing features of expenditures on rural development and social services in India is the very poor effectiveness of such expenditures. Among employment programmes, the EGS being implemented in Maharashtra is relatively well acclaimed. The scheme includes a guarantee to provide employment to all adults over eighteen years of age living in villages and small municipal towns in Maharashtra. The guarantee is only for un-skilled manual work within the district. Acharya (1990) observes that the guarantee aspect is not well known except in areas where voluntary groups are active. The EGS has been providing, on an average, about half a million jobs per year in rural Maharashtra, though there are considerable variations across seasons, years and districts. The EGS is intensive in its use of unskilled labour as 60 per cent of expenditure is to be spent on its wage component and is therefore self-targeting in nature. It is also an important source of employment for women, with estimates varying from

39 (Programme Evaluation Organization 1980) to 51 per cent (Dandekar 1983). The EGS stabilizes rural incomes, as is evident from increased participation during the lean season and drought years.

Estimates of employment provided through this programme range from a low of 25 person-days (Programme Evaluation Organization 1980) to 160 days (Dandekar 1983). The EGS is estimated to have eliminated around 7 per cent of unemployment in 1987-8 (Mahendra Dev 1995) and one-third of underemployment (Osmani 1991) in Maharashtra. In terms of its contribution to household income, the estimates range from 21 per cent (Deshpande 1988) to 65 per cent (Dandekar 1983).

However, the participation in EGS has not helped beneficiaries to cross the poverty line. The EGS in fact has not served to reduce the head count ratio, though it has served to reduce the intensity of poverty (Mahendra Dev 1995). In fact, the very necessity of the scheme over two decades after it was initiated, along with the relatively high levels of rural poverty in Maharashtra, at 36 per cent in 1993-4 as per NSSO data using Expert Group methodology (Malhotra 1997) serve to illustrate the limited impact that the scheme has had on the general poverty situation in the state.

Social Assistance Schemes

One of the components of the budget head of social services is social security and welfare. Tamil Nadu and Kerala are two states which have implemented a variety of schemes for the benefit of the destitute and weaker sections of the population. The social security schemes in Tamil Nadu include old age pensions, Destitute Widows Pension, Destitute and Deserted Women's Pension, Destitute Agricultural Labourers Pension, Marriage Assistance for Orphan Girls and Daughters of Poor Widows, Accident Relief, Family Benefit Scheme, Survivor Benefit Scheme, etc. Guhan (1993) had estimated that 732,000 poor households out of an estimated 4.4 million, about 17 per cent, have been protected from contingencies which could have made them poorer. It is also significant that out of the total beneficiaries, at least 57 per cent were women, mainly deserted women, widows, working mothers, and brides belonging to poorer households. Guhan's estimates further show that pensions would have covered

28 per cent of the poor, Survivor Benefit Scheme and maternity assistance about 63 per cent, and marriage grant 90 per cent. The expenditure incurred (of around Rs 400 million) constituted 1.5 per cent of the revenue expenditure of the government in 1989–90.

The main drawbacks of the Social Assistance Schemes in Tamil Nadu include: the inadequacy of amounts disbursed (Rs 75 per month, subsequently enhanced to Rs 100 per month) to enable the individual to cross the poverty line, narrowly and rigidly defined eligibility criteria, leading to a high rate of rejection of eligible applicants (Easwara Prasad 1995), high opportunity cost of obtaining information and applying for assistance.

Nutrition Programmes

Nutrition programmes in India, follow two broad approaches — one represented by the PDS, with its wide and untargeted coverage, and more specific targeted programmes such as the Integrated Child Development Scheme (ICDS) and state-sponsored programmes for the benefit of vulnerable sections of the population. The problems associated with the PDS, such as lack of targeting, leakages, and irregular and inadequate supplies, have rendered it an ineffective instrument for ensuring protection of the nutritional entitlements of the vulnerable population. It is estimated that the PDS would at most supply 10 per cent of the required calories (Harriss–White 1995). The PDS not only does not meet the requirements of the poor but also operates against their interests by raising open market prices (Radhakrishna and Indrakant 1987). The worst affected are the daily-wage and migrant labourers, and those without proper residential addresses and therefore not covered by the PDS.

The nutrition programmes implemented by Tamil Nadu have been much acclaimed. The Chief Minister's Nutritious Meal Programme, introduced in 1982, is the largest such programme, providing midday meals to children in the age group of 2–15 years in their schools and nurseries. Old age pensioners have also been considered eligible for midday meals since 1983. An evaluation of the impact of the Midday Meal Scheme in Coimbatore district (Harriss 1991), reports that the programme has not led to an increase in the height of children but that there have been substantial gains for female children. The Tamil Nadu

Integrated Nutrition Project, operating in all districts, is a more comprehensive programme covering nutrition needs for children in the 6–36 months age group as well as pregnant women and nursing mothers. Among these schemes, the Tamil Nadu Integrated Nutrition Project is considered to be better targeted (Subba Rao 1992).

Guhan (1994) has assessed the efficacy of different social security measures by using five indicators, viz. coverage ratio, transfer efficiency, targeting efficiency, benefit-cost ratio, and impact efficiency.[2] Comparing the efficacy of the EGS and PDS, he finds that the targeting efficiency of EGS (90 per cent) is high as compared to PDS (40 per cent). The relatively better targeting in EGS translates into a better benefit-cost ratio (21.6) as compared to PDS (11.2). However, the wider coverage in the PDS leads to a better impact ratio despite higher leakages (35 per cent) as compared to EGS (10 per cent).

The social assistance programmes in Tamil Nadu had a coverage ratio of 33 per cent for old age pensions, and 60–70 per cent for maternity assistance and Survivor Benefit Schemes. The targeting efficiency in these programmes is high on account of the fact that benefits are small enough for the non-poor to desist from infiltrating, no ceilings are placed on the number of beneficiaries assisted, and there is no problem of moral hazard. Transfer efficiency of these programmes is also high because the schemes are implemented by regular government staff to avoid additional expenditure and post-office payments reduce the scope for corruption.

EDUCATION AND HEALTH

A characteristic feature of the education and health sectors in India is the gross underutilization of social infrastructure (built

[2] Coverage ratio indicates coverage of the programme of the contingency or need to which it is addressed; transfer efficiency is the proportion of likely net benefit to one unit of gross expenditure, after allowing for programme and administrative overheads; targeting efficiency is the proportion of transfer that reaches its target group after making allowance for the share going to the non-target group explicitly or due to leakages; benefit-cost ratio is the product of transfer efficiency and targeting efficiency; impact-ratio is the product of coverage ratio and benefit-cost ratio.

at considerable public cost) by the people for whom it is meant. This is considered to be the combined effect of low levels of government expenditure on social sectors and the distorted pattern in which it is spent, resulting in poor quality of services being rendered in public schools and hospitals.

Capital expenditure, which goes towards the building of infrastructure, constitutes a very small proportion (less than 5 per cent) of the expenditure incurred across Indian states on social services, education and health. Wide variations exist in the social infrastructure built up in the states, as well as in the efficiency with which they function. This is reflected in the varying utilization of such infrastructure, particularly by the population in rural areas.

The percentage of illness episodes reported to the primary health centres reflects their utilization, while the high levels of non-enrolment and drop-outs, especially among low income households, reflect the poor utilization of education facilities. A large proportion of drop-outs as well as those not enrolled cited 'not interested' as a reason for such behaviour, which according to Minhas (1991) reflects the poor quality of the facilities provided. The drop-out rate in 1987–8 varied from 16 per cent in Kerala to 79 per cent in Bihar.

In view of the above, it is necessary to investigate the nature of linkages between the infrastructure, per capita expenditure, and attainment in the education and health sectors. Infrastructure represents the fructification of capital expenditures incurred in the past, whereas per capita revenue expenditure goes towards the maintenance of various facilities in schools and health facilities. The ranking of Indian states according to education and health infrastructure, attainment, and per capita government expenditure for two time points, 1983–6 and 1988–91 is given in Table 7.5. The indicators included in the infrastructure and attainment indices are listed in the Appendix 7.1. The indices have been constructed using the principal components method, first reported in Prabhu and Chatterjee (1993).

Rank correlation coefficients have been computed, separately, for education and health sectors for two time periods, 1983–6 and 1988–91.The rank correlation coefficients between education and health infrastructure, and real per capita expenditure and attainment are given below:

TABLE 7.5

RANKING OF STATES ACCORDING TO SOCIAL INFRASTRUCTURE PER CAPITA EXPENDITURE AND ATTAINMENT: 1983–86 AND 1988–91

State	1983–86						1988–91					
	Education			Health			Education			Health		
	SI	PCE	ATN	SI	PCE	ATN	SI	PCE	ATN	SI	PCE	ATN
1. Andhra Pradesh	12	10	11	8	10	8	10	11	11	8	13	8
2. Assam	2	4	14	9	8	10	2	7	9	9	6	10
3. Bihar	4	14	6	14	15	12	5	14	14	14	15	11
4. Gujarat	13	3	9	4	7	9	14	4	4	3	8	9
5. Haryana	15	6	5	13	2	7	12	6	8	13	7	7
6. Karnataka	9	8	8	7	9	4	15	9	7	7	9	6
7. Kerala	10	1	1	2	6	1	9	2	1	1	4	1
8. Madhya Pradesh	8	13	12	15	11	13	8	15	12	15	11	15
9. Maharashtra	11	5	2	3	3	3	11	3	3	4	5	3
10. Orissa	3	12	10	12	13	14	3	12	10	12	12	14
11. Punjab	5	2	4	1	4	2	4	1	5	2	2	2
12. Rajasthan	14	11	15	10	1	11	13	8	15	11	1	12
13. Tamil Nadu	7	7	3	6	5	6	7	5	2	5	3	5
14. Uttar Pradesh	6	15	13	11	14	15	6	13	13	10	14	13
15. West Bengal	1	9	7	5	12	5	1	10	6	6	10	4

Source: Prabhu and Chatterjee (1993).

Rank Correlation Coefficients

Education

1983-6

Education Infrastructure and Attainment   = 0.0643

Per Capita Education Expenditure and Attainment = 0.5357

1988-91

Education Infrastructure and Attainment   = 0.0857

Per Capita Education Expenditure and Attainment = 0.7929

Health

1983-6

Health Infrastructure and Attainment   = 0.8179

Per Capita Health Expenditure and Attainment   = 0.5429

1988-91

Health Infrastructure and Attainment   = 0.8179

Per Capita Health Expenditure and Attainment   = 0.5321

The above computations show a high correlation between per capita education expenditure ranks and attainment ranks. However, the correlation between education infrastructure ranks and attainment ranks is very poor for both the time points considered. In the case of the health sector, the situation is the reverse. Infrastructure ranks are highly correlated with attainment ranks even as the correlation between per capita expenditure ranks and attainment ranks is relatively lower, at 0.54 and 0.53 in the first and second time periods respectively. It is also interesting to note that the rank correlation of health infrastructure with health attainment is remarkably consistent, at 0.82 in both the time points.

The results of the regression analysis are similar. The component scores obtained by various states in attainment indices are related to the scores in infrastructure development and real per capita revenue expenditures. The results are as follows:

Year   Equation R^2

1985-6 EDCNL ATTN = 0.934 - 0.049 INFRAED + 0.025* REVED   0.334
            (1.058)   (-0.107)   (2.936)

1990-1 EDCNL ATTN = 0.002 + 0.152 INFRAED + 0.024** REVED   0.579
            (0.003)   (0.064)   (4.613)

1985-6 HLTH ATTN = 2.923** - 0.062*INFRAHLTH - 0.016 REVHLTH 0.385
            (6.483)   (-2.469)   (-1.118)

1990-1 HLTH ATTN = 2.690* - 0.072* INFRAHLTH - 0.006 REVHLTH 0.593
            (6.630)   (3 - 3.347)   (-0.527)

Figures in parentheses are t values
*   significant at 5 per cent level
** significant at 1 per cent level

The contrast between educational and health attainment is sharp. In the health sector, the coefficient of infrastructure development is statistically significant, while the coefficent of per capita expenditures is statistically insignificant. In the education sector, the converse is true with education expenditure emerging as important in influencing attainment levels. The relative importance of infrastructure, which implies capital expenditure for health attainment, is stressed by the World Bank as well (World Bank 1995).

The regression analysis shows that economic growth as well as public provisioning constitute two equally important routes in influencing poverty levels. The results seem to suggest that SDP growth is meaningful only if it is accompanied by rural development and social sector expenditure.

The above analysis raises several important issues. The deceleration in social-sector expenditures, particularly since the mid-1980s, poses questions regarding the priority given to human development in Indian states. The relative importance of per capita revenue expenditures for educational attainment and that of infrastructure for health attainment also highlight the areas on which greater attention needs to be paid for improving human development outcomes.

Appendix 2

Attainment Indices
and Infrastructure Indices

The indicators used for the Attainment and Infrastructure indices for 1983–6 and 1988–91 are given below.

ATTAINMENT INDICES

Education Attainment Indicators

1. Literacy Rate (7+), 1984–5, 1990–1
2. Female Literacy Rate, 1984–5, 1990–1
3. Average number of years of schooling

The average number of years of schooling of a cohort was calculated as follows in three simple steps:

i. Current enrolment ratio in secondary schools* 4 years
ii. [(Enrolment ratio in primary schools four years earlier) minus (current enrolment ratio in secondary schools)] * 5 years
iii. In the third stage, the number of years obtained in steps i and ii were added to obtain the average number of years of schooling.

This exercise was carried out with primary school enrolment ratios in 1980–1 and 1984–5 and secondary school enrolment ratios in 1984–5 and 1987–8 for the two time points.

Health Attainment Indicators

1. Crude Death Rate (3 years average), 1984–6 and 1988–90
2. Infant Mortality Rate (3 years average), 1984–6 and 1988–90

INFRASTRUCTURE INDICES

Education Infrastructure Indicators

1. No. of primary schools and secondary schools per 100 sq kms — 1985–6 and 1989
2. No. of primary schools and secondary schools per lakh population
3. No. of teachers (primary + secondary — both trained and untrained — per 10,000 students in primary and secondary schools — 1985–6 and 1987–8

Health Infrastructure Indicators

1. No. of dispensaries per 100 sq kms — 1985 and 1989
2. No. of primary health centres per 100 sq kms — 1985 and 1989
3. No. of hospital beds per lakh population — 1985 and 1989
4. No. of dispensaries per lakh population — 1985 and 1989
5. No. of primary health centres per lakh population — 1985 and 1989
6. No. of doctors per lakh population — 1985 and 1987
7. No. of nursing persons per lakh population — 1985 and 1987

Sources of Data

CSO, Statistical Abstract of India
CMIE, Volume II — States various issues

8

People's Own Perception and Assessment of Poverty

INTRODUCTION

Poverty, in a broad sense, describes the whole spectrum of deprivation and ill-being. In a more narrow sense, for purposes of measurement and comparison, it is defined as low income, or more specifically as low consumption, which is more stable and easier to measure. The second definition is generally known as income-poverty. Drèze and Sen (1995) make a similar distinction between 'poverty' which they describe, 'not merely as the impoverished state in which people live, but also to the lack of real opportunity' and 'economic poverty' which indicates 'low income, meager possessions and other aspects'.[1]

Chambers further distinguishes between poverty and other forms of deprivation. He describes poverty as 'lack of physical necessities, assets and income. It includes income-poverty but is more than being income poor. Deprivation refers to a lack of what is needed for well-being and for leading a full and good life. Its dimensions are physical, socio-economic, political and psychological. Well-being is the experience of leading a good-quality life. Thus, well-being and ill-being refer to experience,

---

[1] Drèze and Sen (1995) refer to the sequence of things a person does or achieves as a collection of 'functionings'. 'Capability refers to the alternative combinations of functionings from which a person can choose. The notion of capability is essentially one of freedom – the range of options a person has in deciding what kind of life to lead. Poverty refers to the lack of real opportunity – given social constraints and personal circumstances – to choose other types of living. Poverty is thus a matter of 'capability deprivation'. Economic poverty which refers to low incomes, meagre possessions and other related aspects also has to be seen in its role in severely restricting the choices people have to lead valuable and valued lives (ibid.: 10–11).

poverty more to physical lack, and deprivation to a much wider range of disadvantages. 'Poverty and deprivation' is short for 'poverty and other forms of deprivation'. (Chambers 1995: 5)

Chambers (1983) enumerates eight criteria for deprivation, of which poverty, defined as the lack of physical necessities, assets and income, is only one. The others include social inferiority, isolation, physical weakness, vulnerability, seasonality, powerlessness and humiliation. In the case of the poor, many of these dimensions may be quite imperfectly correlated with income-poverty. For instance, vulnerability may increase even if there is an increase in income, and for the poor, there may be a trade-off between income and security. Seasonality of employment is another dimension, the implications of which may be underplayed in the conventional treatment of poverty.

Using income-poverty as an indicator or proxy for other forms of deprivation is often misleading. This is because:

Income-poverty starts as a proxy or correlate for other deprivations, but then subsumes them. What is recorded as having been measured — usually low consumption — then masquerades in speech and in prose as the much larger reality. It is then but a short step to treating what has not been measured as not being real. Patterns of dominance are then reinforced: of the material over the experiential, of the physical over the social; of the measured and measurable over the unmeasured and unmeasurable; of economic over social values; of economists over disciplines concerned with people as people. It then becomes the reductionism of normal economics, not the experience of the poor, that defines poverty (Chambers 1995: 8).

Mukherjee (1993) points out that the use of measured income as an indicator of poverty poses several problems in the case of rural households. These households have diverse and complex livelihood strategies, which overlap and fluctuate everyday. The economic evaluation of many of these activities is a difficult task. Using income as a single criterion of poverty ignores the complex inter-relationship between the different strategies and processes which influence poverty. Many dimensions of poverty and deprivation are outside the purview of economic measurability but may be important indicators of a household's well-being.

Apart from the nature of information collected, the method by which it is generated is also important. Conventional questionnaire-based field approaches assumes a certain relation between the outsider (researcher), his knowledge and categories, and those of the poor. This is what Chambers calls the reversal 'from the knowledge, categories and values of outsider professionals to those of insider local people' (Chambers 1994b: 1262).

According to Jodha (1988), 'the concepts and categories used to identify and classify rural realities are often too restrictive to encompass the details of petty but collectively significant components of rural characterization' (ibid.). The same problem applies to measures and yardsticks which are used. This calls for supplementing formal procedures with qualitative approaches and incorporating categories and norms used by the respondent for the identification and assessment of variables affecting him/her. Various gaps in information arise from conventional field approaches, because outside researchers generally lack the understanding of rural reality. Examples of such 'gaps' which can be reduced with participant observation are enumerated in Tables 8.1 and 8.2.

TABLE 8.1

EXAMPLES OF CONCEPTS/CATEGORIES AND YARDSTICKS/NORMS
USED TO IDENTIFY AND MEASURE VARIABLES AND FACETS OF
RURAL REALITY LIKELY TO BE BYPASSED

Concepts and norms	Aspects covered	Facets bypassed
Household income	Cash and kind inflows (including imputed values of major non-traded items)	Ignores time context and transaction partner context of income-generating activity; disregards flow of low value self-provisioning activities with significant collective contribution of sustenance of the people.
Farm production	Production from all farm enterprises	Series of intermediate activities (often considered as consumption activities), which facilitate the final output from farm enterprises in self-provisioning societies.
Food consumption basket	Volume and quality of formally recorded food items	Ignores seasonally varying streams of self-provisioning items/services.

Concepts and norms	Aspects covered	Facets bypassed
Household resource endowment	Only privately owned land, labour and capital resources	Ignores household's collective access to common property resources; and access to power and influence too.
Factor/ product market	Competitive, im-personal interac-tive process of framework	Ignores distortions, imperfections, etc., due to factors like influence, power, affinities and inequities
Farm size grouping	Based on owned or operated landholdings (often standardized for productivity and irrigation)	Ignores totality to asset position including household's access to common property resources, its workforce which determines households' ultimate potential to harness land resources and environment for sustenance.
Labour input	Labour as standard unit expressed in terms of man-hours or mandays, etc. (differentiation based on age and sex not withstanding	Disregards heterogeneity of labour of same age/sex in terms of differences in stamina and productivity; ignores differences in intensity of effort of a self-employed worker and a hired worker. (Inappropriate imputa-tion of value of the labour of self-employed worker is done on the basis of wage rate of hired or attached labourer).
Capital formation	Acquisition of assets	Ignores accretionary process and petty accreditations which are important collectively
Deprecia-tion of assets	Book-keeping-value based reduction in the worth of the asset	Ignores continued usability and recyclibility.
Efficiency/ productivity norm	Quantity and value of final produce of an activity (based on market criteria)	Ignores totality of the operation of the system directed to satisfaction of multiple objectives rather than a single criterion.

Source: Jodha (1988).

TABLE 8.2
EXAMPLES OF 'COMMUNICATION GAPS'
(UNDER THREE CATEGORIES)

(1) Possible differences in connotation of same concept as understood by respondent and researcher

Concept	Connotation As Per	
	Researcher	Respondent
Food consumption	Total food	Major food items excluding petty self-provisioning
Produce	Total	Final produce excluding items harvested during the intra-season period
Manday	Formal work hour 8–10 hours, etc.	Total work time often more than 8–10 hours
Hired labour	Hired+exchanged	Only hired
Unemployment	Involuntary unemployment	Disguised unemployment treated as full unemployment

(2) Possible gaps in yardsticks guiding respondent's quantitative responses and researcher's recording of responses which may make it difficult to establish perfect equivalence between the reported and recorded quantities.

	Item	Researcher
Length/ area	Modern units (metre, hectares, inches, etc.)	Traditional-foot-lengths, steps, arm-lengths, finger widths
Weight/ volumes	Modern measures such as kilogrammes, quintals, litres, etc.	Cart-loads, bag fulls, volume based measures (barrels, etc.)
Production	Modern measures, quintals, etc.	Self-sufficiency periods of subsistence-requirement, e.g., total production equal to 6 months of requirement, etc.
Time	Precise-days, hour, etc.	Vague in terms of proportion of a day or a week, etc., i.e. half-a-day, 3/4 of a day, etc.

*(3)   Degree of precision/vagueness associated with responses as they
are given and recorded*

Item	Recording by researcher	Reporting by respondent
Labour input	Exact days/hours	Ranged units, e.g. 5–7 hour, 10–12 days, etc.
Grain yield	Exact quantities in modern measures/units (quintals/kg, etc.)	Range; e.g. 5–6 bags or 50–55 quintals, etc.
Input use/ output sold	Exact quantities	Range in terms of proportion: 1/3 to 2/3 of bag, etc.

Source: Jodha (1988).

Jodha's main concern has been to see how the poor's own
perceptions and categories inform conventional field research and
how apparent differences between the two can be reconciled.
Others have found distinct advantages in qualitative approaches
which derive from the perceptions of the poor themselves. In the
questionnaire approach, both enumerators and respondents tend
to be poorly motivated and complex causality can only be dis-
cerned indirectly. In comparison, participatory approaches, which
involve learning from the poor, present a plurality of methods.
With triangulation and cross-checking, the reliability of conclusions
can be quite high. Local participants and analysts are usually
committed to getting complete and accurate details, and change
and causality can be interpreted quite directly from their personal
experience (Chambers 1994b, 1994c).

Participatory methods of poverty assessment lead to what Chambers calls a 'reversal of frames'. Instead of concepts and categories
generated by outside researches, methods such as participatory
rural appraisal lead to an understanding of the rural reality based
on the villager's own perceptions and knowledge of his environment. Participatory rural appraisal uses a growing family of approaches and methods enabling 'local people to share, enhance
and analyse their knowledge of life and conditions, to plan and to
act' (Chambers 1994c: 1437). Apart from participatory rural appraisal, these include activist participatory research, agro-ecosystem

analysis, applied anthropology, field research on farming systems, and rapid rural appraisals.

Beginning in 1988, participatory rural appraisal methods have been widely used in India by NGOs, government agencies and institutes. Since then, the use of the participatory rural appraisal has spread to four broad sectors: natural resource management, agriculture, poverty and social programmes, and health and food security (ibid.). According to Chambers participatory poverty assessments score over conventional approaches in terms of cost, speed with which results can be obtained, reliability, insights into causal processes and local resources, and by enabling people to participate in order to overcome poverty. World Bank participatory poverty assessments in Ghana, Zambia and Kenya were designed to answer the questions: 'Who is poor? Why are they poor? What needs to be done to reduce the number of the poor?'. These studies went beyond these questions and investigated who defines poverty, the criteria used, and their priorities. The studies provide many insights into people's priorities and problems which may not emerge in a conventional survey (Chambers 1995).

Hurriedly carried out participatory approaches could themselves lead to wrong conclusions. Also, participatory approaches themselves may not be free from cultural biases and other serious problems. Mukherjee (1993) points out that participatory exercises in the identification of poor households may suffer from the problems of different settings not lending themselves to comparison, cultural biases, deliberate manipulation, and the overlooking of intra-household distributional issues. He suggests that these difficulties could be dealt with through careful triangulation and complementary exercises.

Wealth ranking, an oft-used method of identifying the poor, could also run into difficulties. Groups may be dominated by a few individuals who may be reluctant to rank themselves, or their close relatives, or even other influential villagers. There may be genuine difficulties in arriving at a set of shared criteria between members of a group or between different groups due to intervening caste/class/gender perceptions. There are major obstacles to women's articulation of interests in areas which fall beyond the public endorsement of their role. Public expression of women's interests in the initial participatory rural appraisals generally revolved around health care, child care, nutrition, domestic work and acceptable home-based activities which generated income.

HOW DO THE POOR PERCEIVE POVERTY?

Participatory studies of poverty reveal that the poor use different criteria to assess their own situation and its change over time. The annual or seasonal availability of food or work, eating two or fewer meals, or the number of meals skipped, are often important criteria in people's own definition of poverty along with dietary variations (Srivastava 1996; Harriss 1992; Prasad et al. 1986). Health needs often receive a high priority. An analysis of the criteria used by local people from several studies in Asia and sub-Saharan Africa show that they use a wide range of criteria in which health and physical disability feature prominently when grouping and ranking their own well-being. Income per se was mentioned, if at all, in a lower order (Chambers 1995: 12–13). Not surprisingly, gender differences in perception were also often quite marked.

In his study of two villages in Rajasthan Jodha (1988) used certain 'unconventional' indicators of change which emerged as anecdotal information collected from villagers during a survey in 1978. He found that villagers identified as many as 38 criteria for changing economic status. These included the absence of homestead land, type of dwelling, separate dwelling space for humans and animals, skipping of a meal by adults during the lean season, cash purchases during festivals and lean seasons, dependence on patrons for credit, seasonal out-migration, attached or semi-attached labour, and several other criteria.

These criteria could be grouped into (i) reduced reliance of the poor on traditional patrons, landlords, and resourceful people for sustenance, employment and income (ii) reduced dependence on low-paid jobs/options (iii) improved mobility and liquidity options (iv) shifts in consumption patterns/practices, and (v) acquisition of consumer durables.[2]

2 According to Jodha, these criteria could be further grouped under three categories more familiar to economists: (i) indicators of enlarging opportunity sets or increasing the number of choices (ii) indicators of consumption activities with high income elasticities; and (iii) indicators of increasing investment in lumpy consumer durables.

Comparing his earlier (1964–6) survey with the subsequent 1982–4 one, Jodha isolated 35 households which were worse off by more than 5 per cent in terms of per capita real (net) income, but reported an improvement on the basis of 37 out of 38 other criteria. Although the sample included all categories of households, the nature of change was also substantiated by those households who were initially below the poverty line.

These criteria (along with others, such as social consumption) have been raised in a number of studies although only a few show remarkable convergence and move in the same direction. The poor attach considerable importance to personal freedom and dignity, but this may come at a cost, often that of greater vulnerability, as patron–client ties and secure employment opportunities decline (Jayaraman and Lanjouw 1998). In Wadley and Derrs's (1989) study of a village in Uttar Pradesh, many of the poor believed that their living standards had stagnated in recent years. Those who spoke of an improvement saw it in terms of greater personal freedom and social dignity rather than reduced hunger or poverty. Similarly, though asset acquisition is considered desirable, the poor may eschew this option if it comes with greater risk and increased indebtedness (Chambers 1995: 15; Jayaraman and Lanjouw 1998).

Mukherjee (1993) used social mapping exercises to study villagers' perceptions of poverty and the criteria they used to rank households according to the levels of poverty/well-being in the two villages in Midnapore district of West Bengal. Both the villages studied were small, consisting of less than a hundred households. The first village, Krishna Rakshit Chak was inhabited mainly by poor Lodha tribals, many of whom had gained small plots of land as a result of the government's land distribution programme.

Villagers in Krishna Rakshit Chak used social mapping exercises to rank the households into three groups. Here the poorest households included those with widows as household heads, with practically no asset, no regular source of income and not enough to eat throughout the year. They also included agricultural labourers with no land or any regular source of income or food. Households just above the extreme poor group included those that had some ownership of land but a large number of dependents. The third group of households had around 4 acres of land and better production from agriculture. Some household members in this group had jobs outside the village. On the whole, members of this group were better off in terms of household income, food availability, and purchasing power. Since villagers checked and cross-checked with one another, the process of triangulation was also implemented.

In the discussions, the villagers identified food availability, land holdings and productivity, state intervention and the dependency ratio as some of the key factors in differentiating households on the basis of poverty. Poor households were dependent on the common property resources for certain types of food, prticularly during the lean season. The villagers therefore placed emphasis on the depletion of resources as one of the key factors responsible for poverty. Annual food availability was important since it was a scarce commodity for most households and was linked to the state of crop production and the capacity of nearby forests and ponds to provide food.

Villagers linked well-being with agriculture, common property resources and state intervention, all of which provided various forms of subsistence. In the agriculturally lean seasons, common property resources provided them with a high degree of sustenance. However, the degradation of common property resources and forests, and the pollution of ponds affected their dependence on these sources. In agriculturally lean years, seasonal employment provided by the forest department had earlier provided some buffer, but this was no longer available. The tiny plots of land distributed by the state government, were sufficient only for growing two or three trees or putting up a small hut, but provided the tribals with a measure of psychological security. While the above criteria, though diverse, could identify the poor in the two villages, income seemed a poor choice, due to the diverse livelihood strategies of the poor and their extreme seasonal variability.

The second village, Kalsigeria, was a remote village inhabited by forty-two Scheduled Caste households. Through mapping, the villagers graded households into three groups on the basis of their poverty or well-being. The extremely poor households had no land, a high dependency ratio and not enough working hands. Some households had widows as household heads. These households were chronically deficit households with not enough food to eat, mainly due to their dependence on the depleted common property resources. The next group, of slightly better-off households, had 1 or 2 acres of land and some working members who could contribute to household income. The third group was comparatively better-off, who had about 4 acres of land, which was generally of better quality. Some households here had members with jobs outside the village. These households were much more comfortable in terms of household income, food availability, and purchasing power.

Criteria used by the rural communities in Midnapore villages for ranking of households were (i) food availability (ii) landholdings — absence, ownership and size (iii) productivity of landholdings (iv) state of agricultural crop — whether good or bad (v) common property resources — its support (vi) ownership of assets other than land (vii) number of dependents/working hands (viii) beneficiaries of state intervention through employment and other programmes (ix) jobs outside the village (Mukherjee 1993: 96).

The study showed that the degradation and depletion of common property resources (forests, ponds, etc.) resulted in increases in poverty. This was because of increased vulnerability and reduced availability of fuel, fodder, food, medicines and other sources of sustenance for the poor. The increased deprivation due to the decline in common property resources was not offset by land-reform programmes that could have given the poor an alternative source of sustenance.

In a wealth-ranking exercise in a village in Bihar (Sarkar 1991), the villagers used a complex set of criteria to group households into four categories. These included the capacity of the family to feed itself from its own produce, ownership of house and well, ownership of draught animals, ownership of consumer durables, outside jobs, absence of alcoholism, contacts with the police, etc. In another study in a Gujarat village (Shah 1990), individuals and focus groups were asked to group a selected list of households. The criteria used as indicators of well-being included health and educational status, land and asset ownership, type of dwelling, part-time jobs, credit-worthiness, and the number of dependents.

In village Tarkullah in Gorakhpur district (Khare 1997), two separate wealth ranking exercises were conducted, in better-off and poor localities. The discussion on grouping individuals in the better-off locality generated very little debate and was dominated by a few influential individuals. But in the poor locality, villagers classified selected households into six categories after intense discussion. The criteria which emerged during the discussion included the ownership of land, agricultural assets like tractors, transport vehicles such as cycles or motorized transport, access to irrigation facilities, external sources of income, government jobs, children going to cities for education or training, family size, and the number of working hands.

The poorest category of households included those without any land and dependent mainly on casual labour. The group was also asked to identify households whose position had changed in the last decade and the reasons for this. It was found that households that had experienced improvements were mainly those whose external sources of income had grown. In the case of households whose condition declined, the main reasons appeared to be a decline in traditional sources of livelihood, an increase in the number of dependents, loss of working hands, illness and alcoholism. One of the discussants, whom the group identified as rich, was a businessman, and he argued that the group had ignored his financial liabilities.

Nisha Srivastava (1997) carried out wealth-ranking exercises in two separate localities (rich and poor, and relatively socially homogenous) in Chitauri village in Allahabad district (UP). About thirty names were randomly selected by villagers and then compiled on the basis of their assessment of the individual's economic status. Villagers' discussions and the reasons provided by them were extensively recorded. Villagers then grouped the cards into three piles: well-off, middle and poor households. One of the significant findings was that the nature of access to health facilities and education figured in the categorization of economic status in both localities (Table 8.3).

It has been questioned whether assessments of poverty by the poor themselves differ markedly from those derived from the conventional, single criterion. Chambers (1994b) cites several studies that compare the results of participatory approaches with more conventional questionnaire-based approaches. In some of these, the results were quite similar, even though the conventional surveys were costlier and results took longer to emerge.

The National Council for Applied Economic Research (NCAER) tested Rapid Rural Appraisal and Participatory Rural Appraisal methods as an alternative or complement to a conventional sample survey. Their participatory rural appraisal, which covered only ten villages, as against 120 in the conventional survey, was found to

TABLE 8.3

CRITERIA USED FOR RANKING GROUPS IN THE PATEL AND
SCHEDULED CASTE HAMLETS, CHITAURI, ALLAHABAD

Well-off	Middle	Poor
7–45 acres of land	up to 7 acres of land	no land or very little land
pukka houses	Basic needs in Roti, kapda and makaan covered	most barely managed two meals a day
all children in private schools	few children went to school	children not educated, did not attend school even if enrolled
could generally afford private doctors and health facilities	could only afford government hospitals	when ill, could at best afford the local quack, the '8 anna doctor'
even had bank balances	irrigation was a major problem	drinking water was a problem
generally from upper and middle castes	included mostly middle castes and a few upper castes	included mostly low castes, with a sprinkling of other castes
a few had regular outside employment or businesses	generally did not employ labour, a few worked occasionally for others	were employed by the rich, employment available only for a few months each year

Source: Nisha Srivastava (1997).

generate valid and reliable data at the village level and also fairly good ratio estimates for some, but not all, variables at the state level (Chaudhari 1993). Chambers (1994b) also reports findings which indicate that the wealth rankings by rural individuals tend to be more accurate than those done by outsiders and are fairly closely correlated among themselves. MYRADA has developed an approach whereby separate groups rank households and then meet to reconcile differences, a method which is then used for selecting households for anti-poverty programmes.

A study conducted by the Rurual Health Services Association (RUHSA) Department of the Christian Medical College, Vellore, used a pre-tested structured schedule to rank 412 households on the basis of a composite index consisting of several criteria on which information was collected during the survey. The indicators included type of house, ownership of assets, dresses per person, and yearly income. Wealth ranking was then also carried out by groups of local men and women who evolved a more elaborate set of criteria. The classifications were similar in 62 per cent of the cases. About half the discrepancies were examined in detail by the researchers and in 92 per cent of these, the community-generated wealth ranking was found to be valid.

GENDER PERCEPTIONS

Studies on poverty (including those that take into account the poor's own perceptions) are limited by the fact that they relate mainly to household-level information provided by males. Intra-household issues are generally ignored. However, there are a growing number of studies which focus on the perceptions of women, children, and the elderly within the household.

Mukherjee (1993) describes a case study to show how perceptions regarding poverty could differ between men and women. Men and women were grouped separately in a hamlet of village Zhadgar of Thane district in Maharashtra and asked to prepare village maps. The women were more hesitant in drawing the maps. One important difference which stood out was the women's depiction of footpaths ordinarily used by them for collecting fuel and water which did not find a place in the maps made by the men. In the wealth ranking exercise which followed, the women indicated that two widow-headed households, where both women suffered from some physical disability, were the poorest. But the men indicated two other male-headed households, where the men were unemployed, as being the poorest. On further probing, the men felt that the two women were not among the poorest because both possessed small plots of land. It thus appeared that among men, lack of possession of land and absence of employment were the most important criteria of well-being, while for the women social and physical disability were more important.

Another important implication of gender perceptions regarding well-being is that men are relatively ill-informed about a range of activities performed by women, which have low visibility and low economic value, but which play a very important role in sustaining poor households. These range from women's role in economic activities, to the collection of food, fuel, fodder and other items, as well as bringing up children. In Mukherjee's study of Krishna Rakshit Chak cited earlier, men who were asked to prepare a food calendar, which accounted for the varieties and amount of foods consumed each month, faltered, but women were much more enthusiastic. They used pebbles and stones to indicate their main food items and relative amount and importance of each, monthwise. They also used leaves and twigs to indicate items of supplementary consumption many of which they collected from the forests and ponds. Though the seasonal decline in cereal intake was partly offset by wild food items, there was a decline in consumption in certain months (March to July). The women were not only more aware of the different kinds of food procured from different sources, they also performed different 'hedging' strategies, switching varieties of food to avoid remaining hungry.

Qualitative participatory rural appraisal studies are also important for exploring the gender deprivation of women in the discrimination they face in getting access to schooling, health services, and food. They are overworked and are at the receiving end of violence, etc. Seasonal calendars of food intake by adult men and women, and young boys and girls often show lower intake by females. Because of their social position, the prioritization of problems faced can be quite different for women as compared to men. For women, social problems and problems relating to access to infrastructure often tend to find a higher priority compared to economic problems (Mukherjee 1993). The specific forms of deprivations endured by women led to a different development agenda, placing special emphasis on their social and economic empowerment.

Srivastava (1997) also used focused group discussions among poor women to make them voice their prioritization of problems. Women in the area were employed only for 40 to 60 days a year as casual labourers, and the difficulties of finding more employment and higher earnings received a clear prioritization of problems. Where male members out-migrated, intermittent inflows compounded several other problems. Women's health needs were identified as another major issue. Crushing overwork and domestic violence were mentioned, but women in the group seemed to internalize these problems and treat them as part and parcel of their lives, something they had to live with.

PEOPLE'S MOVEMENTS AND THE ROLE OF VOLUNTARY AGENCIES FOR POVERTY ALLEVIATION

Poor people develop complex strategies to cope with poverty and deprivation.[3] The collective response of the poor to conditions which engender poverty and deprivation are almost as complex as their individual responses.[4] Collective response develops through diverse forms of social, political, and economic organizations in which different types of catalytic agents play a potential role. At the local level, collective responses to social indignity, poor conditions of employment, low wages, and other forms of social and economic deprivation seem to be more widespread than at first assumed. Recent field studies in UP and Bihar, for example, have documented these forms of organizations and struggles and their impact on the conditions of the poor (cf. Lieten and Srivastava forthcoming; Lerche 1995; Singh 1992).

Wider forms of organization of the poor, articulated through social and political organizations, have taken people's own experience as a starting point and launched sustained movements for environmental protection and sustainable livelihoods, tenurial security, land reforms, social dignity, improved working conditions, and higher wages. Sustained movements have also been launched against social problems such as alcoholism and illiteracy.[5] Many

---

[3] Harriss (1992) distinguishes between two types of responses by the poor to deal with 'shocks': coping and survival strategies. 'Coping' strategies protect social reproduction. They are considered ineffective if they result in a long-term drop in consumption, permanent loss of productive assets, or large scale permanent out-migration. The latter responses are considered as 'survival' strategies, which are threats to biological reproduction rather than 'coping'.

[4] These include resistance in the fashion of what Scott calls the 'weapons of the weak' — the constant struggle between the poor and those who extract surpluses from them. These acts are mostly described as individualistic and include 'foot-dragging, dissimulation, desertion, false compliance, pilfering, feigned ignorance, slander, contempt, arson, sabotage . . . ' (Scott 1987: 343–4).

[5] The range and impact of pro-poor organizations is too large to be dealt with in any detail here. Mass movements led by left-oriented political parties helped by their subsequent rise to power in West Bengal and Kerala have followed a conscious agenda of organizing landless labourers and peasants, and

of these movements, with women at their core, have arisen out of women's social experiences.[6] The interlinkages between the social, economic and political empowerment of the poor are quite intricate. In some cases, improvements in social dignity and the bargaining power of the rural poor, in labour and lease markets, for instance, has been an offshoot of the shifts in the political balance of power in their favour, rather than a result of any conscious strategy to improve their well-being.[7]

The link between the mobilization of the poor and public policy is tenuous but it does exist. There are numerous instances of people's movements bringing about a change in public policy. A number of examples can be cited — peasant movements leading to land-reform policies; labour movements leading to wage legislation; ecological movements leading to a reconsideration of forest policies and joint forest management; rehabilitation policies; women's movement

---

land reforms. Though the trajectories of development have been quite different in the two states (with many shortcomings), there has been a fairly remarkable impact on the condition of the poor. (Lieten 1992, 1996; Ravallion and Datt 1996; Kannan 1995; Sengupta and Gazdar 1997; Ramchandran 1997). Radical left movements among the rural poor and tribals in Bihar, Andhra Pradesh and other areas has also impacted favourably on their freedom, dignity and bargaining power (Sharma 1995). Apart from trade unions in the organized sector, some mass and trade union organizations have organized contract labourers, rural labourers and other workers in the informal sector, and in some cases, such as the Chhatisgarh Shramik Sangathan in Madhya Pradesh, have linked economic and social issues and the issues of workers and their households in both industrial and rural settings. At the other extreme, even *jati and biradari* organizations of the poor, have organized themselves around issues of social dignity and rejection of demeaning forms of labour.

[6] Since the early 1970s in particular, there have been a number of women's movements which have addressed themselves to the separate concerns of women as well as wider social and economic concerns. Women have been in the forefront of ecology movements such as *Chipko* in Garhwal, joint cultivation rights in Bodhgaya, unequal wage payments in Nalgonda (Andhra Pradesh) (Agarwal, 1989). In many of these movements, women have focused on gender exploitation both within and outside the family. Women have linked up their struggle for economic betterment and ecological sustainability with issues like alcoholism, women's illiteracy, domestic violence and the division of labour within the household.

[7] The Bahujan Samaj Party (BSP), for instance, has a limited social agenda, which includes social dignity for the Dalits, and a stand against social atrocities. But, the widening political base among the Dalits, and their rise to political power, has led to a shift in the balance of political forces and greater political empowerment has improved their bargaining power.

against alcoholism leading to a ban on liquor consumption in Haryana and Andhra Pradesh; and the campaign for the right to information and transparency in rural development projects leading to legislation, ordinances, and government orders on the right to information in a number of states. Thus, apart from direct gains, people's movements may lead to legal entitlements for the poor through their impact on public policy and thus enlarge the scope of further potential gains.

Since the early 1970s, there has also been a more rapid growth of non-governmental organizations (NGOs) in rural and urban areas. Though NGOs have an uneven coverage in different parts of the country and adhere to different objectives and philosophies, many of them take the felt needs of the poor as their starting point and work towards the objective of their economic, social and economic empowerment. As pointed out earlier, organizations like MYRADA and PRIA have pioneered participatory learning and other approaches in which outside researchers facilitate group processes to enable the rural people and the poor to rank themselves, prioritize their problems, and work out solutions in various diverse areas such as natural resource planning, micro planning, watershed planning and health planning.

Activities of many of the NGOs are focused on the poor in the urban areas. For example, the Society for Promotion of Area Resource Centres assists people in poor communities to gain access to shelter and basic amenities and acquire wealth through community based savings and credit schemes. Formed in 1984, its activities have centred on pavement and slum dwellers in Mumbai, supporting the formation of collectives among them. It has provided pavement dwellers with practical learning experience on how to gain knowledge regarding their own conditions, supported the formation of Mahila Milan which began as a collective of women pavement dwellers in Bombay, and set up resource centres accessible to people who needed them. The NGO has also negotiated a group policy with an insurance company for over 400 pavement dwellers, and convinced formal credit institutions to lend to poor people through NGOs on the basis of savings collateral (Ravi Srivastava 1997).

While several NGOs take separate account of women's concerns, their number is typically small, about 15 per cent of the total. These are concentrated in the southern and western regions

(World Bank 1991). Despite diverse ideological orientations and strategies, many of these take into account the deprivation felt by poor women and have developed strategies for their economic and social empowerment. The Working Women's Forum (WWF), an organization consisting of poor women in the informal sector, started in 1978 in Madras (now Chennai), has since spread to urban and rural areas in other states as well. Credit was identified as a key constraint for poor, self-employed women workers. The Forum began by organizing women into small neighbourhood loan groups. Then they identified different trades and their economic viability, to provide a unit for loan provision, collection, and monitoring. Initially, subsidized loans provided by nationalized banks were utilized for the purpose. Since interface with institutional credit was difficult, the Working Women's Credit Society was set up with poor women workers as shareholders.

Other major constraints facing women in the areas of appropriate technology, health needs, social legislation, and police harassment were also taken up through appropriate organizational initiatives. The organizational process of the Working Women's Forum involved a reversal in hierarchy and learning whereby the existing forms of co-operation, i.e. rotating credit groups, mutual aid clubs, neighbourhood groups, kin links, etc. were identified and they formed the basis of the new collectivities, i.e. the neighbourhood group (Azad 1986). Project formulation and expansion were based on felt needs and the participation of women evolved in stages (ibid.).

The Self-employed Women's Association (SEWA) was first registered as a trade union in 1972. It is a confluence of three movements: the labour movement, the co-operative movement, and the women's movement. The Self-employed Women's Association members are either self-employed workers who earn a living through their own small business or through their own labour. The SEWA union has struggled against low wages, exploitation by contractors, lack of social security, corruption and many other issues affecting the working conditions of its members. It has supported the establishment of sixty-five worker co-operatives with over 22,000 workers. Many of these have been established in drought prone rural areas, where labour out-migration for employment has been endemic. Its supportive services include the SEWA bank, which assisted more than 20,000 women with credit during

1993; health care through a co-operative of health workers, dais, doctors and pharmacists; housing services; and a work security-cum-life insurance scheme in collaboration with United Insurance, with over 7000 members.

Before starting work, SEWA activists carefully assess the needs of the poor women through planned action research programmes (Bhowmick and Jhabwala 1996). These are used to identify women's basic needs, their skills and available local resources which would have remained unrecognized and untapped without careful assessment. If promoting employment through self-employment is adopted as a goal, the strategy is to develop local organizations that would be run by women producers. Building women's capacity for self-management was an inherent part of the strategy. Increased economic empowerment in the research areas also led to changes at the individual, household, community and public policy levels though not without struggles and some reversals (ibid.). The critical constraints in empowering women are solved not only at the workplace but also by evolving community approaches for child care, etc.

Thus, even though NGOs suffer from small and uneven coverage and different orientations, they are well positioned to use participatory approaches in which the poor identify their own situation, their resources such as skills, technology, organizations and networks, and the area resources. They are also able to bring these together in a way which increases their economic, social and political empowerment.

CONCLUSION

People perceive poverty and well-being in terms of categories and criteria which reflect the manifold interrelated strategies that make their social reproduction possible and which reflect their constraints and trade-offs. Naturally, these differ between areas and localities, between groups of people, and between men and women. Participatory strategies claim to have achieved a measure of success in reconciling differing perceptions within the same village or locality.

When people collectively recognize the attributes of their poverty and its causes, it can form the starting point for the development of collective strategies to overcome poverty. In this process, political parties, mass organizations, unions, NGOs, and various other forms of collective co-operative organizations can play a catalytic role. The inter-relationship between economic, social and political empowerment, on the one hand, and public policy on the other, is quite complex. While strategies of social mobilization follow diverse paths, some have been able to use people's felt needs and priorities as a spring-board to overcome poverty. These are based on human, physical, natural, and financial resources which are available locally.

Epilogue

Although a good deal of the analysis contained in this book is informed by the prevailing paradigm of income-poverty, its main intent is to go beyond it, and focus on a more comprehensive view of 'human poverty'. This concept of poverty was elaborated in a paper (commissioned for the *Human Development Report*, UNDP, 1997), prepared by Sudhir Anand and the 1998 Nobel Laureate in Economics, Amartya Sen.

Human poverty has been defined as 'the denial of opportunities and choices most basic to human development — to lead a long, healthy, and creative life and to enjoy a decent standard of living, freedom, dignity, self-esteem and the respect of others'. This understanding of poverty perceives the poorest as active agents struggling against impoverishment. Therefore eradication of poverty entails strengthening, what Amartya Sen, has called 'capabilities' of the poor, and simultaneously create opportunities in society to enable them to make full use of it. Strengthening capabilities, therefore, is crucial for helping the poor to confront and cope with not only a paucity of income but also a host of other adversities as well, such as disease, disaster and discrimination. A sound anti-poverty strategy should, not only aim to increase incomes, but also provide the poor with a variety of assets — personal, social, political and environmental to help them overcome human poverty.

The concept of human poverty also entails the recognition of gender inequality as an essential part of poverty. Measures of income-poverty are usually made at the household level and do not capture intra-household disparities. A gendered approach to human poverty would involve examining how resources such as food, education, health services, and productive assets are distributed within the household. Intra-household distribution of these assets is a valuable pointer to how well capabilities can be strengthened through public and private interventions.

It is encouraging that the Central Statistical Organisation has embarked on conducting time-use surveys, which will provide quantitative information pertinent to intra-household equity. These surveys should be complemented with qualitative and participatory approaches to gain a good understanding of how the poor perceive their predicament and what avenues they are likely to exploit to break out of poverty

The ending of all forms of discrimination and marginalization based on class, caste, gender, religion, race or ethnicity, already a part of fundamental rights guaranteed under the Constitution, would go a long way towards eliminating some of the main causes of human poverty. The Supreme Court of India has proved to be an effective spur to public action by widening the interpretation of the fundamental right to life and liberty (Article 21 of the Constitution) to include the right to livelihood, the right to education, and the right to a healthy environment.

Fifty years after the adoption of the Universal Declaration of Human Rights, and after nearly as many years of fighting poverty with less than satisfactory results, the time might have come to adopt a rights-based approach to poverty eradication. A rights-based approach focuses not only on the protection (appropriate in the case of civil and political liberties) but also on the promotion of a more comprehensive set of rights through positive public action. These would include rights to education and health which are essential to increase people's 'capabilities'. There is an advantage in perceiving these necessities of human life as an integral part of human rights, which would imply a recognition that poverty is a brutal denial of human rights (UNDP 1998). Even though the right not to be poor may not be amenable to enforcement through standard judicial processes, it is nonetheless valuable to perceive poverty as a violation of human rights. As states and the international community, reflecting 'the spirit of our age and the realities of our time' (in the words of the 1993 World Conference on Human Rights Vienna Declaration) begin to take human rights seriously, there is a greater likelihood that the duty cast upon states, civil society, and the international community to act against the persistence of poverty will not be shirked for long any more.

Bibliography

Background Papers Commissioned by UNDP – India, 1997

Meenakshisundaram, S.S., 'A Note on the Implementation and Impact of Anti-Poverty Programmes'.

Prabhu, K. Seeta, 'Human Poverty Index for Indian States – A Note'.

—— 'Public Provisioning for Poverty Alleviation'.

Radhakrishna, R., 'Food Security, Nutrition and Poverty in India'.

Shariff, A., 'Relative Income Deprivation and Capability Poverty in Rural Households: Inter-state and Inter-group Differentials in India'.

Srivastava, R., 'People's Own Perception and Assessment of Poverty'.

Tendulkar, S.D., 'Poverty: Concepts and Measures'.

—— 'Poverty in India'.

Select Bibliography

Acharya, S. (1990), *Maharashtra Employment Guarantee Scheme: A Study of Labour Market Intervention*, New Delhi: ILO-ARTEP.

Acharya, S.S. (1989), *Socio-Economic Impact of 1987 Drought in Rajasthan*, Department of Agricultural Economics, Udaipur: Rajasthan Agricultural University.

Agarwal, Bina (1989), 'Rural Women, Poverty and Natural Resources: Sustenance, Sustainability and Struggle for Change', in *Economic and Political Weekly* (India), 28 October 1989, no. 24, pp. WS-46/WS-65.

Anand, S. and M. Ravallion (1993), 'Human Development in Poor Countries: On the Role of Private Incomes and Public Services', *Journal of Economic Perspectives*, vol. 7 (1), pp. 133–50.

Ministry of Rural Areas and Employment, Annual Reports, 1994 to 1997.

Ardener, E. (1975), 'Belief and the Problem of Women', in S. Ardener (ed.), *Perceiving Women*, London: Dent.

Azad, Nandini (1986), *Empowering Women Workers: The W.W.F. Experiment in Indian Cities*, New Delhi: UNICEF.

Bardhan, P. (ed.) (1990), *Conversations between Economists and Anthropologists*, Delhi: Oxford University Press.

Bernadas, C.N. Jr. (1991), 'Lesson in Upland Farmer Participation: The Case of Enriched Fallow Technology' in Jaro, Leyte, Philippines, *Forests, Trees and People Newsletter*, no. 14, October, pp. 10–11.

Bhalla, G.S. (1994), 'Policies for Food Security in India' in G.S. Bhalla (ed.), *Economic Liberalisation and Indian Agriculture*, New Delhi: Institute for Studies in Industrial Development.

Bhowmick, Sharit and Renana Jhabwala (1996), 'Rural Women Manage their own Producer Co-operatives: Self-Employed Women's association (SEWA)/ Banaskantha Women's Association in Western India', in Carr et al. (eds), *Speaking Out: Women's Economic Empowerment in South Asia*.

Bhowmick, Sharit and Meena Patel (1996), 'Empowering Marginalised Workers: Unionisation of Tobacco Workers by the Self-Employed Women's Association (SEWA) in Kheda, Gujarat', in Carr et al. (eds), *Speaking Out: Women's Economic Empowerment in South Asia*.

Bidinger, P.D. et al. (1990), 'Economic, Health, and Nutritional Consequences of the Mid-1980s – Drought on a Tank-Irrigated, Deccan Village in South India', Resource Management Programme, Economics Group, Progress Report 98, Hyderabad: ICRISAT.

Boyce, J.K. (1986), 'Kinked Exponential Models for Growth Rate Estimation', *Oxford Bulletin of Economics and Statistics*, 48 (4), pp. 385–91.

Carr, Marilyn, Martha Chen and Renana Jhabwala (eds) (1996), *Speaking Out: Women's Economic Empowerment in South Asia'*, London: Intermediate Technology Press.

Chambers, Robert (1983), *Rural Development: Putting the Last First*, London: Longman Scientific and Technical.

—— (1992), 'Poverty in India: Concepts, Research and Reality', in Harris et al. (eds).

—— (1994a), 'The Origins and Practice of Participatory Rural Appraisal', *World Development*, vol. 22, no. 7, pp. 953–69.

—— (1994b), 'Participatory Rural Appraisal (PRA): Analysis of Experience', *World Development*, vol. 22, no. 9, pp. 1253–68.

—— (1994c), 'Participatory Rural Appraisal (PRA): Challenges, Potentials and Paradigm', *World Development*, vol. 22, no. 10, pp. 1437–54.

—— (1995), 'Poverty and Livelihoods: Whose Reality Counts', UNDP, mimeo.

Chaudhary, S.K. (1993), 'Studies on Efficacy of RRAs/PRAs as a Complement/Substitute to Sample Surveys', New Delhi: NCAER (mimeo).

Cornia, G.A. and F. Stewart (1993), 'Two Errors of Targeting', *Journal of International Development*, vol. 5, no. 5, pp. 459–96.

Dandekar, K. (1983), *Employment Guarantee Scheme – An Employment Opportunity for Women*, Pune: Gokhale Institute of Politics and Economics.

Deshpande, S.K. (1988), *Local Level Management of a Rural Anti-Poverty Programme: A Case Study of the Employment Guarantee Scheme of Maharashtra*, Bangalore: Indian Institute of Management.

Dholakia, R.H. (1994), 'Regional Dimension of Acceleration of Economic Growth in India', *Economic and Political Weekly*, 27 August, pp. 2203–8.

Drèze, J. and A.K. Sen (1989), *Hunger and Public Action*, Oxford: Clarendon Press.

—— (1995), *India: Economic Development and Social Opportunity*, Delhi/ Oxford: Oxford University Press.

—— (1997), *Indian Development: Selected Regional Perspectives*, Delhi: Oxford University Press.

Dubey, A. and S. Gangopadhyay (1998), 'Counting the Poor – Where are the Poor in India?', Department of Statistics, GOI, New Delhi.

Duggal, Ravi, Sunil Nandaraj and Asha Vadair (1995), 'Health Expenditures Across States – Part I', *Economic and Political Weekly*, 15 April, pp. 834–44.

Easwara Prasad, E.S. (1995), 'Social Security for Destitute Widows in Tamil Nadu', *Economic and Political Weekly*, vol. 28, no. 41, 9 October, pp. 2207–13.

Economic Times (1997), 'Ministry Fails to Spend Target Amount on Basic Needs Plan', 24 March 1997, p. 1.

Finance Ministry/UNDP/Harvard Centre for Population and Development Studies Project (IND/92/006): Strategies and Financing for Human Development, 1992–7.

Food and Agriculture Organization (1996), 'The Sixth World Food Survey', Rome: FAO.

Gangopadhyay S., L.R. Jain and A. Dubey (1997), 'Poverty Measures and Socioeconomic Characteristics: 1987–8 and 1993–4', Report submitted to Department of Statistics.

George, P.S. (1984), 'Food Security in South Asia', *Economic and Political Weekly*, vol. 29, no. 18 April 1994, p. 1092.

Gill, Gerard (1991), 'But How does it Compare with the Real Thing?', RRA Notes no. 14, pp. 5–14.

Gillespie, S. and G. McNeill (1992), *Food, Health and Survival in Developing Countries*, New Delhi: Oxford University Press.

Gopalan, C. (1995), 'Towards Food and Nutritional Security', *Economic and Political Weekly*, vol. 30, no. 52, December 1995, pp. A-134–41.

Government of India (1966), *Report of the Education Commission*, New Delhi.

— (1991), *Report of the Committee for Review of National Policy on Education* (Ramamoorthy Committee), New Delhi.

— (1996), 'Economic Survey: 1995–96', Ministry of Finance, Economic Division, New Delhi.

— (1997) 'Annual Administration Report of Department of Education', Ministry of Human Development, Department of Education, New Delhi.

— (1998), 'National Programme of Nutritional Support to Primary Education (Mid-day Meals Scheme)'. A discussion paper, Ministry of Human Development, Department of Education (EE Bureau), New Delhi.

Guhan, S. (1993), 'Social Security for the Poor in the Unorganised Sector: A Blueprint for India', in K.S. Parikh and R. Sudarshan (eds), *Human Development and Structural Adjustment*, Madras: Macmillan.

— — (1994), 'Social Security Options for Developing Countries', *International Labour Review*, vol. 133, no. 10, pp. 35–53.

— (1995), 'Social Expenditures in the Union Budget', *Economic and Political Weekly*, vol. xxx, nos 18 and 19, May 6–13, pp. 1095–1102.

Hanumantha Rao Committee Report on 'Drought Prone Programmes'.

Harriss, B. (1991), *Child Nutrition and Poverty in South India: Noon Meals in Tamil Nadu*, New Delhi: Concept Publishers.

— (1992), 'Rural Poverty in India: Micro-level Evidence', in Harriss *et al.* (eds).

Harriss, B., S. Guhan and R.H. Cassen (1992), 'Poverty in India: Research and Policy', Bombay: Oxford University Press.

Harriss-White Barbara (1995), 'Economic Restructuring: State, Market, Collective and Household Action in India's Social Sector', *The European Journal of Development Research*, vol. 7, no. 1, pp. 124–47.

Herring, Ronald (1983), *Land to the Tiller: The Political Economy of Agrarian Reform in South Asia*, New Haven: Yale University Press.

Hill, Polly (1986), *Development Economics on Trial: The Anthropological Case for a Prosecution*, Cambridge: Cambridge University Press.

International Institute for Population Sciences (IIPS) (1994), *National Family Health Survey: 1992-93*, Mumbai.

— (1994), *National Family Health Survey: Tamil Nadu*, Mumbai.

Jayaraman, Raji and Peter Lanjouw (1997), 'Rural Living Standards in India: A Perspective from Longitudinal Village Studies', Background paper to the World Bank Report No. 16483-IN, 'Achievements and Challenges in Reducing Poverty', 27 May.

— (1998), 'The Evolution of Poverty and Inequality in Indian Villages',

World Bank Paper Series 1870, Poverty and Human Resources Development Research Group, Washington D.C.: The World Bank.

Jodha, N.S. (1988), 'Poverty Debate in India: A Minority View', *Economic and Political Weekly*, Special Number, November, vol. XXIII, nos 45–7, pp. 2412–28.

Kannan, K.P. (1995), 'Declining Incidence of Rural Poverty in Kerala', in *Economic and Political Weekly*, 14–21 October, vol. XXX, nos 42 and 43, pp. 2651–62.

Khare, Sandeep (1997), 'Qualitative Assessment of Poverty in Tarkullah Village of Gorakhpur', Report prepared for the World Bank Study on Qualitative Assessment of Poverty in Some of India's Poor regions (mimeo).

Krishnaji, N. (1997), 'Human Poverty Index: A Critique', *Economic and Political Weekly*, vol. 32 (35), pp. 2202–5.

Krishnan, T.N. (1994), 'Access to Health and Burden of Treatment in India: An Inter-State Comparison', Discussion Paper Series 2, UNDP Research Project on Strategies and Financing Human Development, CDS, Thiruvananthapuram.

— (1996), 'Hospitalisation Insurance', *Economic and Political Weekly*, 13 April, Research Paper for Finance Ministry/UNDP/Harvard Centre for Population and Development Studies Project (IND/92/006): Strategies and Financing for Human Development, 1992–7.

Lerche, Jens (1995), 'Is Bonded Labour a Bound Category? Reconceptualising Agrarian Conflict in India', *Journal of Peasant Studies*, vol. 22, no. 3, April, pp. 484–515.

Lieten, G.K. (1992), *Continuity and Change in Rural West Bengal*, New Delhi: Sage.

— (1996), *Development, Devolution and Democracy, Village Discourse in West Bengal*, New Delhi/London: Sage.

Lieten, G.K. and Ravi Srivastava (forthcoming), *Unequal Partners: Power Relations, Devolution and Development in Uttar Pradesh*, New Delhi: Sage.

Mahendra, Dev (1995), 'Alleviating Poverty: Maharashtra Employment Guarantee Scheme', *Economic and Political Weekly*, vol. XXX, nos 41 and 42, 14–21 October, pp. 2263–76.

Malhotra, R. (1997), 'Incidence of Poverty in India: Towards a Consensus on Estimating the Poor', *Indian Journal of Labour Economics*, vol. 40, no. 1, January–March, pp. 67–102.

Marjit, S. and S. Mitra (1996), 'Convergence in Regional Growth Rates: Indian Research Agenda', *Economic and Political Weekly*, vol. 32, no. 35, pp. 2202–5.

Martorell, R. and T.J. Ho (1984), 'Malnutrition, Morbidity and Mortality', *Population and Development Review, A Supplement to Vol. 10*, pp. 49–68.

Mascarenhas, James (1991), 'Participatory Rural Appraisal and Participatory Learning Methods: Recent Experiences from MYRADA and South India', Forests, Trees and People, Newsletter no. 15/16.

Meenakshi, J.V. (1986), 'How Important are Changes in Taste? A State Level Analysis of Food Demand', Economic and Political Weekly, vol. 31, no. 50, 14 December, pp. 3265-9.

Meenakshisundaram, S.S. (1994), 'Interface Between Bureaucrary and Elected Representatives', Occasional Paper No. 6, National Institute of Rural Development, Hyderabad.

— (1994), 'Decentralisation in Developing Countries', New Delhi: Concept Publishing Company.

Minhas, B.S. (1991), 'One Estimating the Inadequacy of Energy Intakes: Revealed Food Consumption Behaviour Versus Nutritional Norms (Nutritional Status of Indian People in 1983)', The Journal of Development Studies, vol. 28, no. 1, pp. 1-38.

— (1991), 'Educational Deprivation and its Role as a Spoiler of Access to Better Life in India', Technical Report no. 9104, New Delhi: Indian Statistical Institute.

Moss, David (1995), 'Authority, Gender and Knowledge: Theoretical Reflections on Participatory Rural Appraisal', Economic and Political Weekly, 1 March, pp. 569-78.

Mukherjee, Neela (1992), 'Villager's Perception of Rural Poverty through the Mapping Methods of PRA', RRA notes no. 15, pp. 21-6.

— (1993), Participatory Rural Appraisal: Methodology and Applications, New Delhi: Concept Publishing Company.

National Council of Applied Economic Research (NCAER) (1992), Household Survey of Medical Care, New Delhi.

— (1993), Comparative Study of Sample Survey and Participatory Rural Appraisal Methodologies, New Delhi: NCAER.

— (1996), Human Development Profile of Rural India, Inter-State and Inter-Group Differentials, Selected Indicators, New Delhi.

National Institute of Adult Education (1993), 'Statistical Database for Literacy – Volume II. Final Population and Literacy 1991', New Delhi.

NSS Report no. 407: National Sample Survey Organisation: Report on Operational Landholdings in India: 1991-92:Salient Features, Department of Statistics, Government of India, New Delhi (1996).

NSS Report no. 407: Employment and Unemployment in India, 1993-94, 50th Round (1996) Other details are the same as those for Report no. 407 which is for the 48th Round.

Office of Registrar General (1997), 'Sample Registration System Estimates 1995', Government of India, New Delhi.

Osmani, S.R. (1991), 'Social Security in South Asia', in E. Ahmad, Jean Drèze, John Hills and A.K. Sen (eds), *Social Security in Developing Countries*, Oxford: Clarendon Press.

Pangore, G. and Lokur, V. (1996), 'The Good Society – The Panipanchayat Model of Sustainable Water Management', Indian National Trust for Art and Cultural Heritage, New Delhi.

Parikh, K.S (1992), 'Importance of Food and Agriculture Policies in the Success of Structural Reforms in India', invited paper, 29th European Association of Agricultural Economists, Germany: Hohentreim.

—— (1997), *India Development Report*, New Delhi: Oxford University Press.

Parikh, K.S and R. Sudarshan (eds) (1993), *Human Development and Structural Adjustment*, Madras: MacMillan.

Pelletier, D.L., E.A. Frongillo Jr., D.G. Schroeder and J.P. Habicht (1995), 'The Effects of Malnutrition on Child Mortality in Developing Countries', *Bulletin of the World Health Organization*, vol. 73, no. 4, pp. 443–8.

Perspective Planning Division (1979), *Report of the Task Force on Projections of Minimum Needs and Effective Consumption Demand*, New Delhi: Planning Commission.

Planning Commission (1993), *Report of the Expert Group on Estimation of Proportion and Number of Poor*, New Delhi: Planning Commission.

Prabhu, K. Seeta (1997a), 'Promotional and Protective Social Security During Economic Reforms', *Review of Development and Change*, vol. II (1), January–June, pp. 24–51.

—— (1997b), 'Social Sector Expenditures in India: Trends and Implications', Background Paper for UNDP (1997b).

—— (1997c), 'Structural Adjustment and Human Development: A Study of Two Indian States', Report Prepared for the UNDP Research Project on Strategies for Financing for Human Development, Thiruvananthapuram, mimeo.

Prabhu, K. Seeta and Somnath Chatterjee (1993), *Social Sector Expenditures and Human Development: A Study of Indian States*, Development Research Group Study no. 6, Mumbai: Reserve Bank of India.

Prabhu, K. Seeta and Sangita Kamdar (1997), 'On Defining Poverty from a Human Development Perspective: An Exploratory Exercise', University of Mumbai, mimeo.

Prabhu, K. Seeta and P.C. Sarker (1997), 'Trends in Social Sector Expenditures in Indian States: Some Disturbing Features', University of Mumbai, mimeo.

Prabhu K. Seeta, P.C. Sarker and A. Radha (1996), 'Gender-Related Development Index for Indian States: Methodological Issues', *Economic and Political Weekly*, vol. XXXI (43), 26 October, pp. WS 72–9.

Prasad, P.H., G.B. Rodgers, S. Gupta, A.N. Sharma, and B. Sharma (1986), 'The Pattern of Poverty in Bihar: Population and Labour Policies Programme', Working Paper no. 152, World Employment Programme, Geneva: ILO.

Pretty, Jules, S. Subramaniam, D. Ananthakrishnan, C. Jayanthi, S. Muralikrishnasamy and K. Ranganayaki (1992), 'Finding the Poorest in a Tamil Nadu Village: A Sequence of Mapping and Wealth Ranking', RRA Notes, no. 15, pp. 39–42.

Programme Evaluation Organisation (1980), *Joint Evaluation Report on Employment Guarantee Scheme in Maharashtra*, New Delhi: Planning Commission.

Radhakrishna, R. (1991), 'Food and Nutrition: Challenges for Policy', *Journal of the Indian Society of Agricultural Statistics*, vol. XLIII, no. 3, pp. 211–27.

Radhakrishna, R. et al. (1996), 'India's Public Distribution System: A National and International Perspective', (Draft), October.

Radhakrishna, R. and S. Indrakant (1987), *Effect on Rice Market Intervention Policies in India: The Case of Andhra Pradesh*, Hyderabad: Centre for Economic and Social Studies.

Radhakrishna, R. and K.V. Narayana (1993), *Nutrition Programmes in India: Review and Assessment*, Hyderabad: Centre for Economic and Social Studies.

Radhakrishna, R. and C. Ravi (1990), *Food Demand Projections for India*, Centre for Economic and Social Studies, 1991.

— (1992), 'Effects of Growth, Relative Price and Preferences on Food and Nutrition', *Indian Economic Review*, vol. 27, special number, pp. 303–23.

Rajaratnam, Jolly, C. Ganesan, Helen Thasian, Nayamoni Babu and Abel Rajaratnam (1993), *Validating the Wealth Ranking of PRA and Formal Survey in Identifying the Rural Poor*, Vellore: RUHSA Department, Christian Medical College.

Ramchandran, V.K. (1997), 'Kerala's Development Achievements', in Drèze and Sen (eds), *Indian Development: Selected Regional Perspectives*, Delhi: Oxford University Press.

Rao, C.H. Hanumantha and R. Radhakrishna (1997), 'National Food Security: A Policy Perspective for India', Plenary paper, XXIII International Conference of Agricultural Economists, 10–16 August, California: Sacramento.

Rao, N., Rurup L., and R. Sudarshan (eds) (1996), 'Sites of Change – The Structural Context of Empowering Women in India', New Delhi: FES and UNDP.

Rao, V.M. (1995), 'Beyond Surpluses: Food Security in Changing

Context', *Economic and Political Weekly*, vol. 30, no. 4, 28 January, pp. 215–19.

Ravallion, Martin and Gaurav Datt (1996), India's Checkered History in Fight against Poverty: Are there Lessons for the Future?, *Economic and Political Weekly*, Special Number, vol. XXXI, nos 35, 36 and 37, September, pp. 2479–86.

Ray, Nandita and D.P. Vasundhara (1996), ' "Like my Mother's House": Women's Thrift and Credit Co-operatives in South India', in Carr et al. (eds)

Report of the Comptroller and Auditor General of India (1995–96) on the Employment Assurance Scheme.

Sarkar, Arup (1991), 'Wealth Ranking in Mahilong, Bihar', RRA notes no. 13, August.

Sawant, S.D. and C.V. Achuthan (1995), 'Agricultural Growth Across Crops and Regions', *Economic and Political Weekly*, vol. 30, no. 12, 25 March, pp. A-2–A-13.

Schiff, M. (1990), 'Nutrition: Alternative Definitions and Policy Implications', *Economic Development and Cultural Change*, pp. 281–92.

Scott, J.C. (1987), 'Weapons of the Weak: Everyday Struggle, Meanings and Deeds', in T. Shanin (ed.), *Peasants and Peasant Societies*, 2nd edn., Oxford: Basil Blackwell.

Secler, D. (1982), 'Small but Healthy' in P.V. Sukhatme (ed.), *Newer Concepts in Nutrition and their Implications for Policy*, Pune: Maharashtra Association for the Cultivation of Science.

Sen, Abhijit (1996), 'Economic Reforms, Employment and Poverty – Trends and Options', *Economic and Political Weekly*, Special Number, September, pp. 2459–77.

Sengupta, Sunil and Haris Gazdar (1997), 'Agrarian Politics and Rural Development in West Bengal', in Drèze and Sen (eds), *Indian Development: Selected Regional Perspectives*, Oxford and Delhi: Oxford University Press.

Shah, Parmesh (1990), 'Economic Classification of a Community Using Locally Generated Criteria', RRA Notes, no. 8.

Shah, Parmesh, Girish Bharadwaj and Ranjit Ambashtha (1991), 'Farmers as Analysts and Facilitators in Participatory Rural Appraisal and Planning', RRA Notes, no. 13, pp. 84–94.

Sharma, A.N. (1995), 'Political Economy of Poverty in Bihar', in *Economic and Political Weekly*, 14–21 October.

Singh, Jagpal (1992), *Capitalism and Dependence: Agrarian Politics in Western Uttar Pradesh 1951–1991*, Delhi: Manohar.

Smith, Sheila and John Sender (1988), 'Investigating Poverty: An Example from Tanzania', RRA Notes, no. 2, October.

Srivastava, Nisha (1997), 'Qualitative Assessment of Poverty in Chitauri Village, Allahabad', Report prepared for the World Bank Study on Qualitative Assessment of Poverty in Some of India's Poor regions (mimeo).

Srivastava, Ravi S. (1996), 'Agricultural Reforms and the Rural Poor in Eastern Uttar Pradesh', Background Paper for the World Bank Country Economic Memorandum 1996.

Subba Rao, K. (1992), 'Interventions to Fill Nutrition Gaps a the Household Level: A Review of Indian Experience', in B. Harriss, S. Guhan and R.H. Cassen (eds), *Poverty in India: Research and Policy*, New Delhi: Oxford University Press.

Sukhatme, P.V. (1982), 'Poverty and Malnutrition', in P.V. Sukhatme (ed.), *Newer Concepts in Nutrition and their Implications for Policy*, Pune: Maharashtra Association for the Cultivation of Science, pp. 11–64.

Sundaram, K. and S.D. Tendulkar (1993), 'National Sample Surveys on Consumer Expenditure and Living Standard Measurement in India', Ch. 5, in David G. Westendorff and D. Ghai (eds), *Monitoring Social Development in the 19902: Data Constraints, Concerns and Priorities*, Avesbury.

—— (1995a), *Living Standard Measurement in India*, Manuscript completed for UNRISD, Geneva.

—— (1995b), 'On Measuring Shelter Deprivation in India', *Indian Economic Review*, vol. xxx, no. 2 (July–December), pp. 1–35.

Suryanarayana, M.H. (1995), 'Growth, Poverty and Levels of Living: Hypotheses, Methods and Policies', *Journal of Indian School of Political Economy*, vol. 7, no. 2, pp. 203–55.

Tendulkar, S. (1983), 'Micro-level Experiments in Socio-economic Development', pp. 87–98 and 'Overview' pp. 537–42 in Centre for Policy Research, *Population, Poverty and Hope*, New Delhi: Uppal Publishing House.

—— (1989), 'An Approach Towards Integrating Large and Small Scale Surveys', Ch. 8, pp. 200–17 in P. Bardhan (ed.), *Conversations between Economists and Anthropologists: Methodological Issues in Measuring Economic Change in Rural India*, New Delhi: Oxford University Press.

—— (1992), 'Connection between Economic and Social Development: An Indian Case Study', pp. 121–61 in UNESCAP, *Social Costs of Economic Restructuring in Asia and the Pacific*, Development Papers, no. 15, Bangkok.

—— (1993), 'Macro-economic Policies and Poverty Reduction', mimeo.

—— (1995), 'Social Welfare, Social Deprivation and Economic Growth: Some Reflections on the Indian Experience', in M. Chattopadhyay,

P. Maiti and M. Rakshit (eds), *Planning and Economic Development in India: Evaluation and Lessons for the Future*, New Delhi: Sage Publications.

Tendulkar, S. (1997), 'Indian Economic Policy Reforms and Poverty: An Assessment', Ch. 12, pp. 248–76 in a forthcoming volume in honour of Manmohan Singh edited by I.J. Ahluwalia and I.M.D. Little, New Delhi: Oxford University Press.

Tendulkar, Suresh D., K. Sundaram and L.R. Jain (1993), *Poverty in India, 1970–71 to 1988–89*, New Delhi: ILO–ARTEP Working Paper (December).

—— (1996), *Macroeconomic Policies and Poverty in India, 1966–67 to 1993–94*, Report submitted to SAAT–ILO, New Delhi.

Tilak, J.B.G. (1995), *Costs and Financing of Education in India: A Review of Issues, Problems and Prospects*, Discussion Paper Series no. 5, Research Project on Strategies and Financing for Human Development, Thiruvananthapuram: Centre for Development Studies.

Tulasidhar, V.B. (1997), 'Resources for Human Development: Notes on Selected Topics', Background Paper for UNDP (1997).

United Nations Development Programmme (1991), (1996), (1997a), *Human Development Report*, New York: Oxford University Press.

—— (1997b), 'India: The Road to Human Development', Paper presented at the 1997 India Development Forum, New Delhi.

—— (1998a), 'Integrating Human Rights with Sustainable Human Development', UNDP Policy Document, New York: UNDP.

—— (1998b), 'Overcoming Human Poverty', UNDP Poverty Report 1998, New York: UNDP.

Wadley, S.S. and B.W. Derr (1990), 'Karimpur 1925–1984: Understanding Rural India Through Restudies', in Bardhan (ed.) Welbourn, Alice, 'RRA and the Analysis of Difference', RRA Notes, no. 14, December, pp. 14–23.

World Bank (1991), *Gender and Poverty in India*, Washington D.C.: The World Bank.

—— (1995), 'India: Policy and Finance Strategies for Strengthening Primary Health Care Services', Report no. 13042–IN, Washington D.C.: The World Bank.

—— (1997), 'India: Achievements and Challenges in Reducing Poverty', Report no. 16483–IN, Washington D.C.: The World Bank.

Name Index

Subject Index